IMAGES
of America

WATERTOWN AND CODINGTON COUNTY

SOUTH DAKOTA

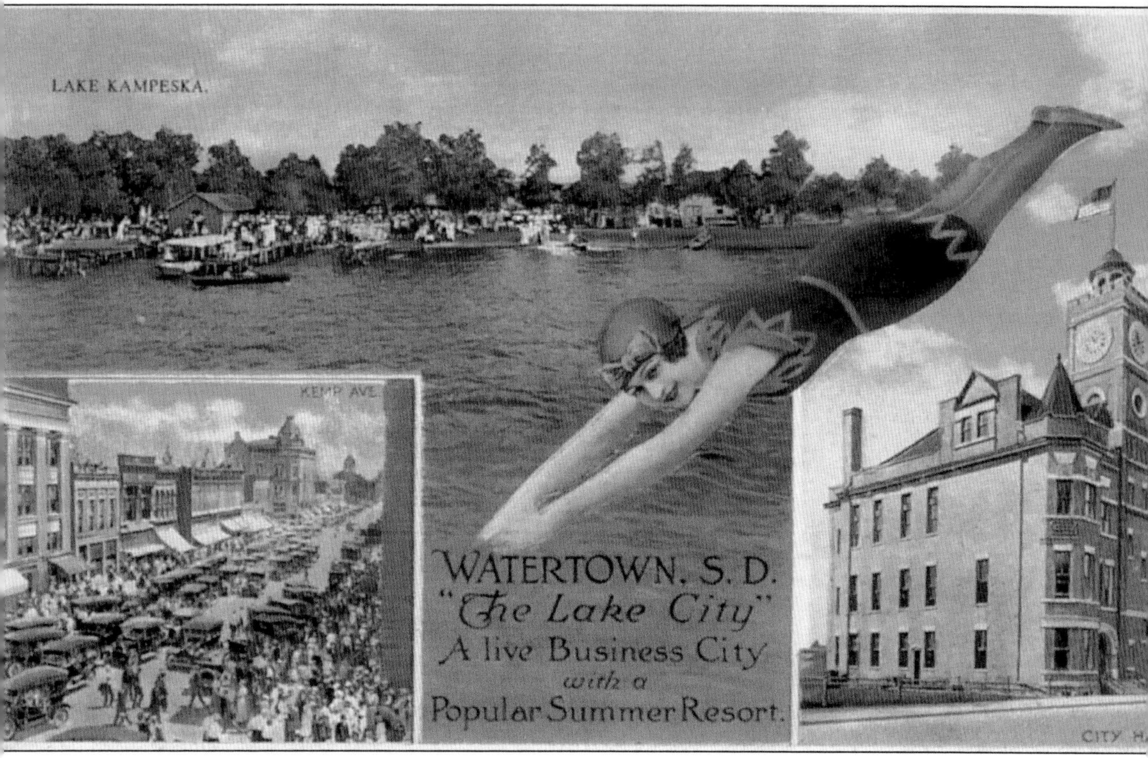

Illustrations of the city hall, a busy Kemp Avenue scene, and recreation on Lake Kampeska are used on this postcard to promote Watertown as "'The Lake City,' A Live Business City with a Popular Summer Resort." T.M. Nodland sent this card from Watertown, to Ada M. Johnson in Duluth, on June 26, 1923. (Courtesy Bud and Arleen Larson.)

IMAGES
of America

Watertown and Codington County

South Dakota

Lisa D. Hanson and Tim Hoheisel

ARCADIA
PUBLISHING

ISBN 978-0-7385-1974-6

Published by Arcadia Publishing
Charleston, South Carolina

Printed in the United States of America

Library of Congress Catalog Card Number: 2002106085

For all general information contact Arcadia Publishing at:
Telephone 843-853-2070
Fax 843-853-0044
E-mail sales@arcadiapublishing.com
For customer service and orders:
Toll-Free 1-888-313-2665

Visit us on the Internet at www.arcadiapublishing.com

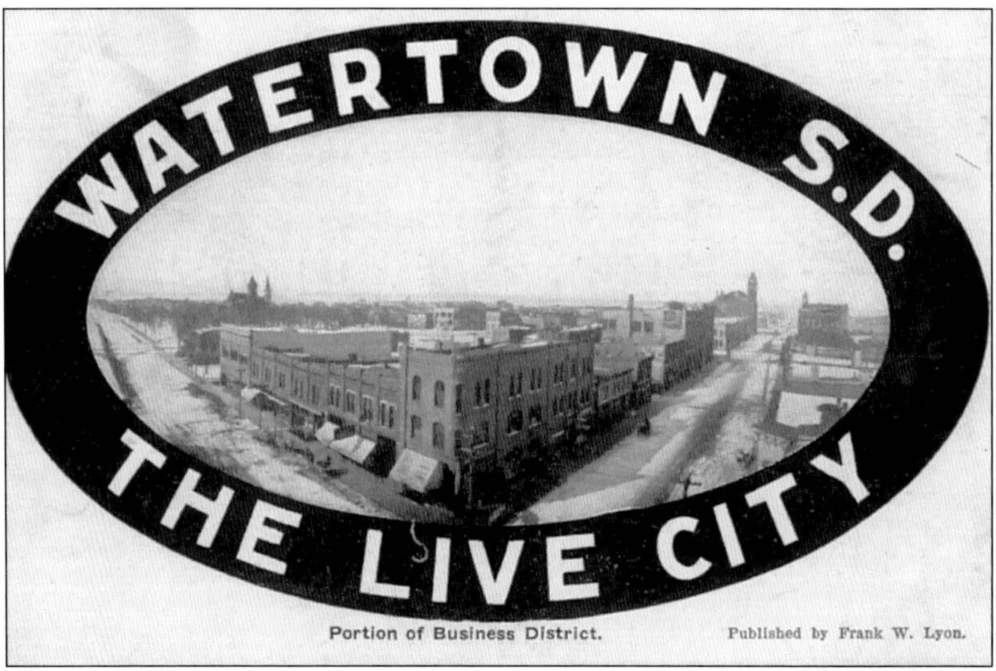

Contents

ACKNOWLEDGMENTS

A number of people need to be acknowledged and thanked for their work on and contribution to this book. First of all, this book would not exist without the hard work and dedication of the assistant director and curator of the Codington County Historical Society, Lisa Hanson. She has worked many hours selecting the photographs and making sure that all of the information in the captions was correct. She has labored tirelessly on this project and deserves the most credit for the completion of the book.

Most of the photographs in the book come from the collection of the Codington County Historical Society in Watertown. These photographs were supplemented with postcard collections of Historical Society members Bud and Arleen Larson, and Ken and Lyn Sheldon. We are grateful that they were willing to share their wonderful collections with us. The photographs from their collections are acknowledged in the captions.

Most importantly, thank you, reader, for buying this book. Proceeds from the sales, including all royalties, go to support the operation of the Codington County Historical Society. Our success depends on your support, and it is important that you know how greatly your support is appreciated.

The mission of the Codington County Historical Society is to preserve, interpret, and disseminate the heritage of Codington County, South Dakota, and this book effectively fulfills all three aspects of the mission. We hope you appreciate this latest installment of historic photos of Watertown and Codington County. Enjoy!

Tim Hoheisel
Watertown, South Dakota
April 2002

INTRODUCTION

It has been 15 years since the Codington County Historical Society last published a relatively broad history of Watertown and Codington County. In that time the museum staff has fielded hundreds of calls from people wanting to buy *A Pictorial History of Codington County, South Dakota* and its predecessor, *The First 100 Years in Codington County, South Dakota, 1879–1979*. Those books were very popular and continue to be requested even though they are out of print. This book does not intend to replace those two volumes, but merely supplement them. This *Images of America* book on Watertown and Codington County published by Arcadia Publishing contains 216 photographs of people, places, buildings, and scenery. With literally thousands of photos to choose from, this book is not intended to be comprehensive. It does intend, however, to show some "new" old photographs of Watertown and Codington County. There is also more detailed information in the photo captions than in previous pictorial history books.

Unlike other larger cities in South Dakota, Watertown was not fortunate enough to be "known" for anything special or unique. Pierre had the State Capitol and became the "Capitol City." Huron had the State Fair and became the "Fair City." Sioux Falls had the Queen Bee Mill, among many other things, and became known as the "Queen City." Aberdeen was the "Hub City" because it was a railroad hub. West River had the Black Hills and gold, which did not need any extra promotion. Even though Watertown emerged as a trade center in northeastern South Dakota, it did not have anything distinctive. Town boosters had a more difficult time promoting Watertown. What Watertown did have was water, literally. Lake Kampeska and Lake Pelican are both within the city limits, and the Big Sioux River bisects the town. Early promotional photographs and postcards showed the lakes and natural scenery of Watertown and proclaimed it the "Lake City." Other promotional postcards showed street scenes of general growth and progress and Watertown became known as the "Live City," a slogan that was used extensively in the 1910s.

The photo postcard on page four is a typical promotional postcard. The building originally known as the Century Block is in the foreground at the southwest corner of Maple Street and Kemp Avenue. The tower in the distance to the west (right) is the former City Hall. The tower in the distance to the south (left) is the former County Courthouse. The photograph itself was taken from the tower of the Grand Opera House and was published by Frank W. Lyon. Early Watertown businessmen and staunch boosters Frank Lyon and L.D. Lyon are renowned for documenting the early history of Watertown through photographs that they used to create postcards and promotional booklets. They did not do this with the preservation of history in mind. They did it to flaunt the "greatness" of Watertown in an attempt to attract settlers. The photograph on the cover of the book is another excellent example of city "boosterism." The words "Boost Watertown" unapologetically embellish the machine in the center of the photo. The Historical Society and researchers use photographs such as these to unravel the early history of Watertown.

The photographs that comprise this book generally range from 1900 through 1960 with most of them being from the early part of the twentieth century. The images are divided into nine chapters making them more manageable for the reader to peruse. Over time many changes occur on the cultural landscape, some are obvious, some subtler. This book offers the reader a glimpse into the early history of Watertown and Codington County through photographs.

Sources consulted in the creation of this book include: *The First 100 Years in Codington County, South Dakota 1879–1979* by the Codington County History Book Committee, 1979; *Pictorial History of Codington County, South Dakota* edited by Joanita Kant, Virginia Allen, and Dr. Stanley W. Allen Jr., 1987; *Heritage Sampler: Stories about People and Places in the History of Codington County*; by Vel Stokke, 1975; "The Early and Territorial History of Codington County; The History of South Dakota," by Wright Tarbell, 1949; *History of South Dakota* by Herbert S. Schell, 1968; and many other city directories and histories of the smaller communities in Codington County.

Like so many cities of similar size, Watertown has not been immune to the negative forces of growth. Big box stores like Wal-Mart, Target, K-mart, and Shopko, the gaudy commercial strip of Highway 212, and cookie-cutter housing developments on the fringes of town have homogenized the city. These forces are unfortunately creating anonymous and undistinguished cities across the country. Richard Moe, President of the National Trust for Historic Preservation appropriately said, "More and more people are seeing that every place in America looks like every place else, and that means that every place looks like no place." Watertown has always possessed a mentality of progress and change. Regrettably the push to modernize has led to the demolition or obscuration of many historic buildings. It is our intention to show readers the appearance and prominence of early Watertown. It is our hope that this book rekindles in current residents some of the enthusiasm of early settlers and pioneers that made Watertown a great city, the "Live City."

One

Commerce and Service

Watertown and Codington County are located in northeastern South Dakota in the heart of the Coteau des Prairie. The total area of Codington County is 688 square miles of mainly agricultural land. There are approximately 38 people per square mile in Codington County, compared to an average of 10 people per square mile for the state of South Dakota.

Codington County and Watertown have always been on the progressive end of the growth scale. In 1900, the population of Watertown was 8,770. Ten years later it almost doubled to 14,092. Fueled by a good farming climate and the railroad, Watertown's heyday of growth was the 1910s. Most of the historic structures still standing in Watertown were built during that period.

Watertown experienced another burst of growth in the 1980s and 1990s. The population of the city was 15,649 in 1980 and is currently 20,237. That is an increase of 4,588, a growth of 23 percent in 20 years. This is the largest population that Watertown and Codington County has ever had. Watertown is now the state's fourth largest city, and may soon surpass Aberdeen, according to population trends and calculations. This growth is attributed to a local farm economy that has remained relatively strong, close proximity to an interstate highway, and a burgeoning tourist industry.

Those businesses and buildings that helped make Watertown what it is today are featured in this chapter. The photographs depict many different businesses, hotels, banks, hospitals, streetscapes, as well as the people who operated these businesses.

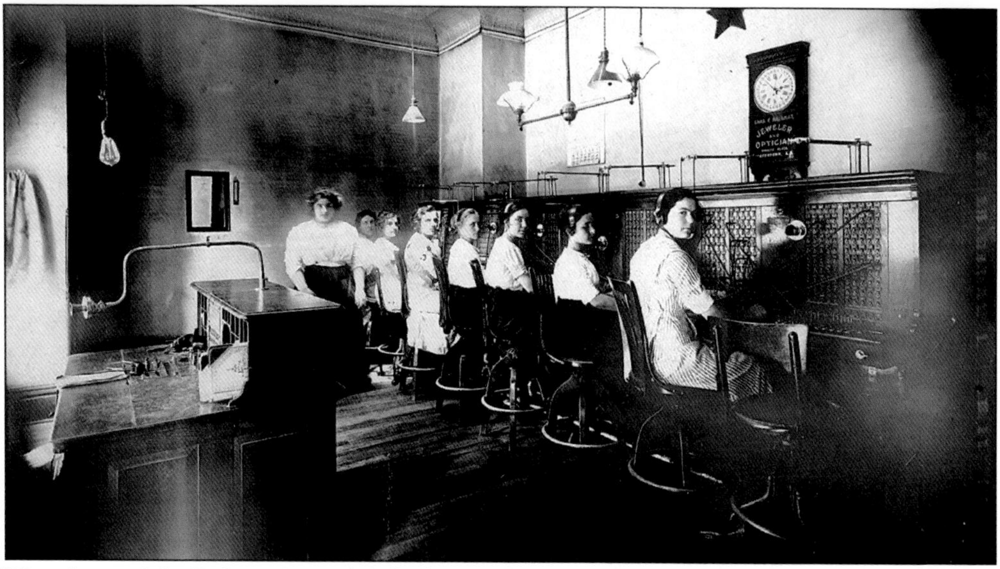

This photo of the Dakota Central Telephone office was taken about 1910, before the company moved to its new location at 23 First Avenue Southeast from its site in Midway Alley. Operators are, from left to right: Maude Jones (chief supervisor), Edith Jacobson, Frieda Dellman, Clara Dellman, unidentified, Ellen Mitchell, Gertrude Joy, and Mary Shield. Dakota Central became a part of the Northwestern Bell Telephone Company in the 1930s. Telephone service in Watertown began in 1887 with the Watertown Telephone Company.

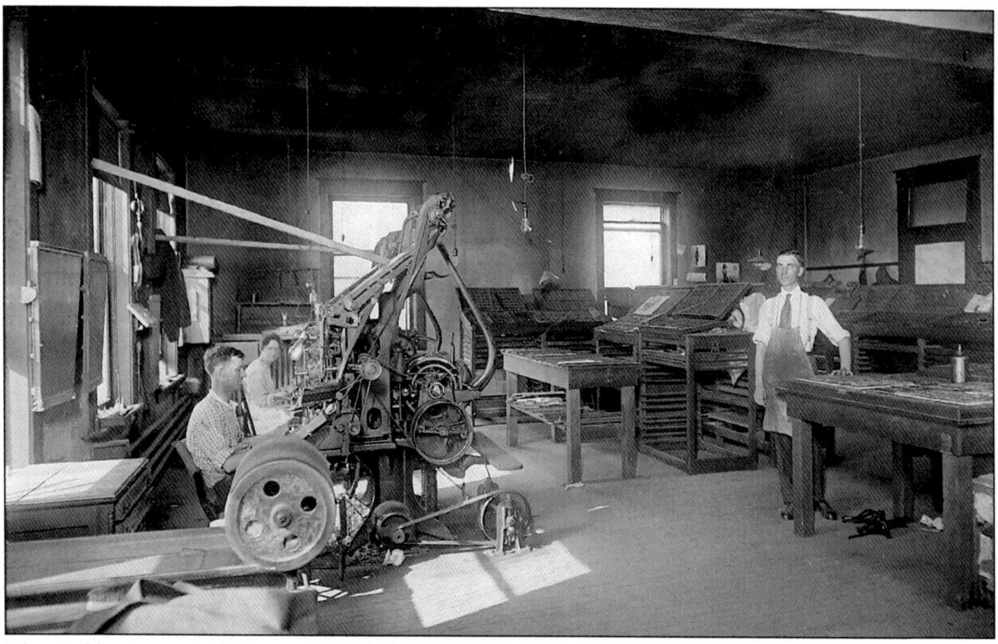

The *Public Opinion*, Watertown's daily newspaper, began in 1882 as a weekly. The paper was published by the Way family since S.X. Way acquired it in 1908, until February 2002, when it was purchased by the United Communications Corporation, of Kenosha, Wisconsin. The employees in this photo of the newspaper printing room from about 1916, as identified on the back of the picture are, left to right: Mr. J.E. Cofe, Elvah Clifgard, and Clarence Halvorson.

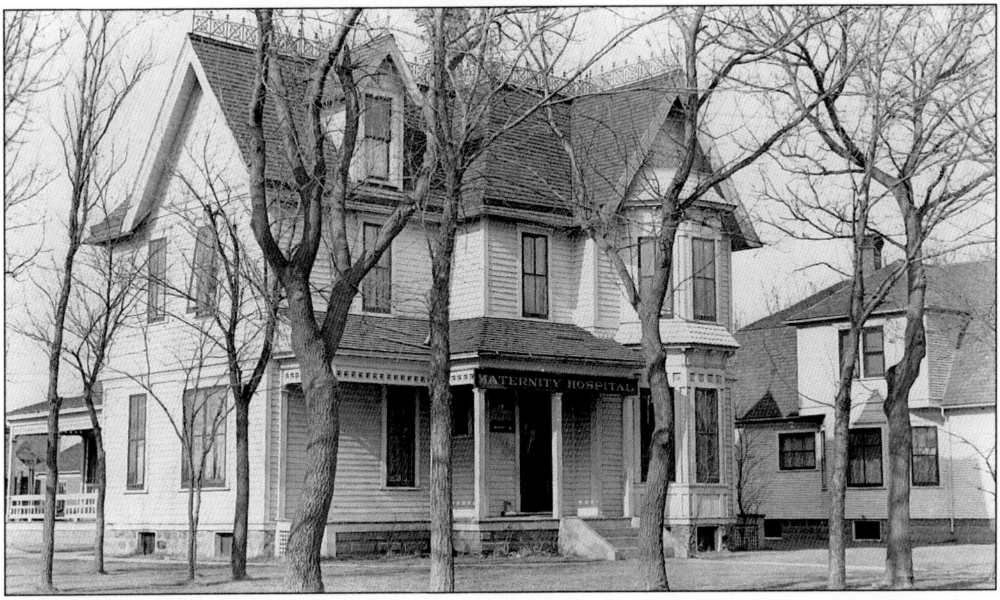

Dr. and Mrs. H.C. Parsons operated this maternity hospital at 223 Fourth Street Southeast from 1910 until about 1916. The December 15, 1910 *Public Opinion* commented, "One of the marks of progress in Watertown this year was the establishing of a hospital for women and children… devoted to the surgical treatment of diseases of women and to the care of mothers during confinement." M.A. Heegaard built the home in 1886, the same year he established a hardware store on North Broadway. The house was replaced with a modern duplex in the 1980s.

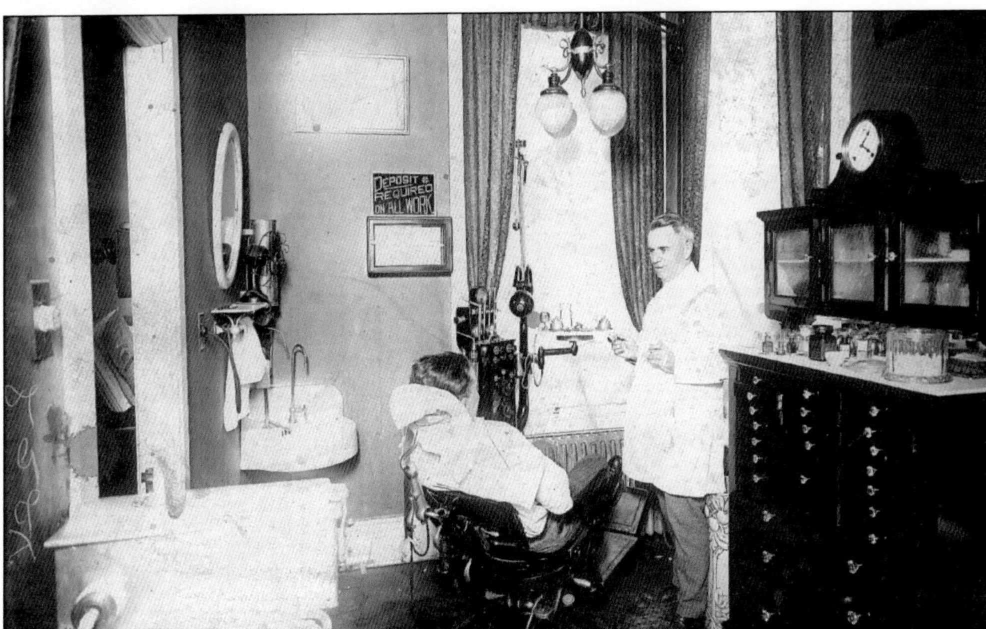

This photo of dentist E.C. Fischer and patient was probably taken about 1903 in his office above the L.W. Cooke Music Store at 18 East Kemp Avenue. Fischer practiced dentistry in Watertown until about 1955. The cabinet at right is almost identical to one on display at the Codington County Heritage Museum at 27 First Avenue Southeast, Watertown.

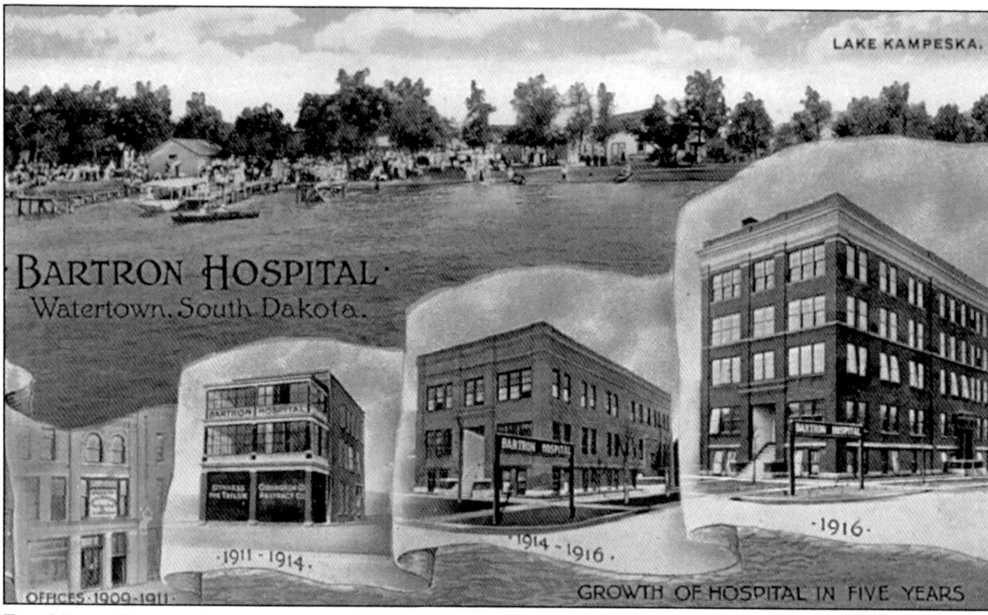

Dr. Harry Bartron's practice grew quickly from the time he first established his offices in Watertown, in the Commercial Bank Building on East Kemp Avenue in 1909. In 1911, Bartron moved his offices to the second and third stories of the Ohtness building formerly on First Avenue Southeast. By 1914, Bartron had built a 40-bed hospital on the southwest corner of the intersection of Second Avenue South and Maple Street, to which he added two stories in 1916. Bartron Hospital became Bartron Clinic in 1957 and moved to its current location at 320 Seventh Avenue Southeast.

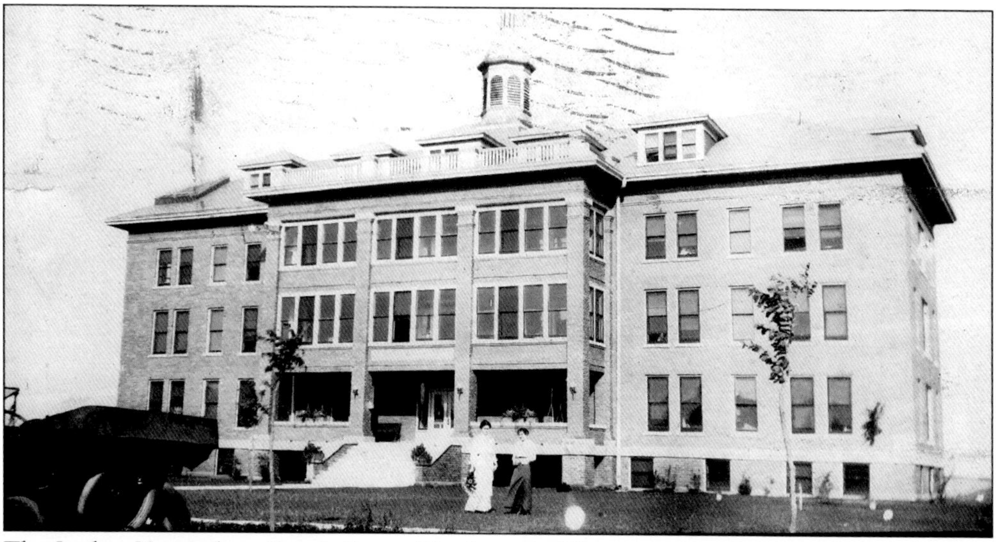

The Luther Hospital on Fourth Street Northeast in Watertown, in this postcard postmarked August 9, 1917, was the result of plans conceived by several area Lutheran ministers in 1909. Construction of the hospital began in 1913 and finished in 1915. The hospital operated a nursing school until a shortage of students and instructors forced its closing in 1946. Luther Hospital became Memorial Hospital in 1951 and eventually merged with St. Ann's Hospital to become Prairie Lakes Hospital in the 1980s. (Courtesy Ken and Lyn Sheldon.)

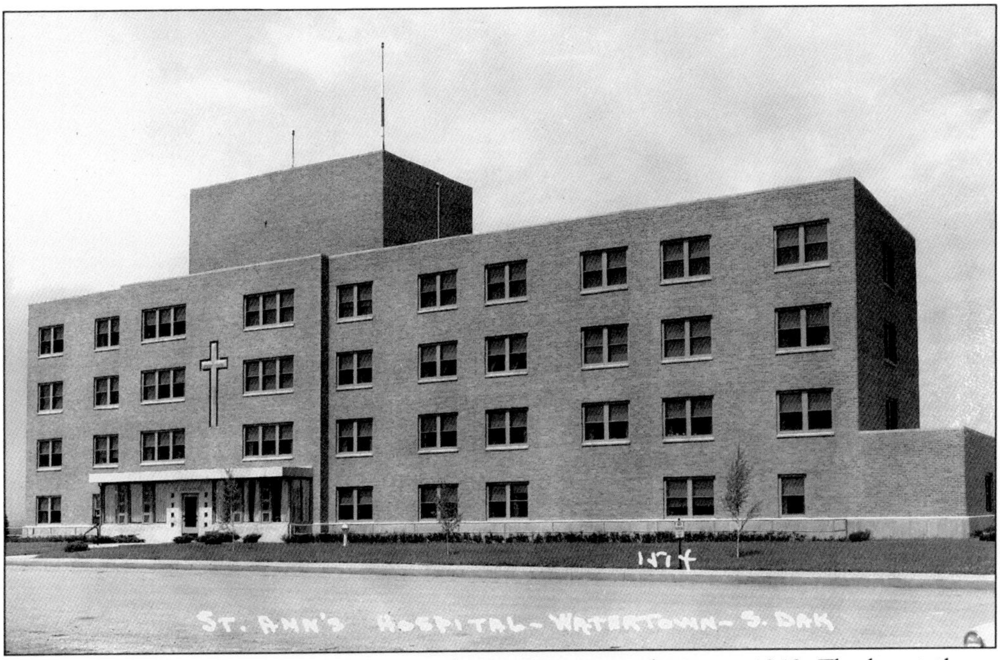

Efforts to build St. Ann's Hospital in northwest Watertown began in 1943. The hospital was dedicated June 4, 1950, and was operated by the Bernardine Sisters until 1973, when advanced age and decreasing numbers prompted the organization to turn over management to the Benedictine Sisters.

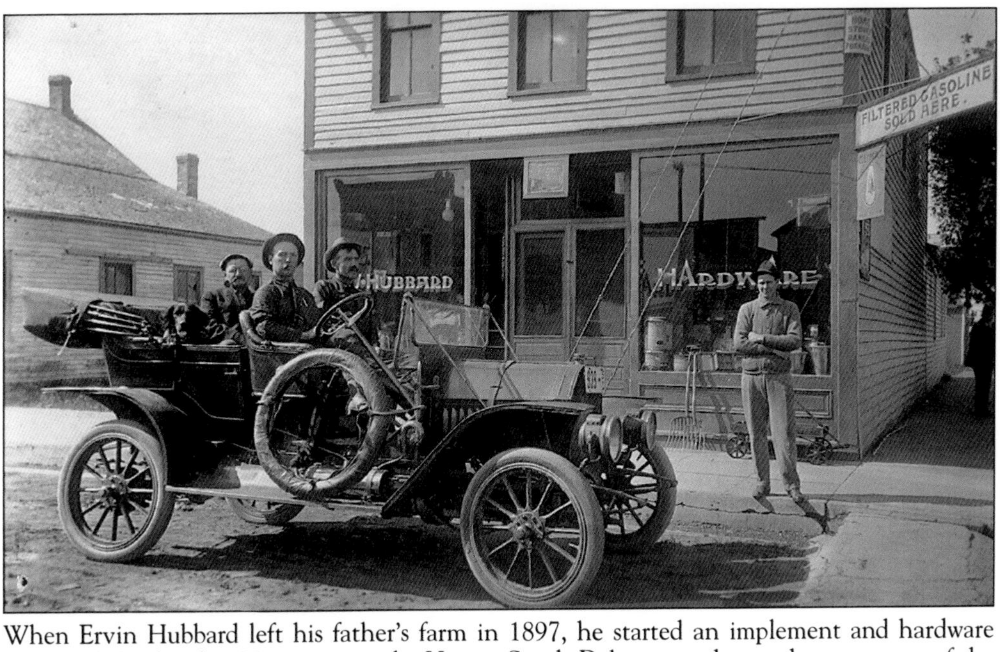

When Ervin Hubbard left his father's farm in 1897, he started an implement and hardware store with his brother Victor in nearby Henry, South Dakota, on the southwest corner of the intersection of Main and Second Streets. John Curley, Vic Hubbard, John Mondloch, and John Aldous are pictured in this postcard from about 1910. Mondloch was a carpenter who built many homes and buildings in and around Henry.

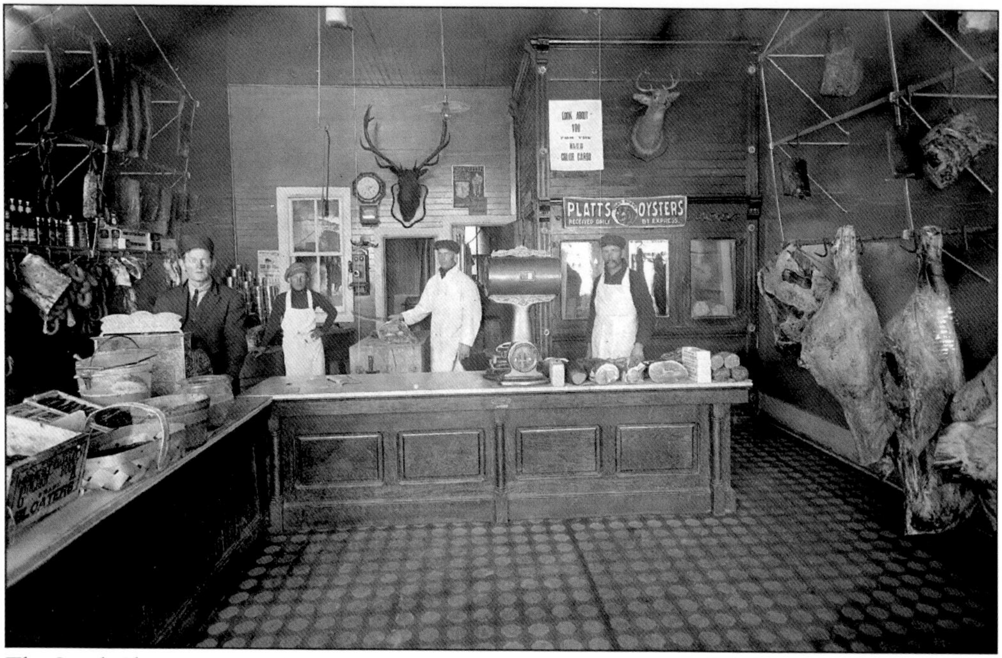

The South Shore meat market in this postcard from about 1919 is unidentified, but it could be the shop of John Henkels & Oscar Claus, who operated in South Shore from about 1916 until about 1930. The Henkels & Claus store was destroyed by fire in 1917. In 1956, the *Watertown Public Opinion* printed a letter from H.T. Ashford, who recalled the Modern Woodmen of America Lodge purchasing oysters in five-gallon kegs from Martin Dahl's meat market for winter oyster suppers in the early 1900s.

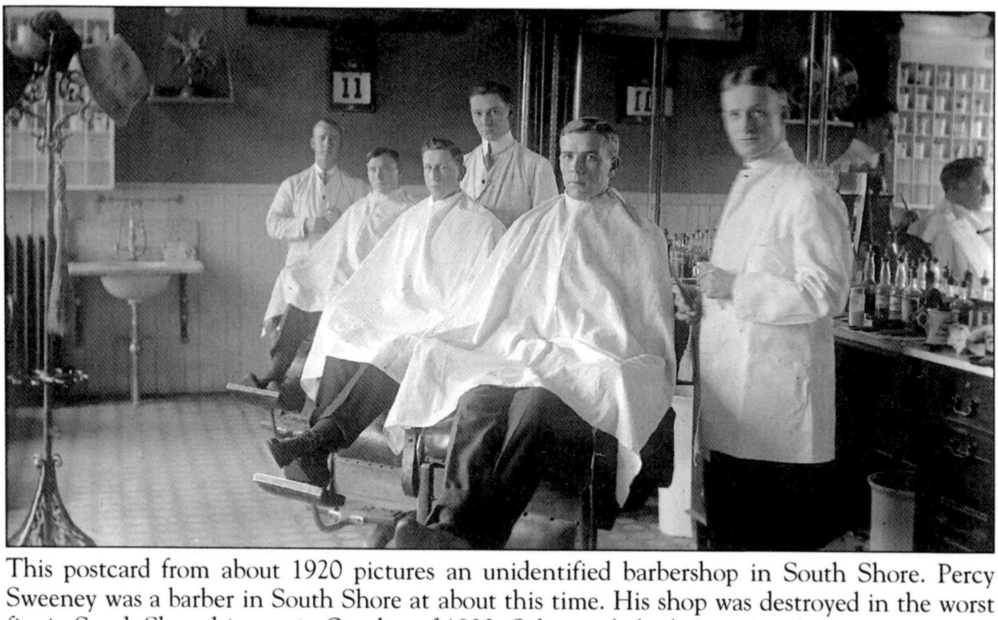

This postcard from about 1920 pictures an unidentified barbershop in South Shore. Percy Sweeney was a barber in South Shore at about this time. His shop was destroyed in the worst fire in South Shore history, in October of 1923. Other early barbers in South Shore, according to Watertown and Codington County directories, were Guy Wilson, Lorn Sorenson, Floyd McDowell, Edward Holtzkamp, Leon Haight, Leonard Haliburton, and Ernest Schmeling.

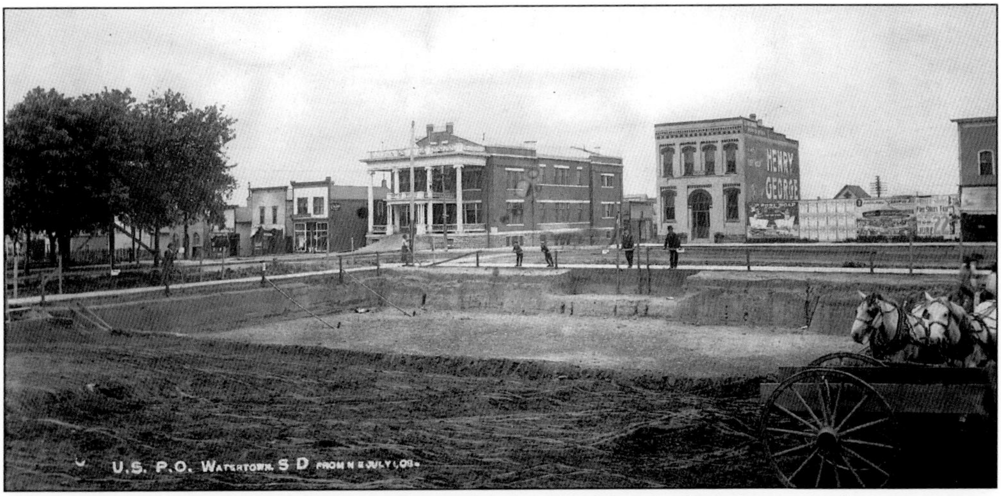

Excavation for the future U.S. Post Office and federal building had just begun at the intersection of Broadway and First Avenue South in this photo from July 1, 1908. Businesses visible on the west side of Broadway, according to a 1908 Dakota Central Telephone Company directory are, from right to left: Watertown Produce Company, Southwick Abstract Company, the Elks Lodge, and M.O. Poulson Pioneer Hardware.

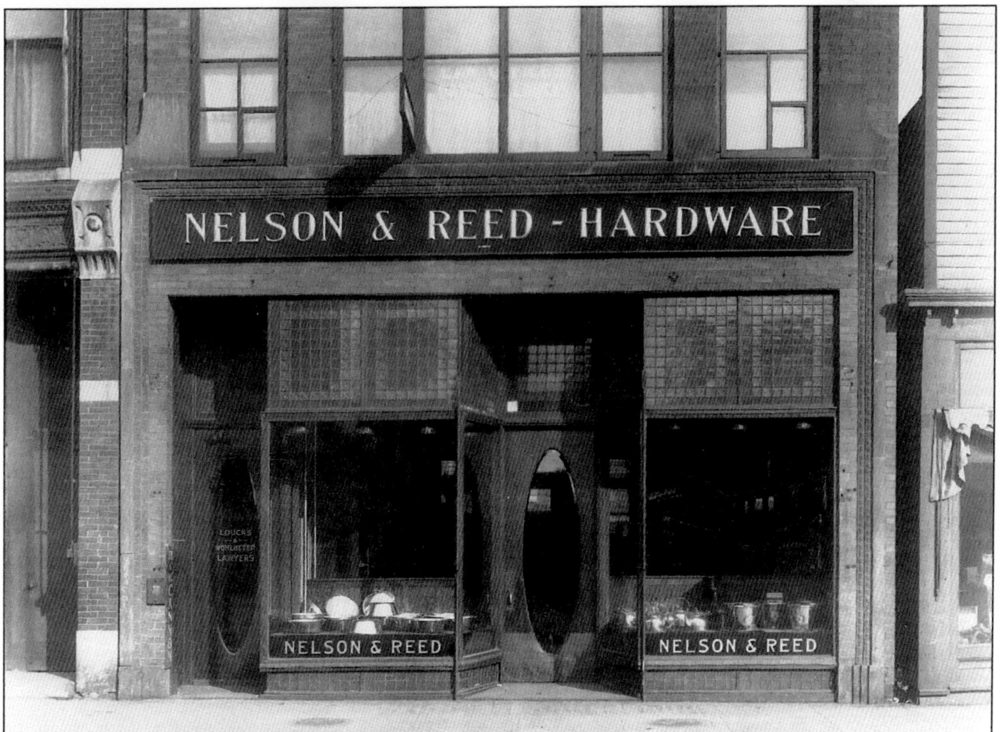

Andrew Nelson and Clyde Reed established Nelson & Reed Hardware, pictured in this photo from about 1922, on South Broadway in about 1914. The Nelson family took over the business in about 1946. Andrew's son Lyle closed the business in 1967. The building at 12 South Broadway is now home to the Kil-Rad Bar, another long-standing Watertown business.

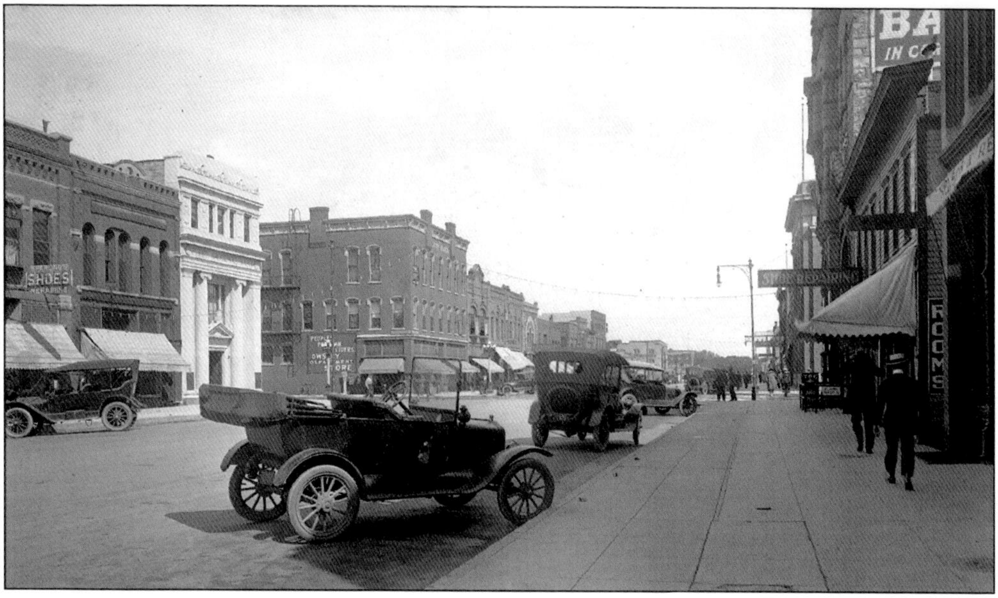

This view of Broadway from about 1920 faces northwest, toward the intersection with Kemp Avenue, and toward the Lamm or Mellette Block, home of the Midland National Life Insurance Company from 1917 to 1951. Midland was organized in 1906 as the Dakota Mutual Life Insurance Company, by six of Watertown's leading men: John B. Hanten, Dr. H.M. Finnerud, Mayor John W. Martin, D.M. Bannister, Frank L. Bramble, and W.B. Cannon. The white building to the left of the Lamm Block is the First National Bank, built in 1916. It became the Medical Arts building in April 1942. (Courtesy Bud and Arleen Larson.)

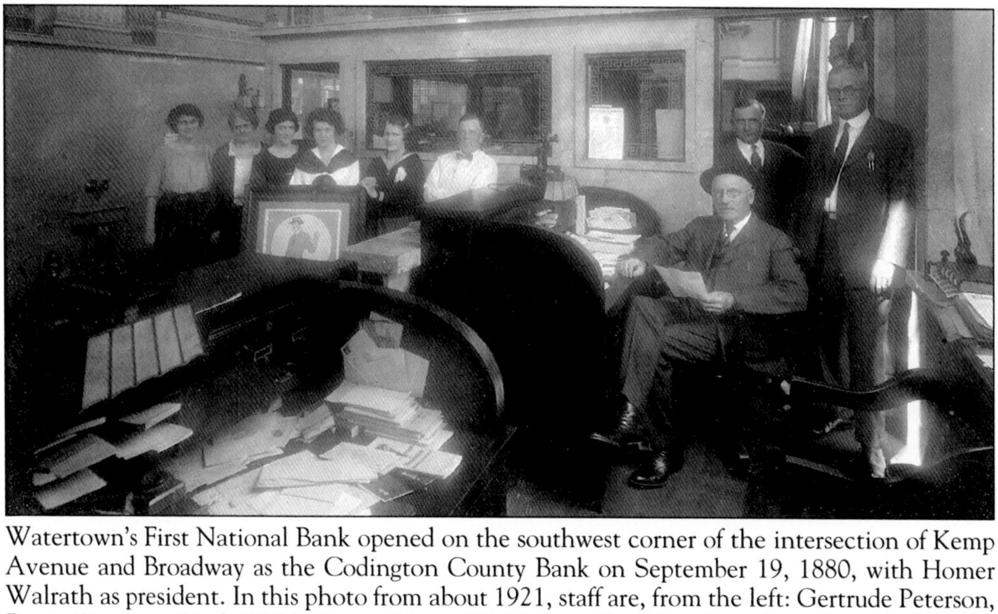

Watertown's First National Bank opened on the southwest corner of the intersection of Kemp Avenue and Broadway as the Codington County Bank on September 19, 1880, with Homer Walrath as president. In this photo from about 1921, staff are, from the left: Gertrude Peterson, Bessie Cosgrove, Ruth Wold, Norma Olson, Ella Nelson, Roy Uhrich, cashier Carroll Lockhart, Vice-President H.J. Fahnestock, and President H.D. Walrath (seated). Olson attended the South Dakota School of Business in Watertown, which turned out many quality workers for Watertown banks and other offices.

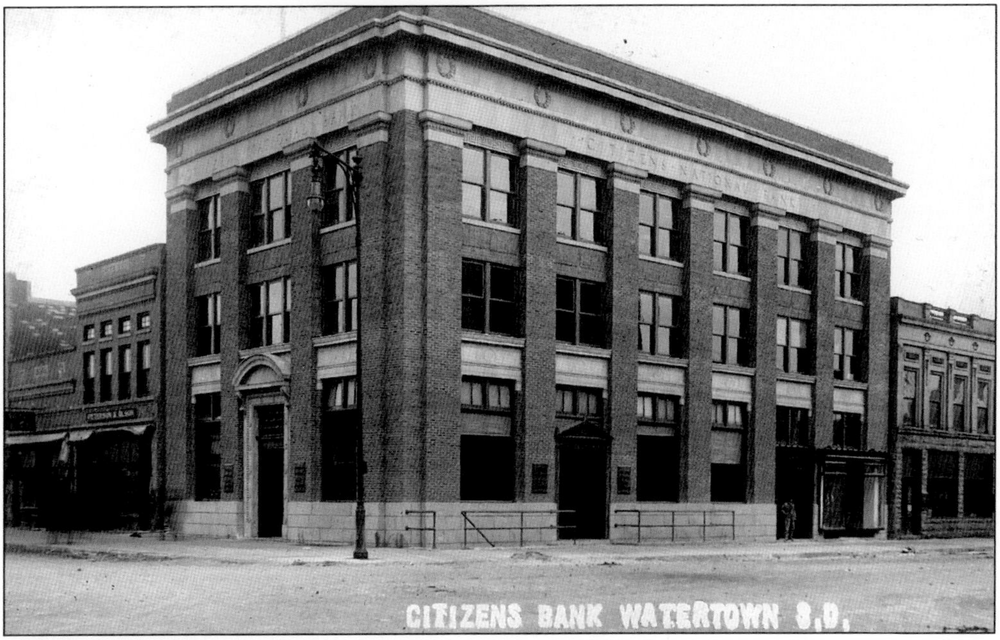

Construction began in 1913 for the Citizens National Bank at the northeast corner of the intersection of Kemp Avenue and Broadway, currently First Premier Bank. The new bank building replaced the H.F.W. Schaller Store building, originally built for the Rice Brothers general store in 1879.

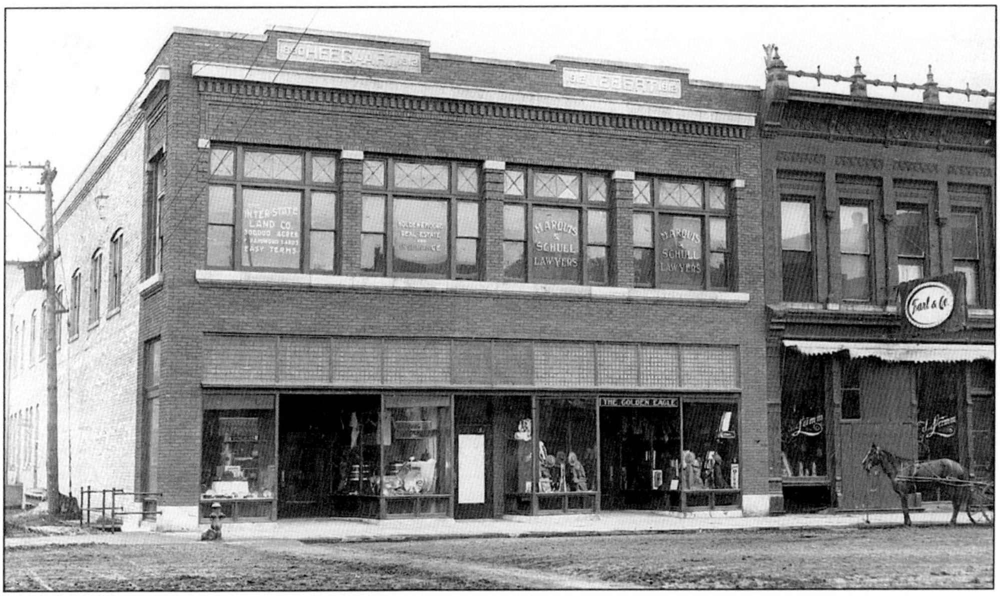

A fire in the Dockensdorf Meat Market at 112 North Broadway on April 28, 1912, practically destroyed it and the two-story Heegard & Company hardware store next door. M.A. Heegaard immediately replaced both fire-scarred frame stores with a fireproof brick building, in partnership with a man named Lebert. Both names can be seen in stone at the top of the building. By 1939, the Harbor Bar was operating in the north half of the building, and now occupies the entire main floor.

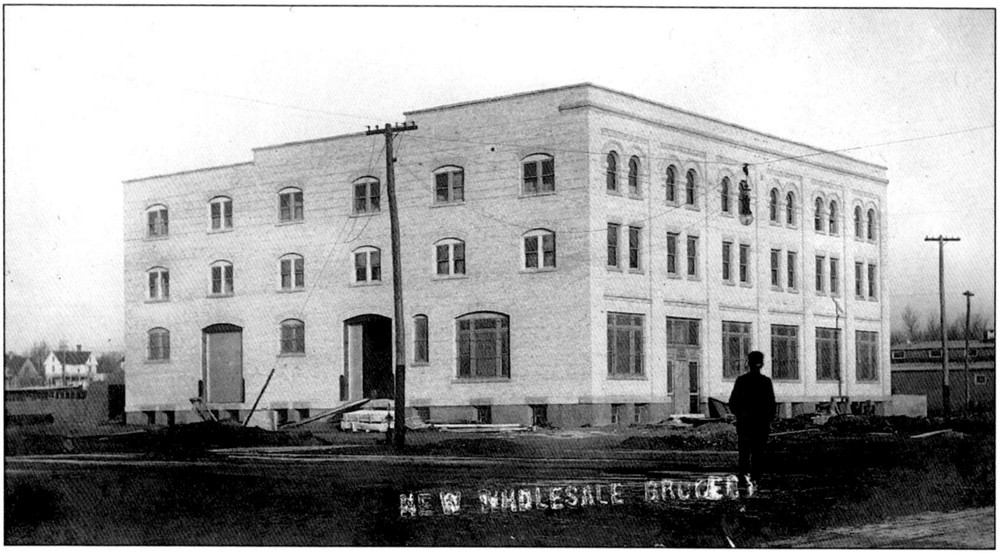

This warehouse was designed by Watertown architect Maurice Hockman, and constructed in 1910 for the Baskerville & Rowe wholesale grocery company. The Winslow-Griffin grocery company had taken over by 1914, but moved to Maple Street in 1932. Hurkes Implement occupied the building from the 1940s until 1967, and Stein Sign Company operated there in the 1970s. The building was remodeled and is now home to a restaurant and brewpub. (Courtesy Ken and Lyn Sheldon.)

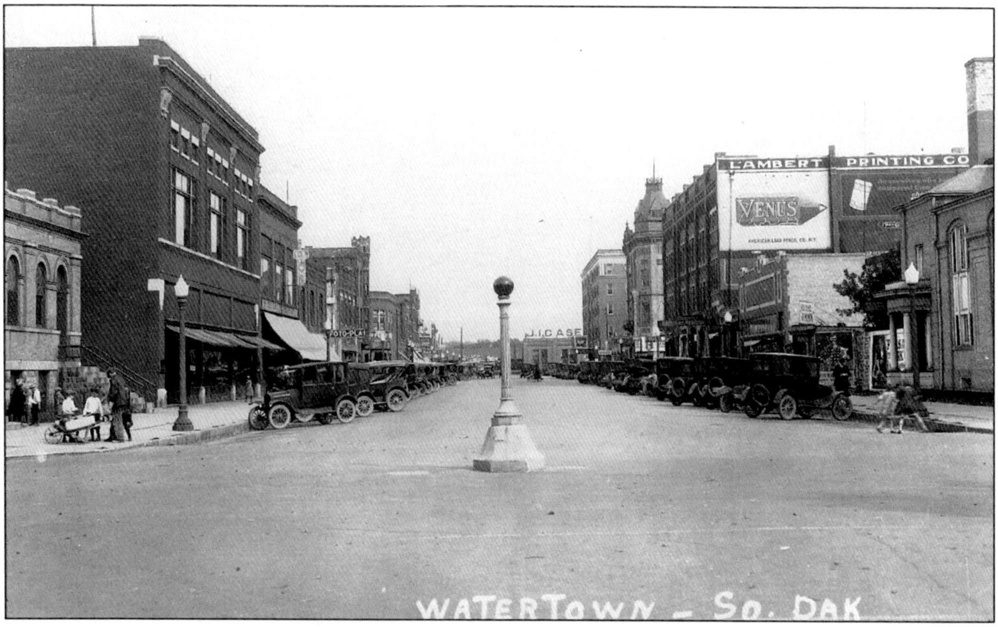

This postcard view of Maple Street, looking north from First Avenue South, dates to about 1920. The two-story building on the left was constructed in 1913 for the H.F.W. Schaller Department Store, which had its grand opening on March 20, 1914. Herberger's bought out Schaller in 1943. Pletan Furniture moved into the building in 1985, after Herberger's moved to the mall in 1978. Also visible in the photo is the Foto-Pla Theater, a few doors down from Schaller's, and the Lincoln Hotel, to the right of the J.I. Case sign. (Courtesy Ken and Lyn Sheldon.)

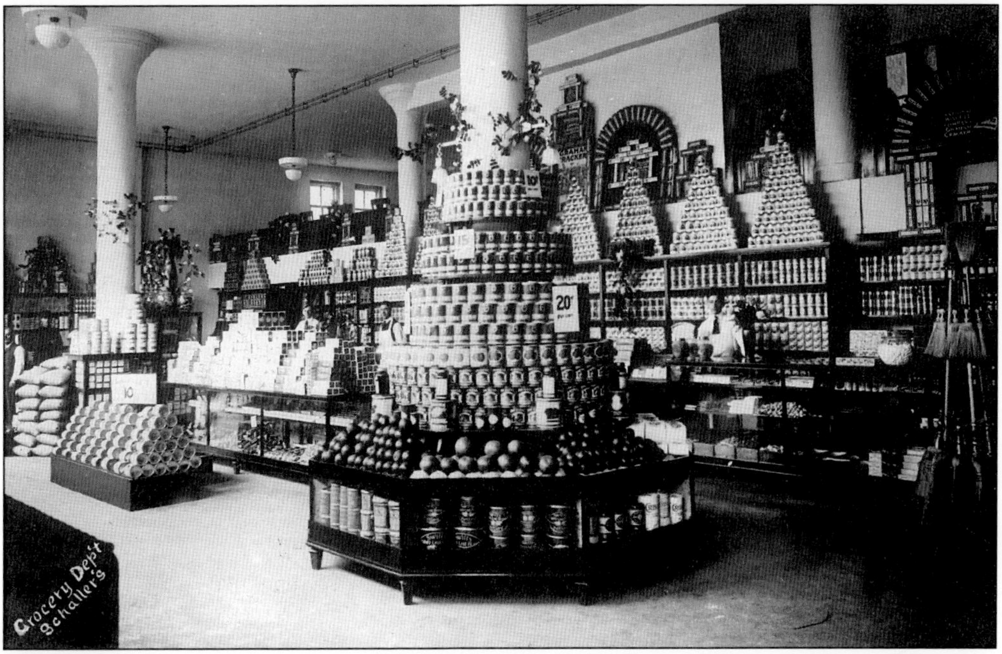

This photo of the Schaller Grocery Department was probably taken about 1910, when the store was located in the Rice Block on the northwest corner of the intersection of Kemp Avenue and Broadway. Many area residents remember the beauty of the Schaller store displays and products. Ida Mulholland, a buyer for the store from about 1914 to 1917, went to New York City to choose many fine product lines for the store. (Courtesy Ken and Lyn Sheldon.)

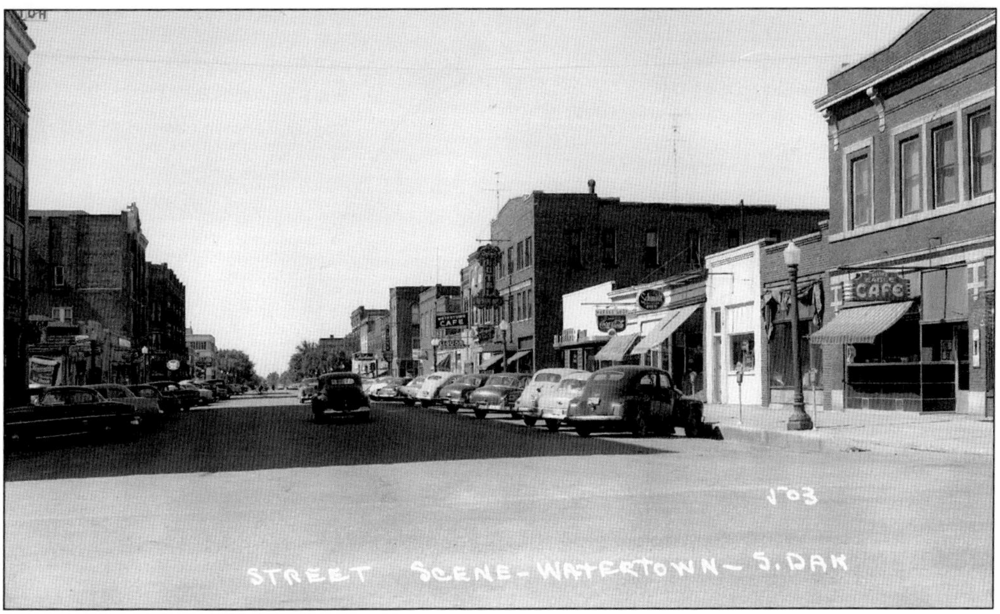

Maple Street, looking south from First Avenue North, about 1952, left to right: Reedy's Eagle Café, Watertown Amusement Company, Mint Liquor Store, Eagle Bar, Waffle Shop, Panatorium Dry Cleaners, Heck's Bar & Lounge, the New Grand Hotel, American Lunch & Billiards, Watertown Café, Cub Nut Hut, a barber shop, and Raschke Bar. (Courtesy Ken and Lyn Sheldon.)

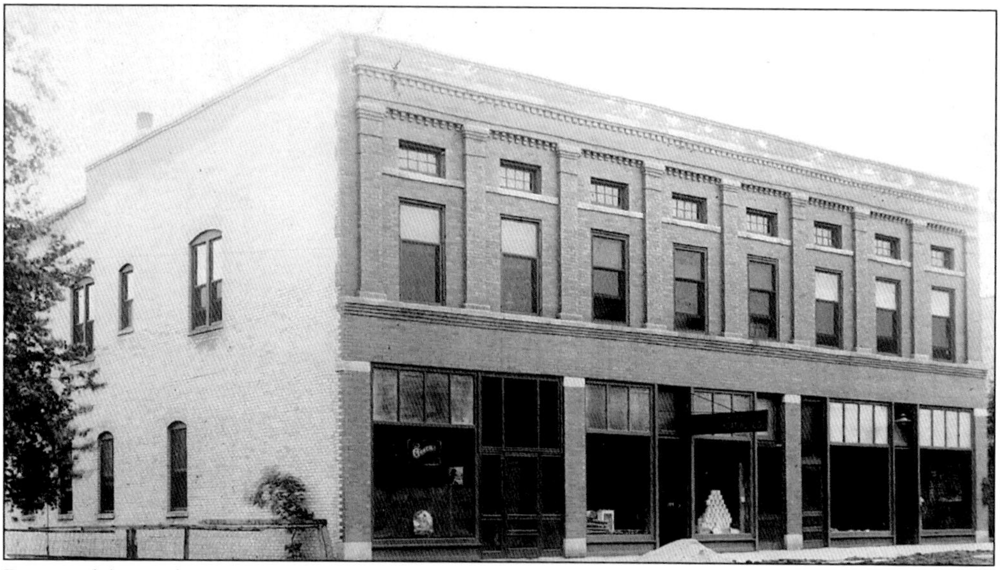

Designed by architect Maurice Hockman, the Smith, Schulner, & Lyon Block at 214–218 East Kemp Avenue was constructed in 1910 for the Louis Schulner Cigar Factory, F.L. Smith Plumbing, and Star Laundry operated by Charles Lyon. Today, Star Laundry is the only original occupant still in operation in the building.

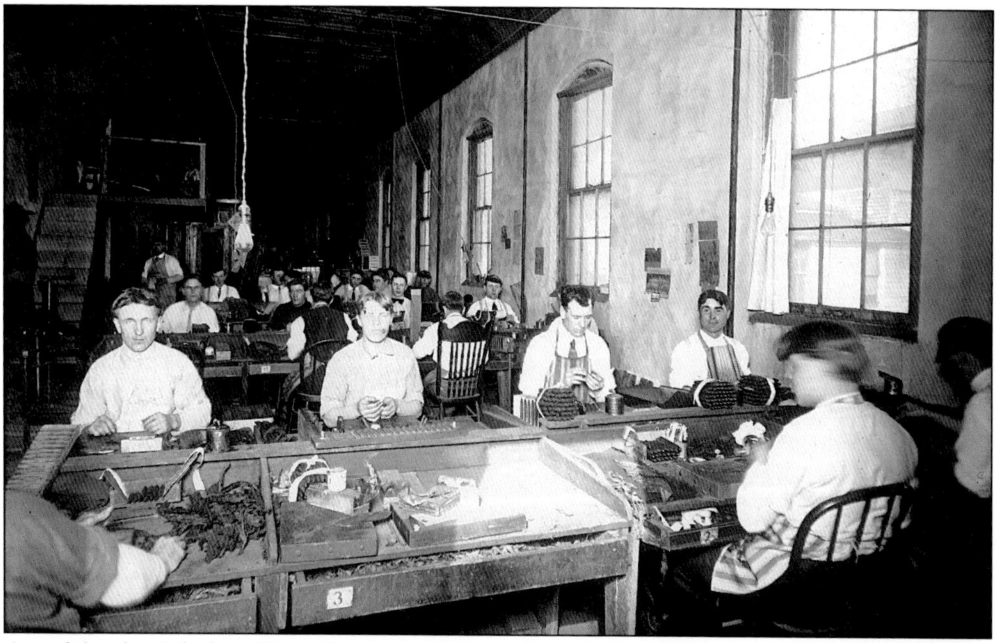

An ad for the Schulner Cigar Factory and its trademark cigar, the Council, in the December 15, 1910 *Public Opinion*, claimed 30 employees for the enterprise. In this undated photo of the Schulner factory, Peter Peterson is third from the left and fourth from left is Paul Krakowski, who started the Watertown Cigar Factory in the 1920s. Cigar manufacturers were a common business in most mid-to-large-size communities in South Dakota, into the 1930s. Watertown had four cigar factories in 1916, and the February 23, 1917 *Public Opinion*, urged St. Patrick's Day celebrants to use local cigars.

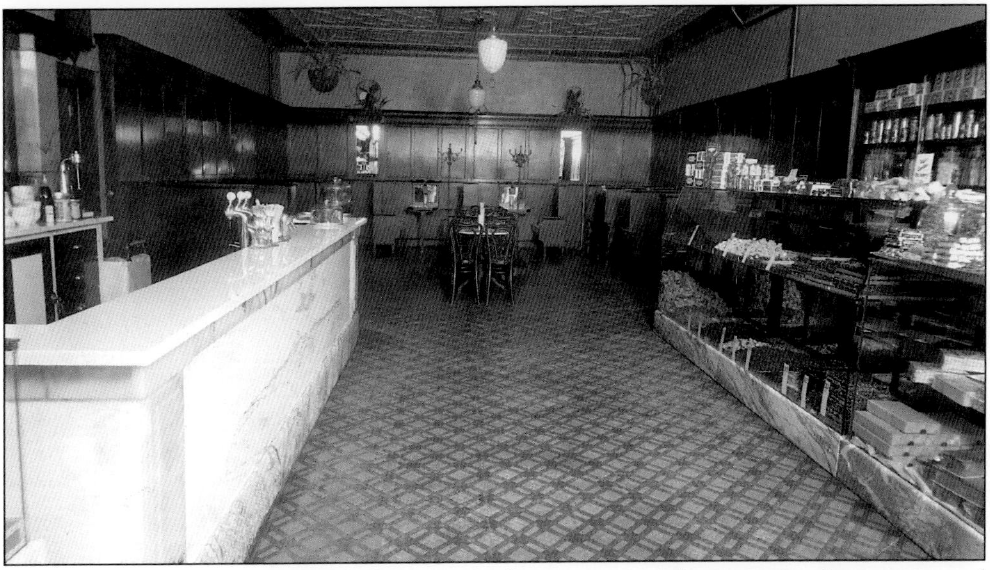

The Sugar Bowl, in this undated photo, was a favorite among the many confectioneries and soda fountains in Watertown. Nick Govis operated the Sugar Bowl at 12 East Kemp Avenue from about 1914 until the early 1920s, when it was succeeded by the well-remembered Palace of Sweets, run by Peter Govis at 14 East Kemp. Sam Latsis soon took over and operated the Palace of Sweets until 1957, though it did make a brief comeback from 1972 until 1975.

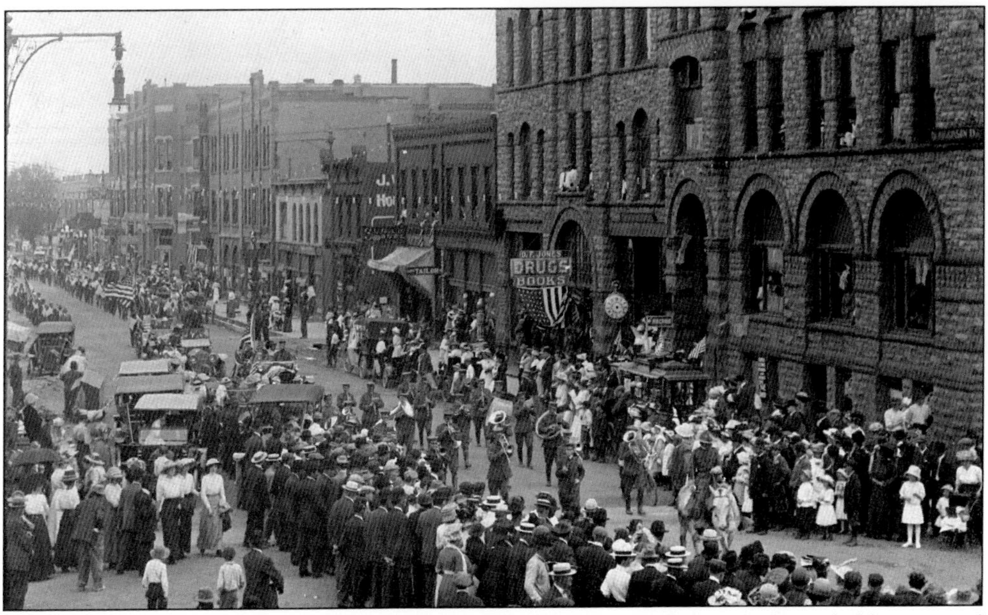

This parade on Kemp Avenue, viewed looking east from the Mellette Block, probably occurred about 1915. The "Drugs" sign in the center of the photo belonged to the D.F. Jones drug store, which had moved to the other side of the street by 1916. The large quartzite stone building on the right is called the Granite Block, and was constructed for the Dakota Loan & Trust Company in 1887. Renowned attorney and state legislator John B. Hanten helped finance the building that is still standing on the southeast corner of the intersection of Kemp Avenue and Broadway, and is one of the most significant historic buildings in the city of Watertown.

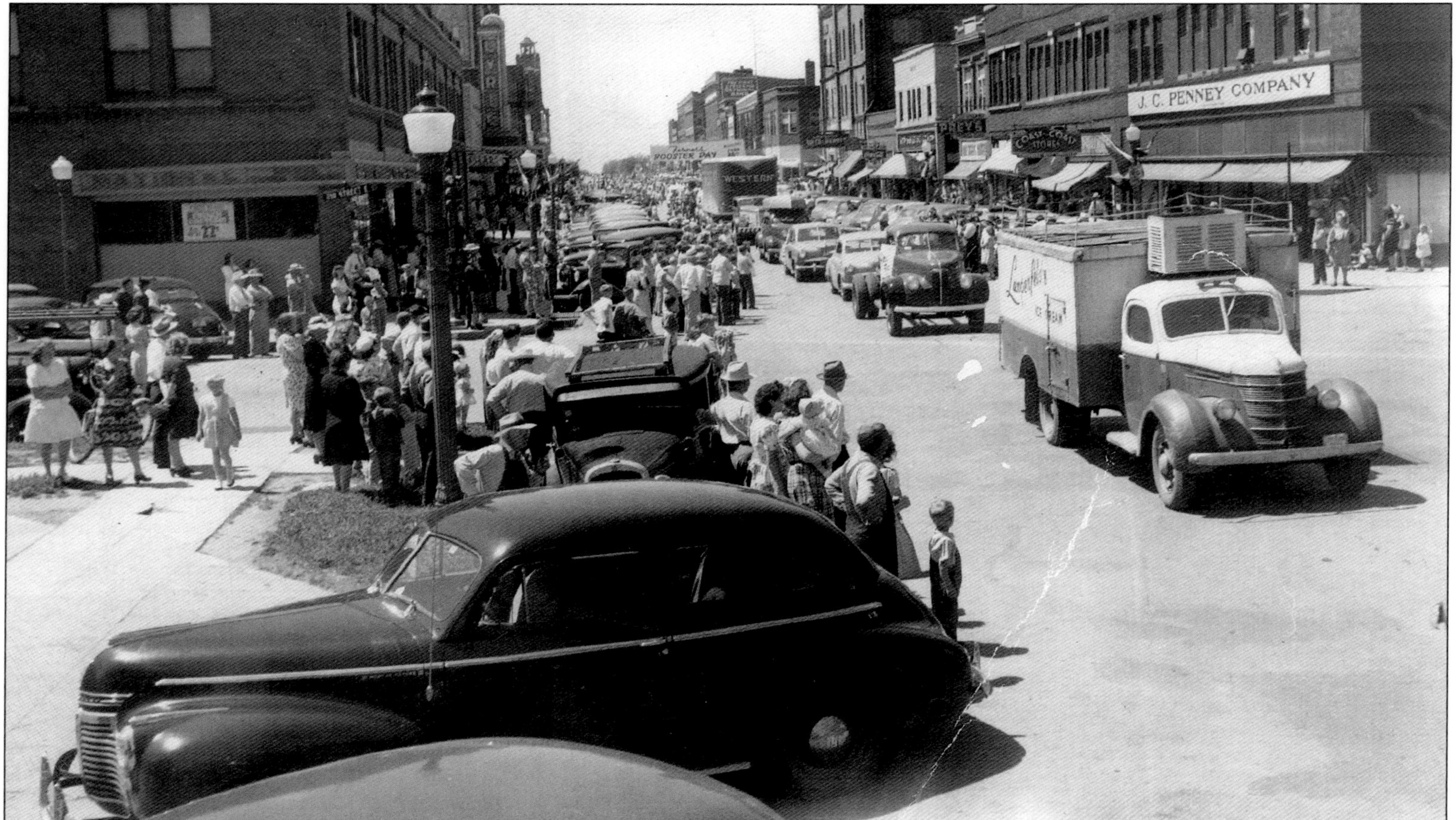

Kemp Avenue was the site of this Farmer's Booster Day parade in the late 1940s. The ice cream truck on the right, at the intersection of Second Street East (running left to right in the photo), belonged to the Langenfeld Ice Cream Company, which moved to Watertown in 1918 from Belle Plaine, Minnesota. The company occupied several different sites throughout the years, until it closed August 31, 1966.

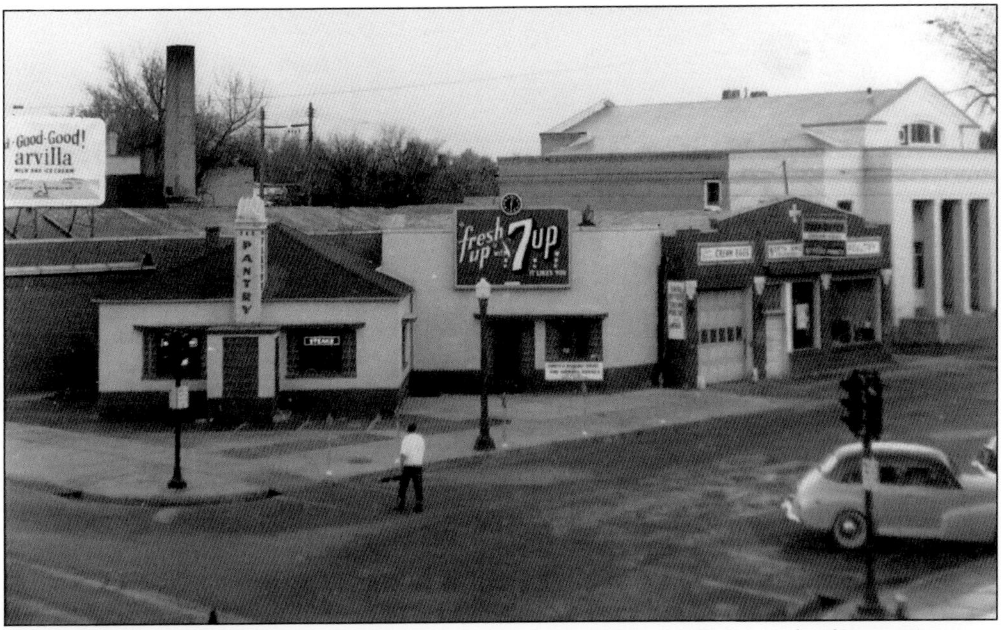

The businesses in this 1940s view of the east side of Second Street East, south of Kemp Avenue, are, from left to right: the Pantry Café, North American Creameries cream station, and Mathiesen, Gergen, & Rhodes Funeral Chapel. The Pantry Café building was originally the Crystal Service gas station, which advertised in 1926 as having a ladies' rest room and tourist information. The Pantry was in operation until 1963. The funeral chapel was originally built for the Presbyterian Church.

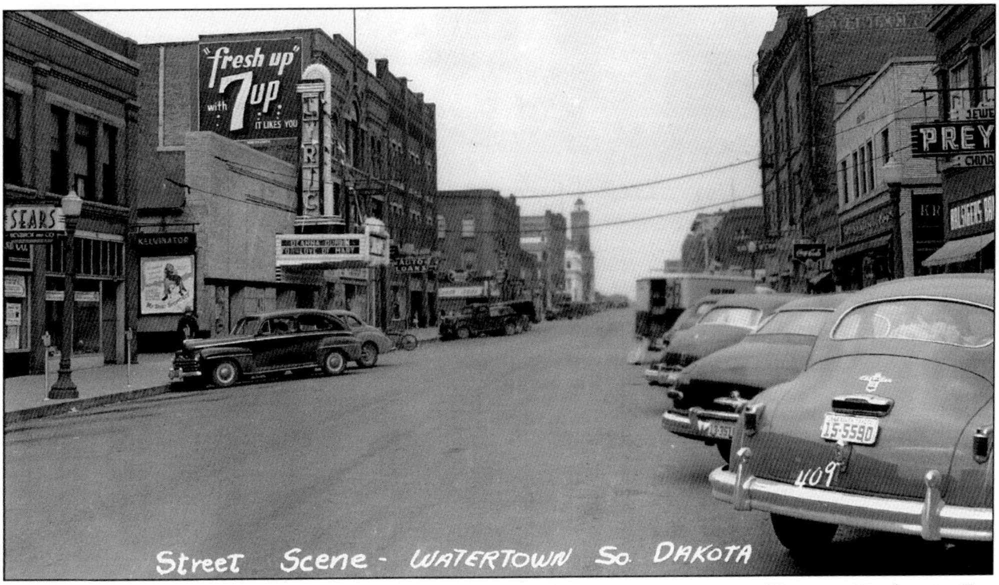

The marquee of the Lyric Theater at 110 East Kemp Avenue is promoting Deanna Durbin in *For Love of Mary* in this view of Kemp Avenue, looking west from around Second Street East in about 1948. The Lyric Theater was remodeled in the 1940s, but closed in the early 1960s. Osco Drug was there from 1965 until 1978, and the building now serves Klein's crafts and framing. The second building from the right in this photo postcard was formerly the Larson clothing store.

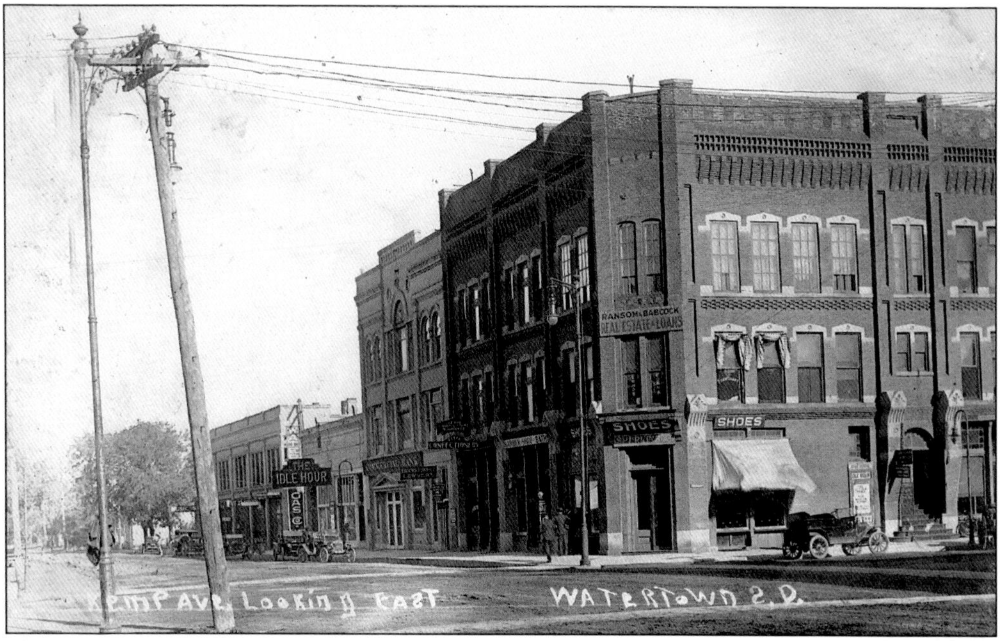

The Goss Block in this view of the south side of Kemp Avenue east of Maple Street from about 1911, was one of the two early opera houses in Watertown, and still stands at the southeast corner of the intersection of Kemp Avenue and Maple Street. It was built in 1888 by druggist Charles Goss to replace the original frame building destroyed by fire in 1887. Many concerts and plays were staged in the beautiful theater on the second and third floors, which was later used as a roller-skating rink. Robert Kreiser's Rexall Drug Store was the longest-standing business in the corner storefront, from about 1914 until 1991. (Courtesy Ken and Lyn Sheldon.)

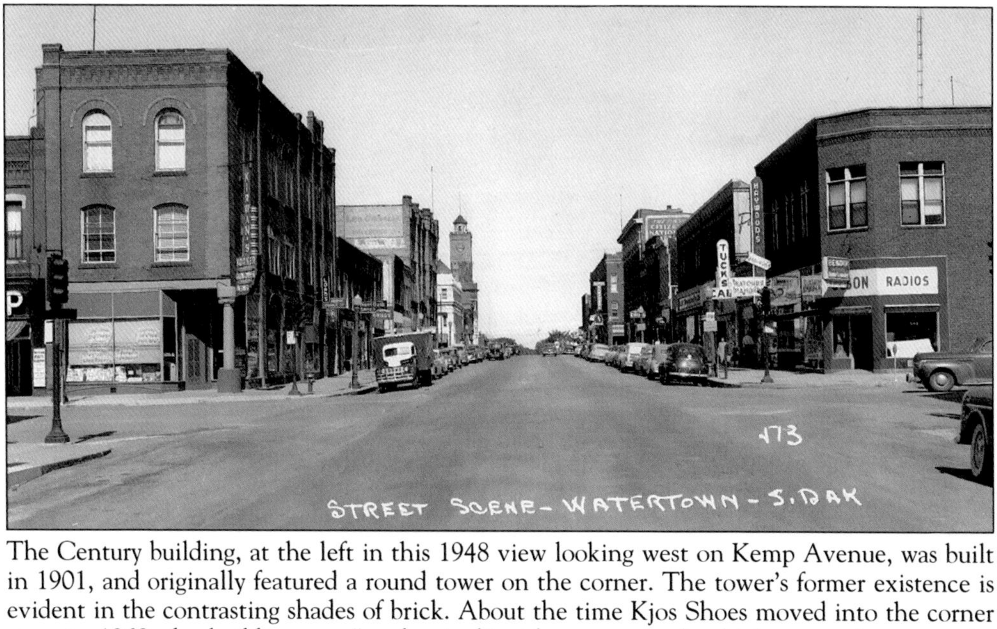

The Century building, at the left in this 1948 view looking west on Kemp Avenue, was built in 1901, and originally featured a round tower on the corner. The tower's former existence is evident in the contrasting shades of brick. About the time Kjos Shoes moved into the corner store in 1968, the building was "modernized" with green metal, which currently covers the entire facade. (Courtesy Ken and Lyn Sheldon.)

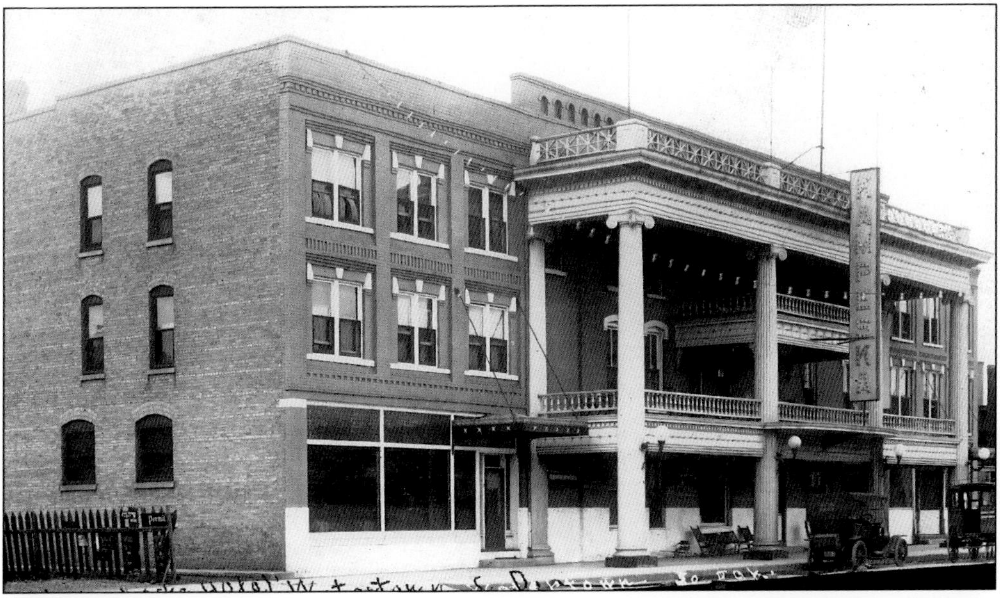

C.C. Wiley constructed the Kampeska House in 1878 at the first site of Watertown, which was at the terminus of the Winona & St. Peter Railroad at Lake Kampeska. The original frame hotel building was moved to the new town site in 1880, on Dakota Avenue, or First Avenue North. As one of the largest structures in the infant settlement it was used for the county courthouse, church services, and town hall. The frame building was soon replaced with brick, and an elaborate pillared porch was added to the hotel in 1906. The Kampeska was the preferred site for many formal club dinners and meetings over the years, until it was razed in April of 1966 to make room for one of several off-street parking lots planned for Uptown Watertown.

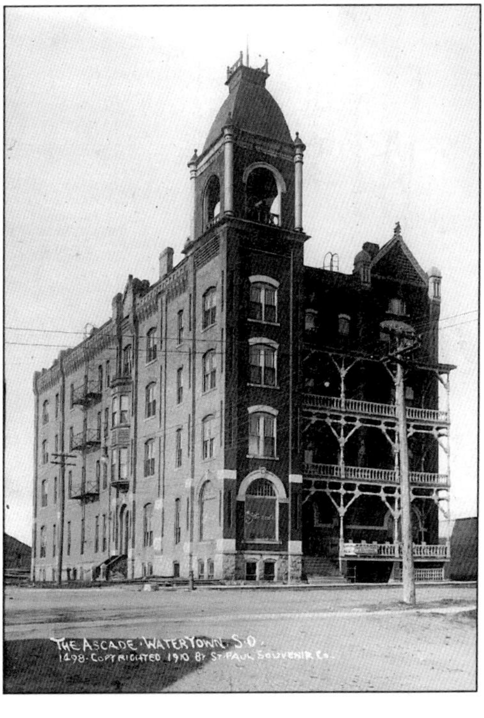

The Arcade Hotel was the vision of a group of men dubbed the "Big Seven," which included C.M. Cannon, Dr. S.W. Stutenroth, C.C. Whistler, and brothers W.R. and D.C. Thomas, and F.G. and Ed Rice. The hotel, which opened grandly on October 10, 1888, was constructed on the northeast corner of the intersection of Kemp Avenue and Second Street West, at a cost of $75,000, triple the planned budget for the structure. Yet, less than 50 years after its opening, the hotel was condemned, and demolition began in 1933. Ernest Cave purchased the property and saved most of the first floor, parts of which are visible in the building Cave built, which is still in use by the family automotive supply company. (Courtesy Ken and Lyn Sheldon.)

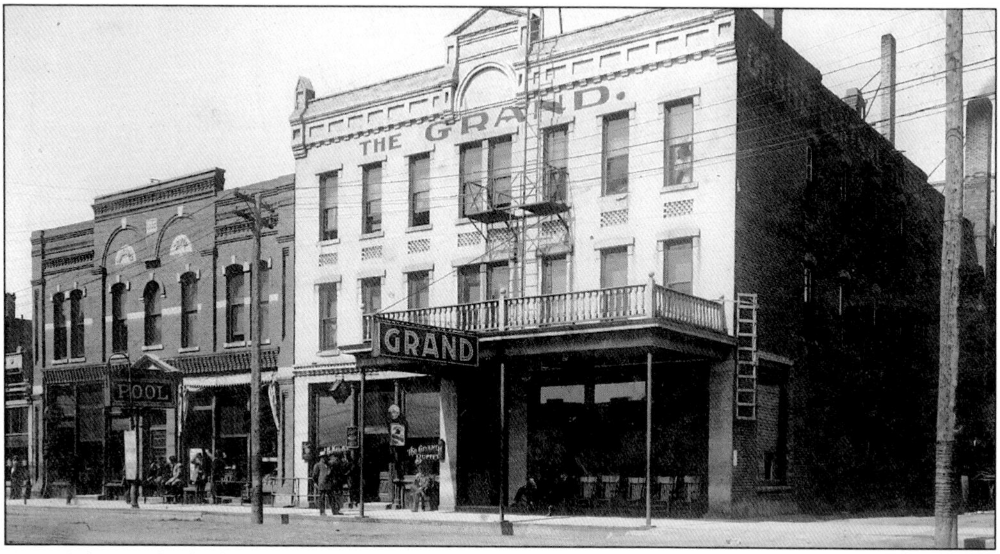

Hans Johnson built the Grand Hotel on North Maple Street in 1886. The hotel changed hands many times, and finally housed a dormitory for the Watertown Business University, before a fire destroyed it. The building to the left of the hotel, on this postcard postmarked August 19, 1910, was constructed for the O.E. Dewey drug store, also in 1886. It once housed the Maple Leaf Café, operated by Cliff and Kathryn Sanders from about 1930 until 1945. Orville Taecker, the current owner, restored the north half of the building after a 1970s fire, but was forced to replace the south half which was too damaged to repair. (Courtesy Ken and Lyn Sheldon.)

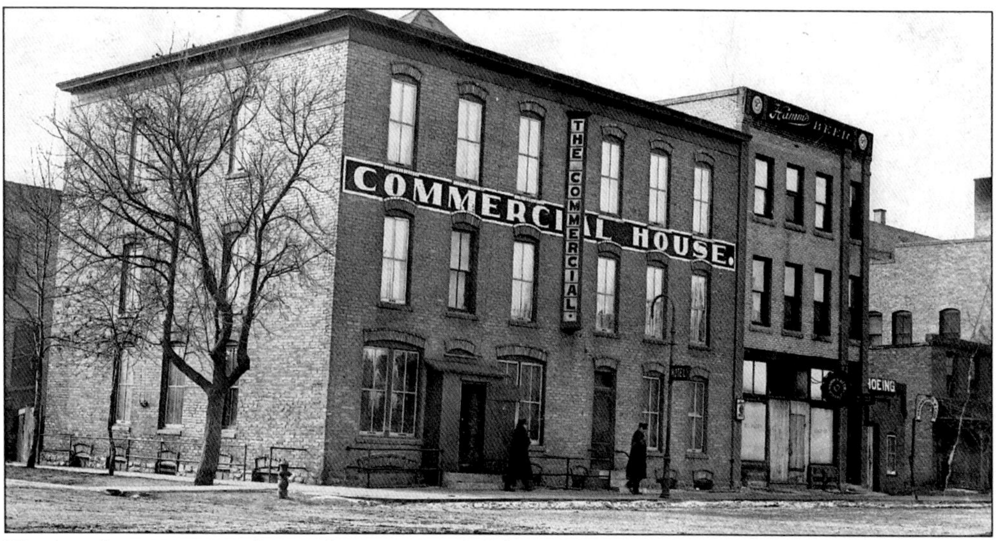

The hotel structure on the southwest corner of the intersection of Second Street East and First Avenue North, on this undated postcard, is pictured here as the Commercial House, but had many names throughout the years. In 1886, Frederick Jones built it as the Jones Hotel, but by 1901, the name was changed to the Commercial House. The hotel became the Royal about 1927, but became the Travelers Inn from 1932 until about 1939. The Public Opinion newspaper company next door then used the building for many years, until it moved to Third Avenue Northwest. The City of Watertown then took the Public Opinion's place, and remodeled the buildings for use as a City Hall.

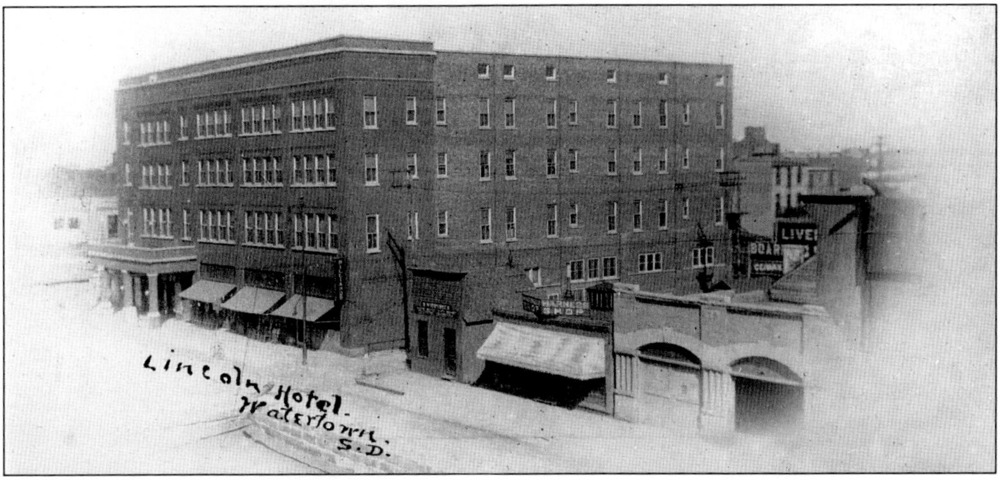

The Lincoln Hotel is probably the best-known hotel in the history of Watertown, and is also considered the last hotel built in Watertown's golden hotel era. Construction of the building started in 1910 on North Maple Street as the new home for the Schaller Department Store, but plans changed and the Metropolitan Theater—a first-class theater modeled after the Metropolitan Opera Theater in New York City—opened on St. Patrick's Day 1911. The new Lincoln Hotel, promoted as "absolutely fireproof," opened shortly after in 1912. A fifth floor was added several years later, giving the hotel a total of 150 Rooms, 70 of which had private bathrooms, a luxury at the time. The hotel closed in 1970, and the solid brick building was demolished in October of 1972.

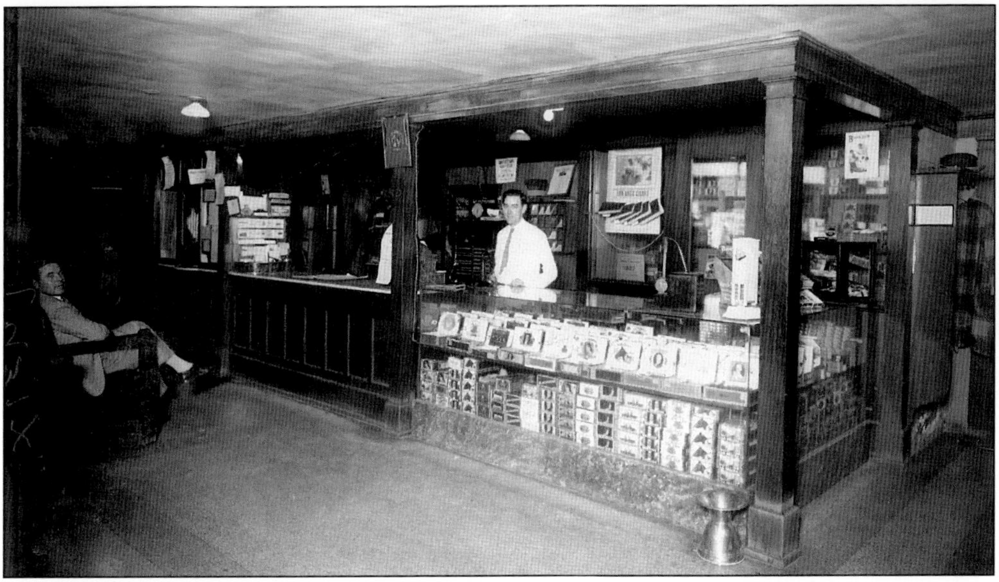

Jerry Drake, pictured here about 1927, at the Lincoln Hotel registration desk and cigar counter, began his career at the Lincoln in about 1916 shifting scenery at the Metropolitan Theater. Drake worked at the hotel until 1940, eventually making assistant manager. In 1937, however, Drake, Al Steinmetz, and Frank Bramble bought the Dakota Warehouse, opening a locker plant there in 1938. Drake bought his partners' interests in 1940 and moved the locker facilities north of the Lincoln Hotel, which was convenient for the many out-of-town hunters who stayed at the Lincoln who needed to freeze their game. Drake soon needed to expand his facilities and bought two lots in south Watertown, near the current junction of U.S. Highways 212 and 81.

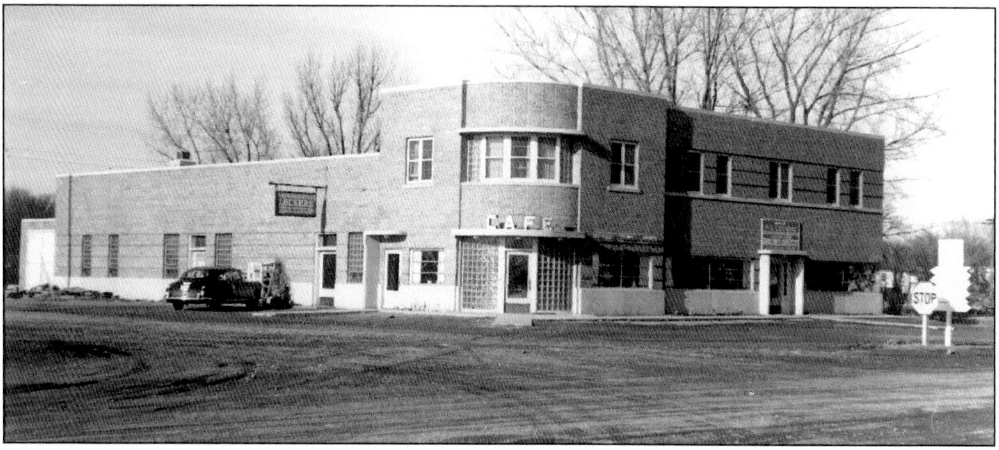

When Jerry Drake moved his locker business to the south part of Watertown, he expanded it to five plants and named it the K-D Locker Plant, which is pictured in this snapshot from about 1950. The advent of home freezers soon made the lockers obsolete, however, so Drake remodeled the plant and opened the Drake Motor Inn July 6, 1956.

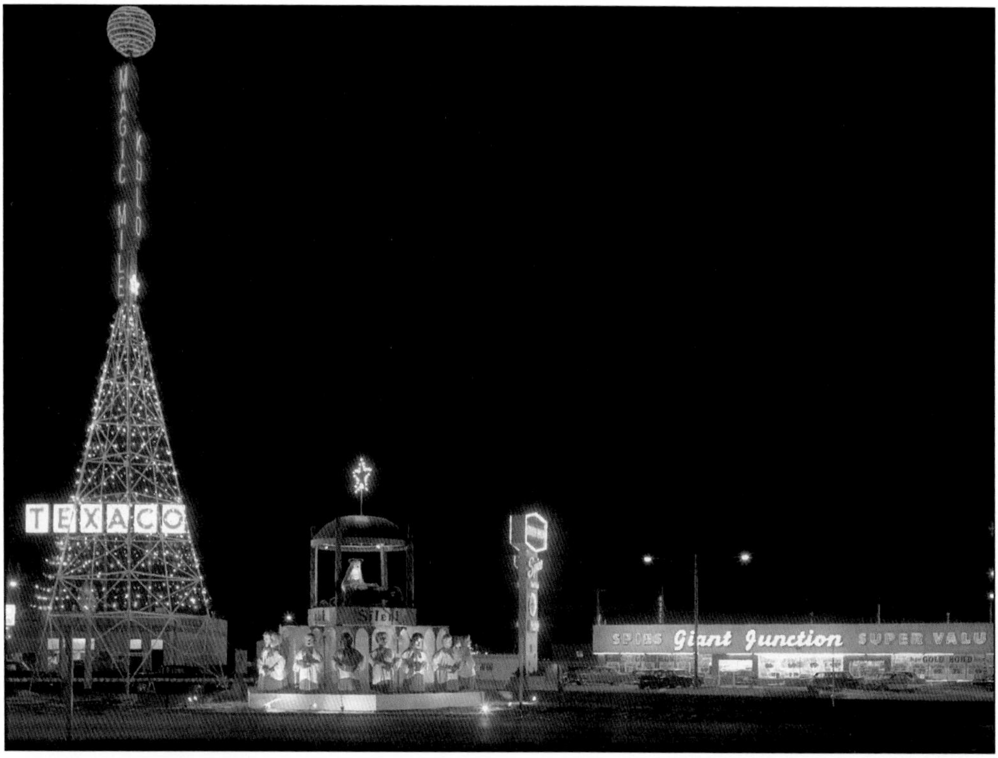

As owner of one of the first businesses on the new corridor of U.S. Highway 212 south of Watertown (the highway previously ran on Kemp Avenue), in the 1950s Jerry Drake spearheaded the Magic Mile Association, which was instrumental in getting Highway 212 widened for better traffic flow. Many new businesses soon sprouted along the major transportation route, and other Watertown businesses, such as the Spies grocery store, moved their businesses from other parts of town to the highway. Spies opened the Giant Junction Super Valu, pictured here at the junction of U.S. Highways 212 and 81 in December of 1962.

Two

Civil Servants and Structures

In the settling of a city, civil structures were some of the first buildings to be constructed. They were typically grandiose buildings that supposedly symbolized the city and demonstrated to visitors and potential residents that the city and county were progressive. In early photographs, they are usually the tallest and biggest buildings in the skyline. Watertown and Codington County were no different. The original Codington County Courthouse was built in 1884. It was razed in 1927 and replaced with a larger building on the same site. The original City Hall was built in 1889 and razed in 1974. The current City Hall is in the former Watertown Public Opinion building on the corner of Second Street East and First Avenue North. The original post office building was abandoned when a new building was built in 1975. The post office building is still standing and is listed on the National Register of Historic Places unlike the original courthouse and city hall. The original library building, the Carnegie Public Library, was built in 1906 and served as the library until 1968. It is currently home to the Codington County Historical Society and Heritage Museum and is also listed on the National Register of Historic Places.

This section pays tribute to the buildings and those hard-working men and women who toil daily with the operation of government business and serve our country in the military.

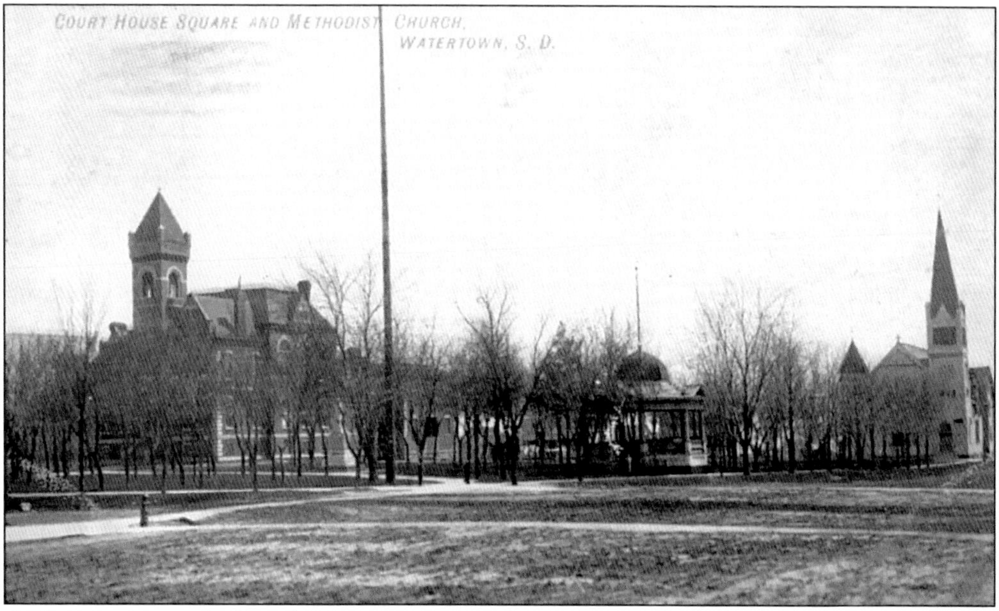

Codington County built its first permanent courthouse, pictured at left on this postcard, in 1884. The county began planning and budgeting for a new courthouse in 1918. The old courthouse pictured here was razed in 1927 to make room for construction of the new courthouse on the same site.

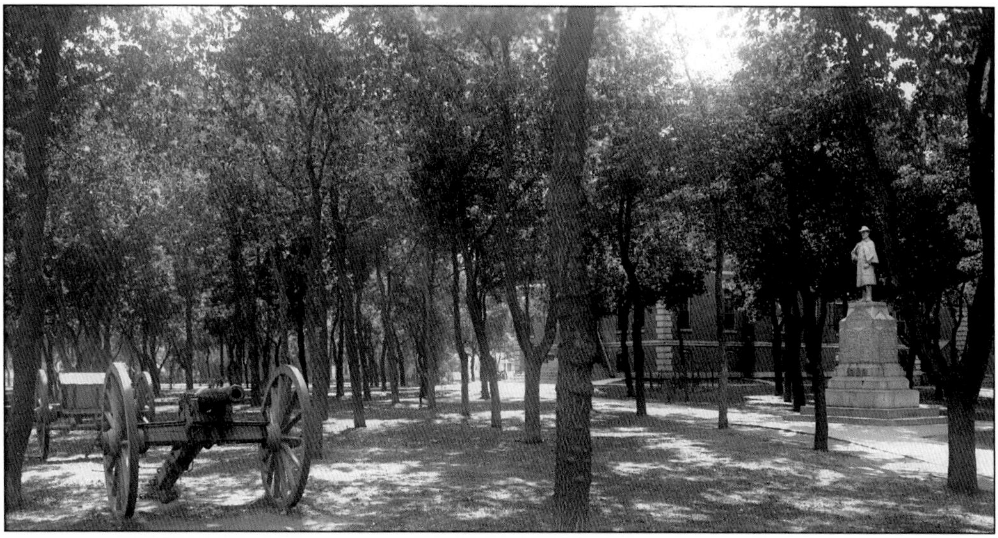

According to an article in the May 26, 1979 edition of the *Watertown Public Opinion*, the cannons in this undated photo postcard of the Codington County Courthouse yard first belonged to a National Guard unit based in Clark in the late 1800s. Just before 1900, the unit decided the pieces were no longer needed, so both were given to the Chief of Ordnance, who was located in Watertown at that time. The cannons were displayed on the Codington County Courthouse lawn for several years. One of the cannons was eventually moved to Mitchell, South Dakota. The other was moved to Mount Hope Cemetery, and was displayed there until 1975. The statue on the postcard, at right, was dedicated in 1900 to honor the members of Company H who fought in the Spanish-American War. (Courtesy Ken and Lyn Sheldon.)

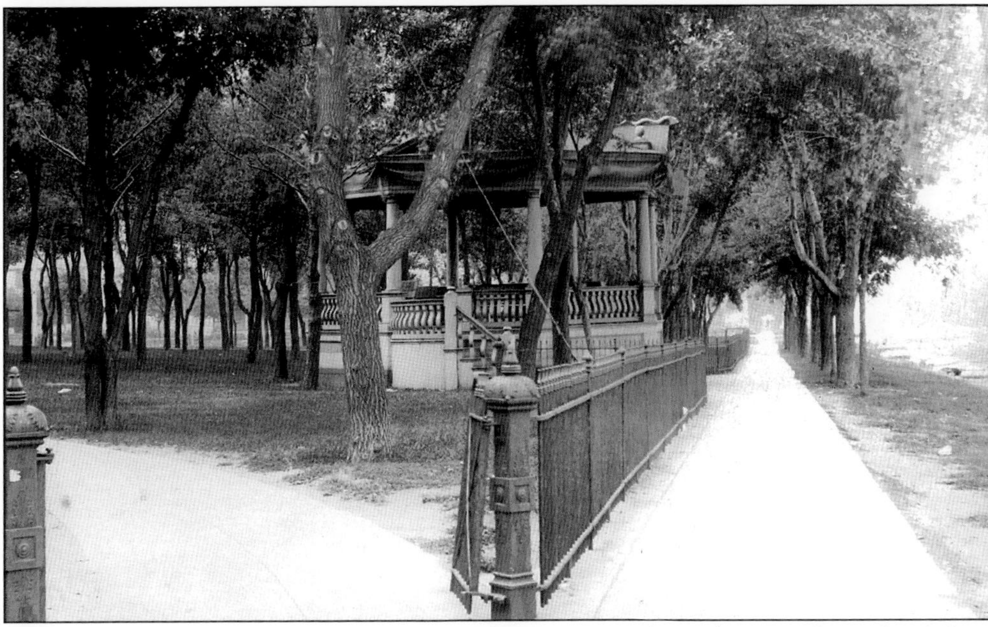

The bandstand on the west side of the Codington County Courthouse lawn, on this undated photo postcard, was a landmark for many years, until it was moved to the Stokes-Thomas City Park at Lake Kampeska. Watertown bands reportedly gave two concerts per week there in the summer, when the bandstand was in the courthouse square. (Courtesy Bud and Arleen Larson.)

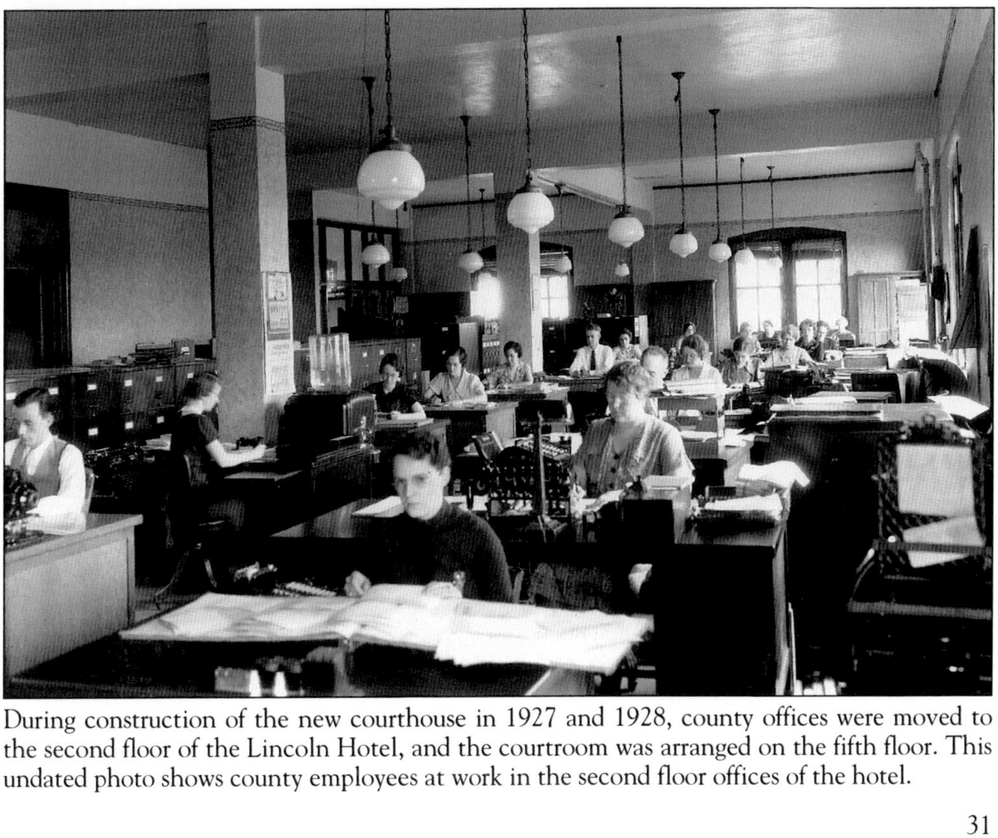

During construction of the new courthouse in 1927 and 1928, county offices were moved to the second floor of the Lincoln Hotel, and the courtroom was arranged on the fifth floor. This undated photo shows county employees at work in the second floor offices of the hotel.

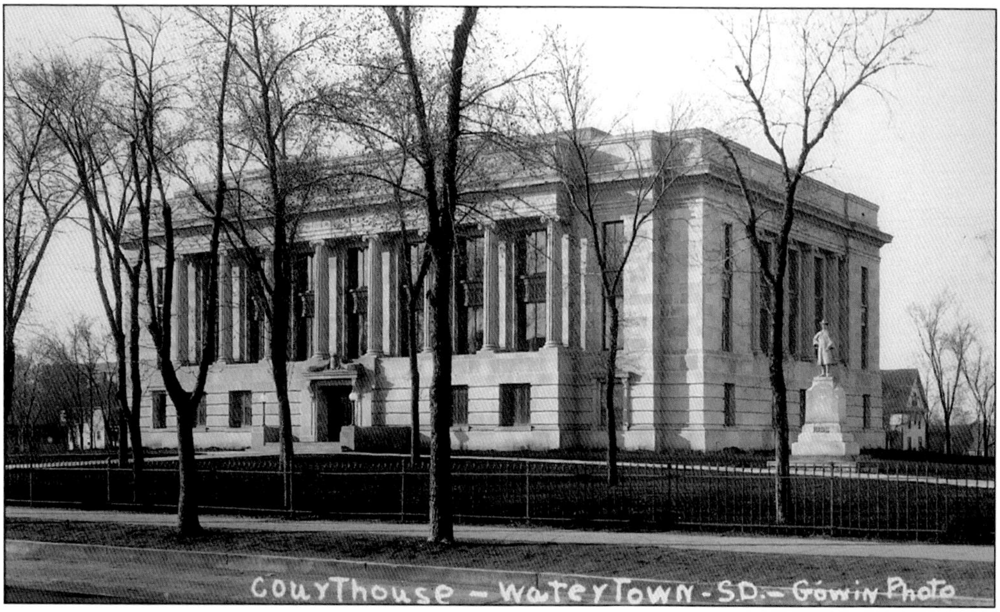

The new Codington County Courthouse was dedicated in festivities stretching over two days, June 19 and 20, 1929. Watertown's Gray Construction Company paired with the architectural firm Freed, Perkins, & McWayne of Sioux Falls to construct the neoclassic courthouse of white Indiana limestone. Artist Vincent Adoratti of New York City was hired to do the two paintings in the cathedral glass-domed rotunda representing "Justice and Power" and "Wisdom and Mercy." The courthouse features brass railings and fixtures, marble hallways, and terrazzo and marble floors.

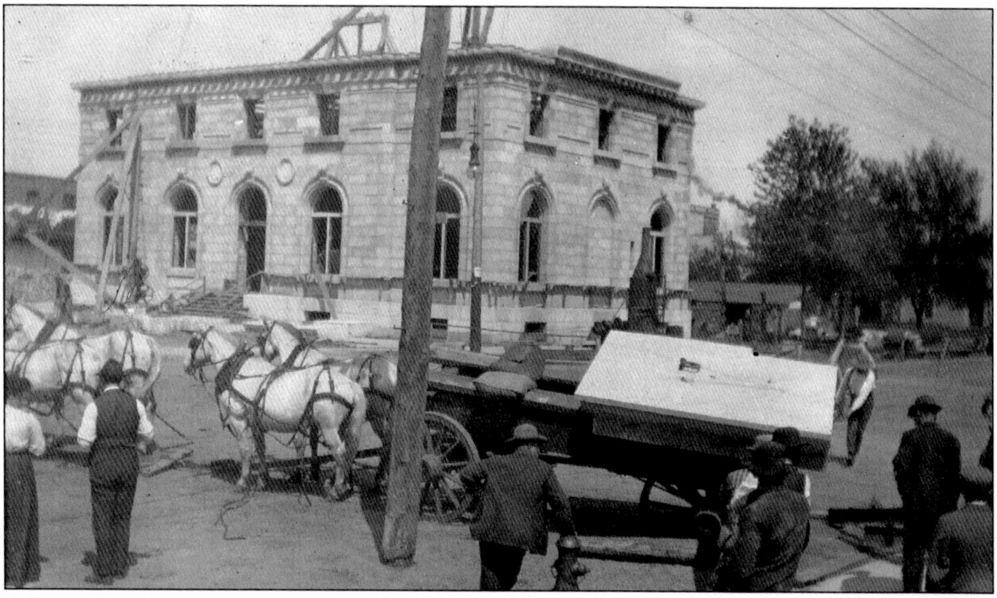

After years of renting space in other business buildings, the United States Postal Service began construction of a new post office in Watertown in 1908. The new post office was constructed of Bedford stone on the northeast corner of the intersection of Broadway and First Avenue North, and cost $90,000. This photo of the ongoing construction in about May of 1909, shows a stone slab for the roof cornice on a horse-drawn wagon.

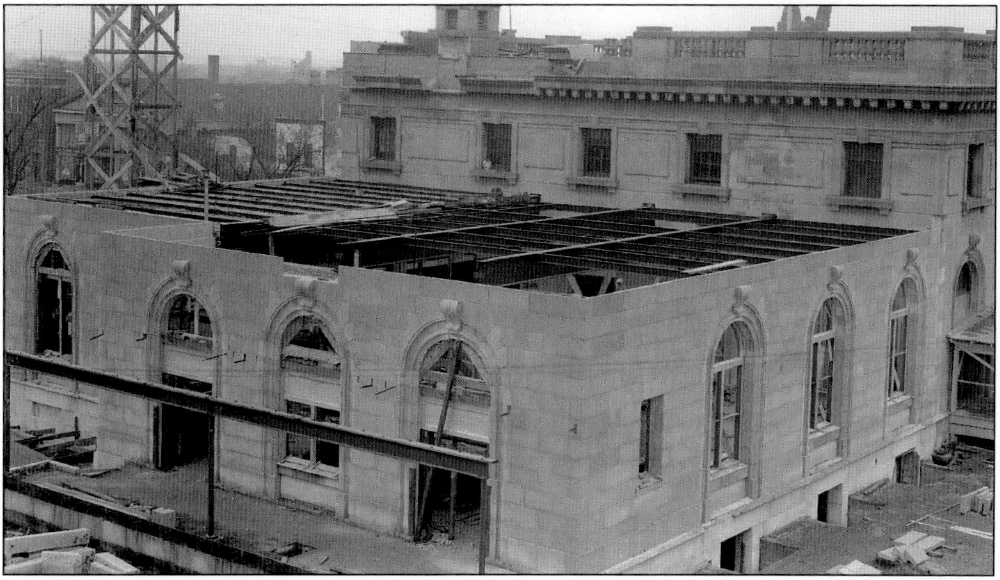

Construction of an addition to the east of the U.S. Post Office began in November 1932 and finished October 1933. This photo shows the state of construction on May 1, 1933. The post office outgrew the building, and moved into its current home, built on East Kemp Avenue, in 1976.

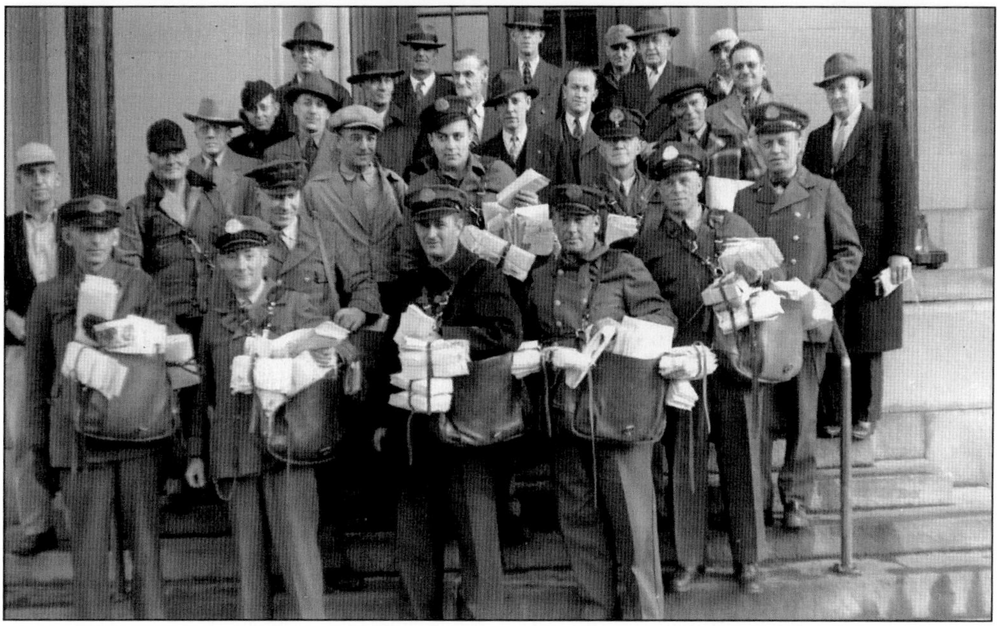

The November 22, 1945 edition of the *Watertown News-Reminder* paper featured this photo and the headline, "'Please Mail Early' Urge These Watertown Postal Workers." The workers, from left to right, top to bottom, were identified as: Carl Lindgren, Jesse Thorpe, Jesse Vincent, Ray Hayford, Leo Craney, Guy Smart, Nic Weber, Jack Lester, George Miller, Wilbur Bartlett, Bill Fish, Lawrence Schiltz, Fred Fehn, Frank Vaux, Paul Dahlberg, Guy Peterson, Verne Wagner, Charley King, Kyle Roe, Glenn Breim, Paul Pitt, George Telleckson, Al Lowry, Harry Blinkensop, Raleigh Gordon, Herb Franklin, Glenn Watkins, Tony Ludzvick. Others employees not in the picture were Alvin White, Bernard Hurd, Homer Kreger, Paul Born, Chet Irwin, George Breim.

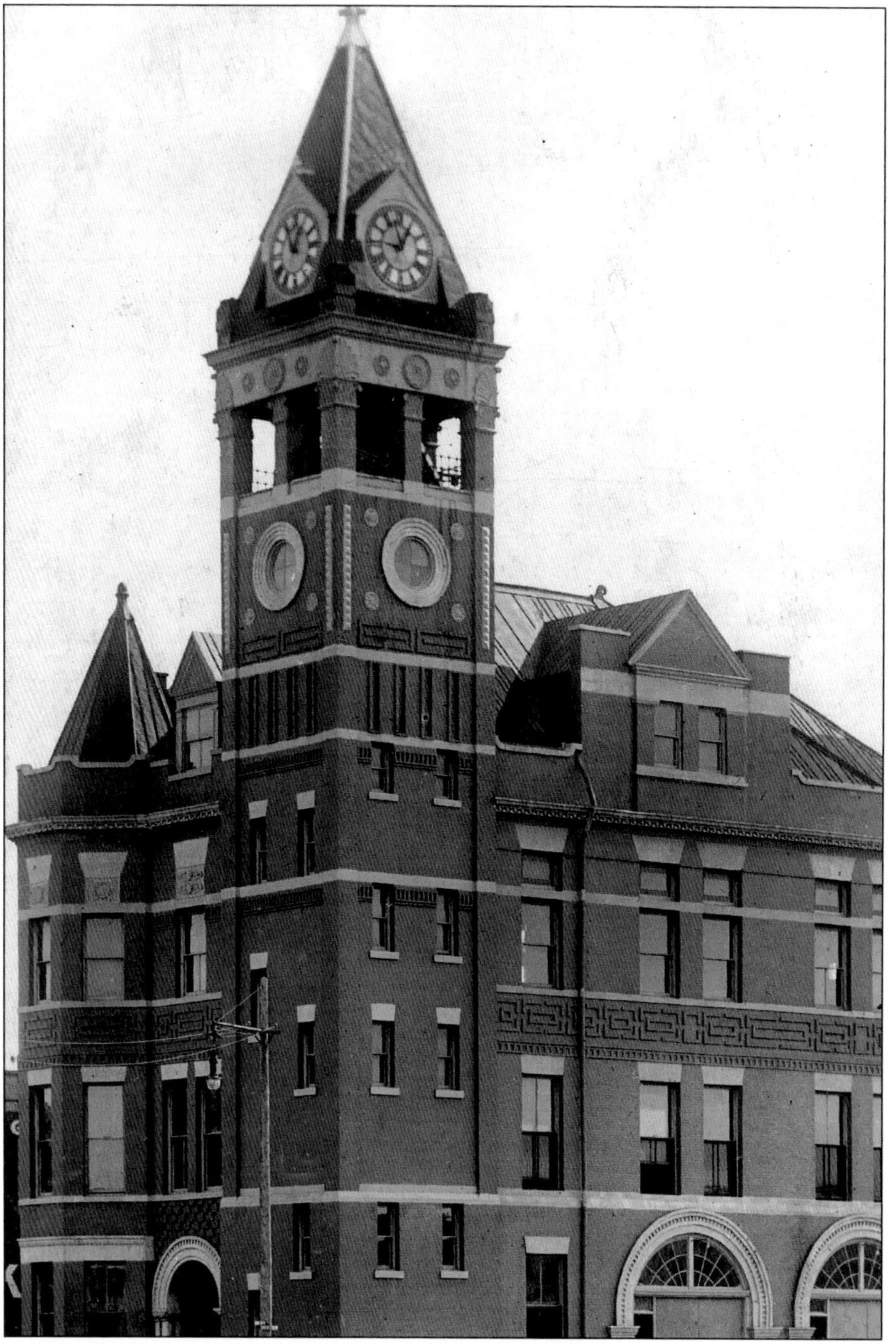

Watertown's first city hall was three stories high, and housed the city jail, fire department, council chamber, public library, public hall, and city offices. Construction began in 1889, according to the designs of architect L.V. Sybrant, on the southeast corner of the intersection of Kemp Avenue and First Street West. When the building was declared structurally unsound in 1974, the city moved its offices to the old *Public Opinion* building on Second Street Northeast, and the old city hall was demolished. A high-rise building containing subsidized apartments for senior citizens opened its doors there in 1975.

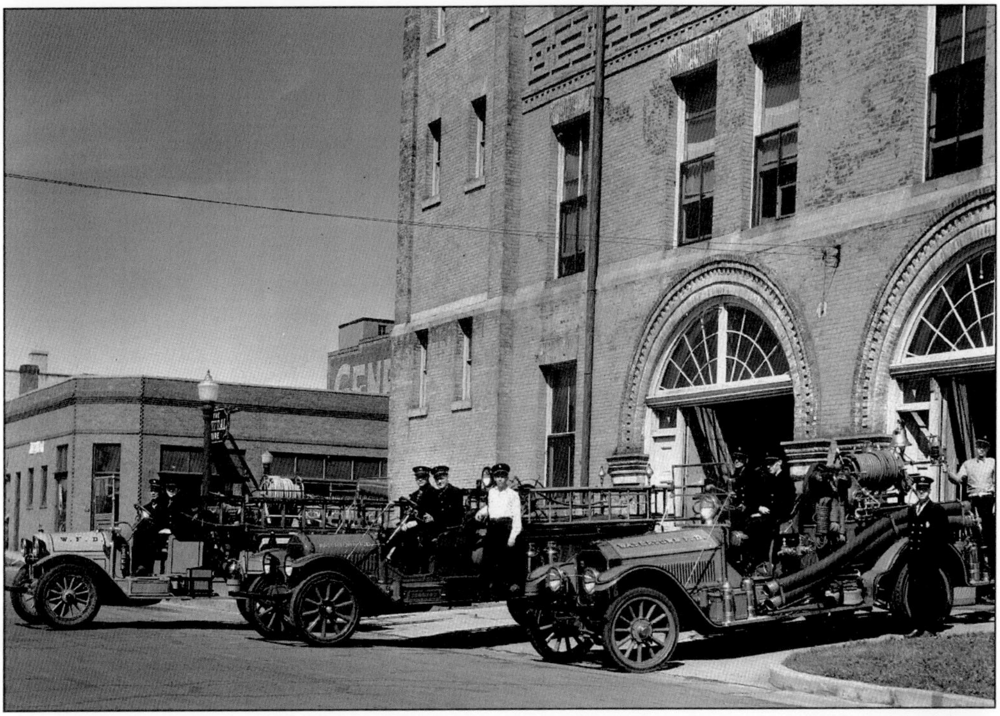

The Watertown Fire Department was housed on the ground floor of the city hall, and had large arched doors on the west side. The first record of fire apparatus purchased by the City of Watertown was a chemical engine, recorded in 1885. Andrew Foley was the first fire chief for the city.

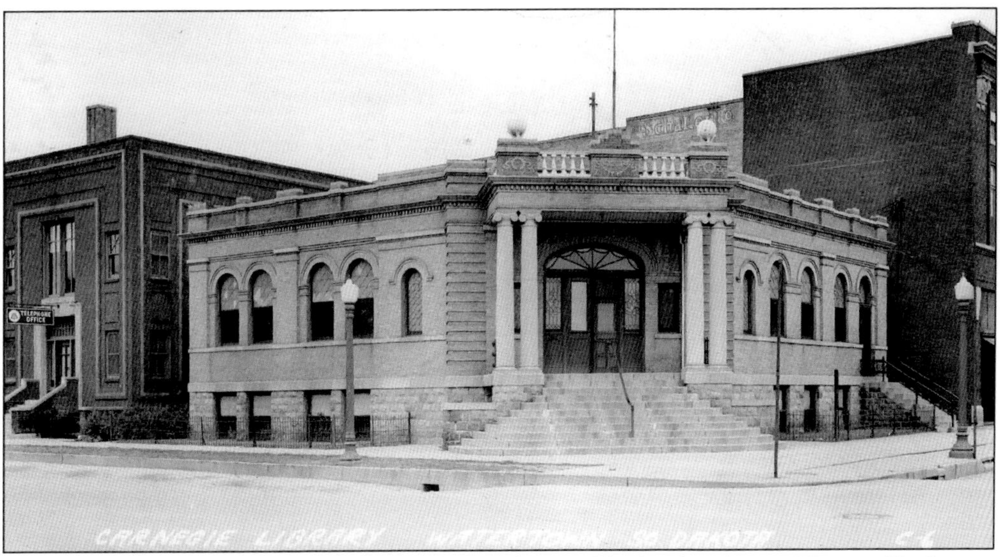

Construction of Watertown's Carnegie Library, designed by local architect Maurice Hockman, began in 1905 and was completed in 1906. The city library was previously housed in the city hall on West Kemp Avenue. The library outgrew the 1906 building in the 1960s, and built a new library close to the new high school. The Codington County Historical Society was organized and started the Kampeska Heritage Museum in the Carnegie building in 1970. The museum was renamed the Codington County Heritage Museum in 1999. (Courtesy Ken and Lyn Sheldon.)

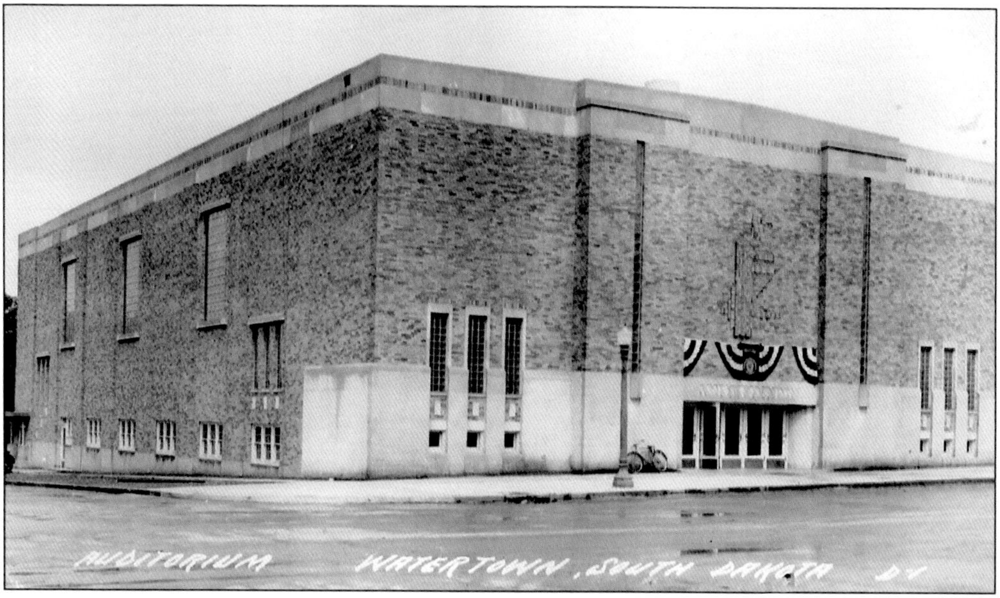

Forty-five percent of the cost of Watertown's $130,000 City Auditorium on South Broadway was provided by the Works Progress Administration. The auditorium was dedicated November 8 and 9, 1939, and was constructed to include housing and facilities for the 34th Signal Corp, with a garage in the west end for the Corp's trucks and mobile equipment. The Watertown High School Arrows' basketball games were played on the auditorium's beautiful maple floor until the new high school and civic auditorium were constructed in the 1960s. The building is still used for various community events.

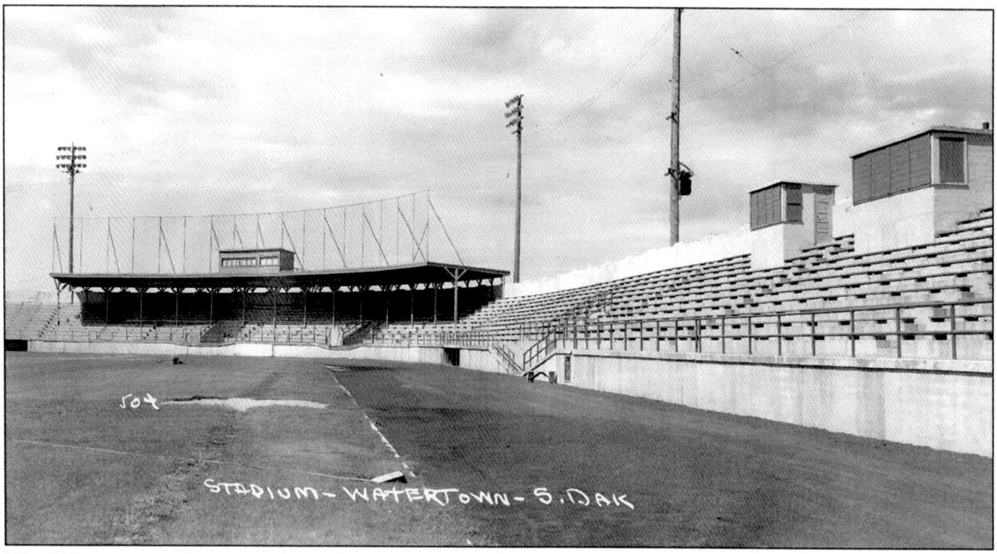

The Watertown Municipal Stadium on West Kemp Avenue, another WPA project, was built in 1940. According to a local story, the structure was originally planned as a band shell, but was built in phases, and was modified for use as an athletic stadium in the last phase of construction. The stadium became the property of the Watertown School District. Dwight A. Miller was superintendent of Watertown schools when the stadium was constructed. (Courtesy Ken and Lyn Sheldon.)

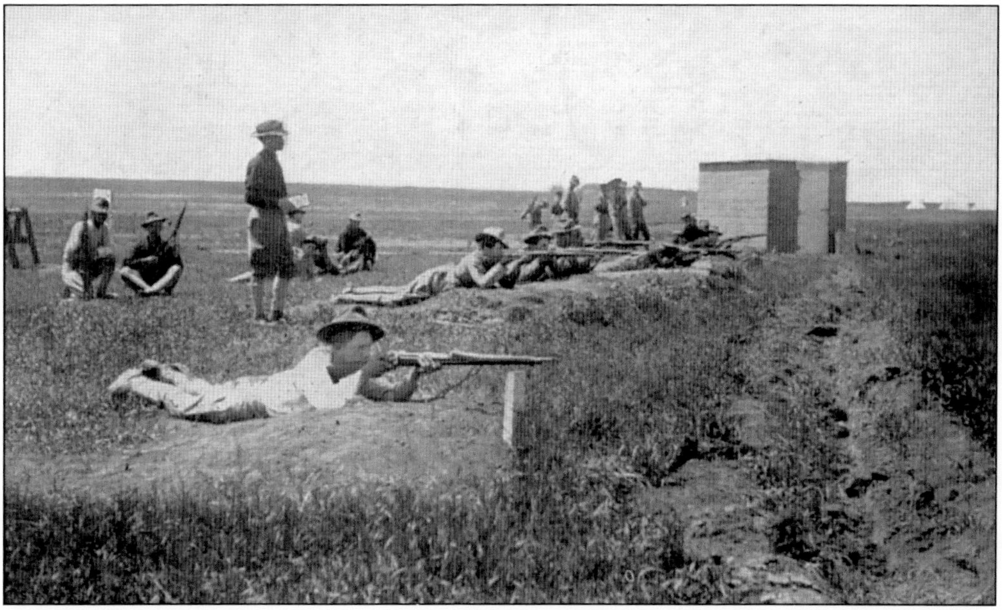

Property for a camping ground for the South Dakota National Guard at Lake Kampeska was purchased by C.B. Williamson in 1903, with $1,000 from Codington County, and smaller amounts solicited from private Watertown businesses and individuals, for a total of $5,860. The property included about 74 acres of land, and was located on the present site of the Municipal Golf Course. The camp, named Camp Roosevelt, was closed after 1912, but officers schools were held there until 1917.

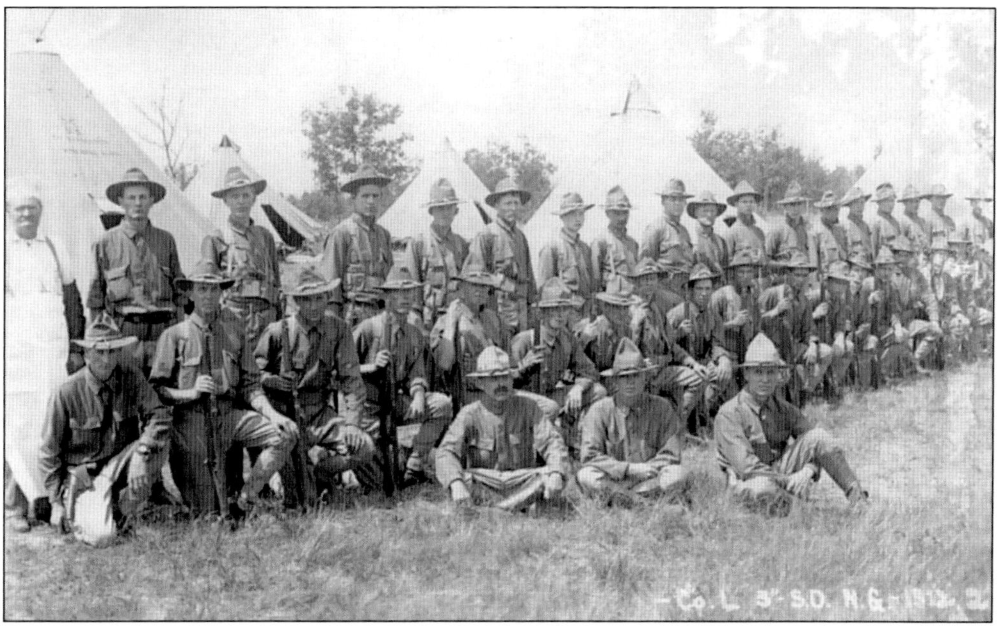

No barracks were constructed at Camp Roosevelt, so the men lived in army tents, as shown in this group photo of the 1912 encampment. None of the men are identified, but the man on the left in the front row of three men seated on the grass, is probably General C.H. Englesby of Watertown, who was appointed Adjutant General of the state by Governor Elrod in 1905.

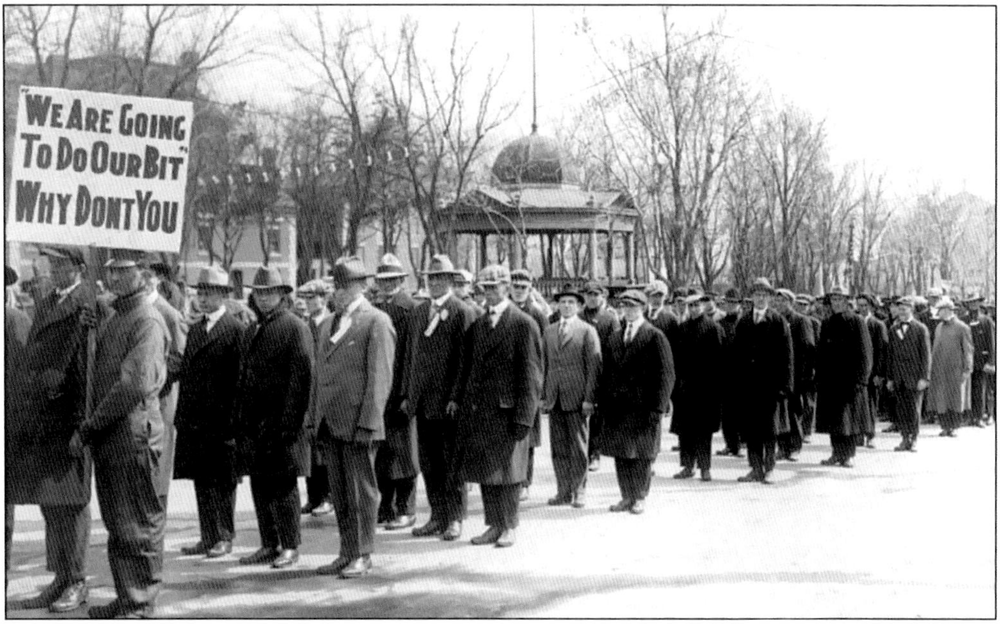

These Codington County men lined up on South Broadway in 1917 to enlist for World War I at the U.S. Post Office. The man on the end of the second row, in a light-colored suit, is Gerhard Gilbert, mayor of Watertown from 1948 to 1954. Note the bandstand on the Codington County Courthouse west lawn in the background.

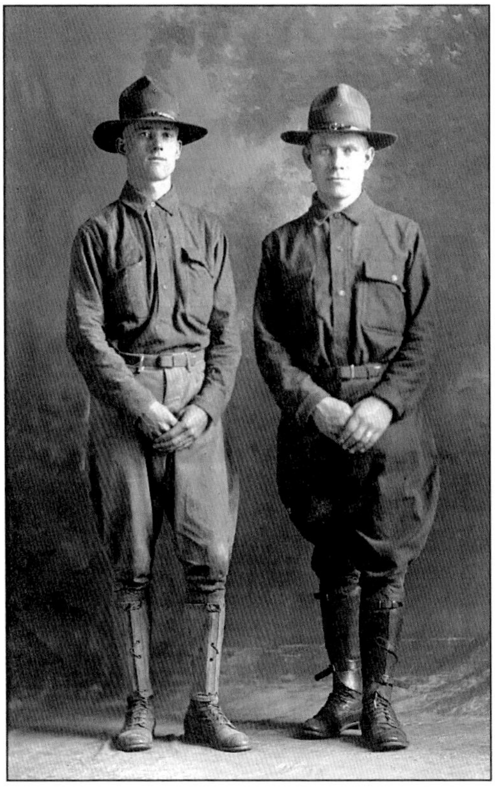

Good friends George Coombes and Carl Swanson, both of Watertown, had this photo taken about 1918, when they were both in the army. The Fourth Regiment of the South Dakota Cavalry headquartered in Watertown in 1917 and 1918, and used the Arcade Hotel as their command center.

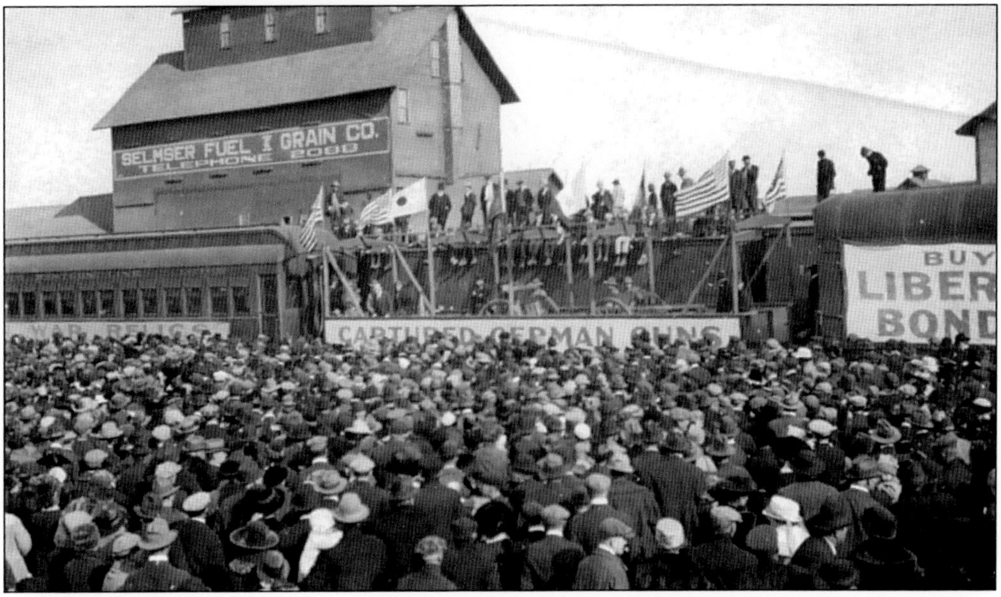

After World War I, railroad cars carrying displays of war relics and captured enemy weapons toured the state, with returning troops. This photo postcard shows a crowd gathered at the Chicago & Northwestern Railroad tracks in front of the Selmser Fuel & Grain Company, to welcome returning troops. Signs on the railroad cars read, from left to right, "European War Relics," "Captured German Guns," and "Buy Liberty Bonds."

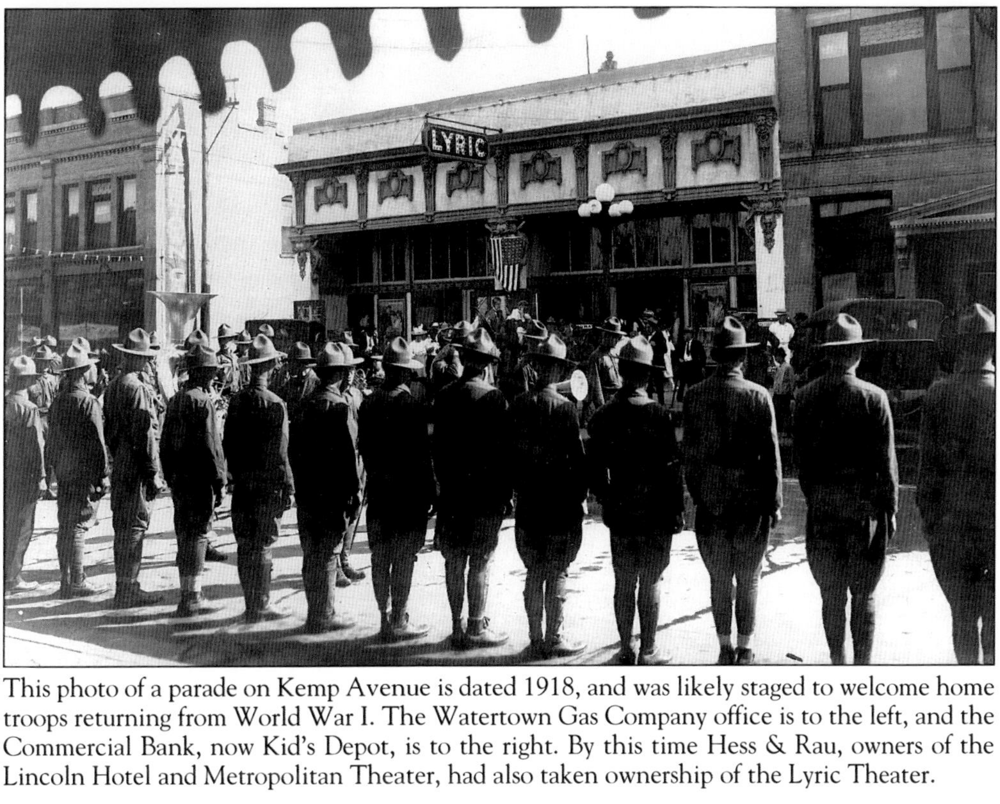

This photo of a parade on Kemp Avenue is dated 1918, and was likely staged to welcome home troops returning from World War I. The Watertown Gas Company office is to the left, and the Commercial Bank, now Kid's Depot, is to the right. By this time Hess & Rau, owners of the Lincoln Hotel and Metropolitan Theater, had also taken ownership of the Lyric Theater.

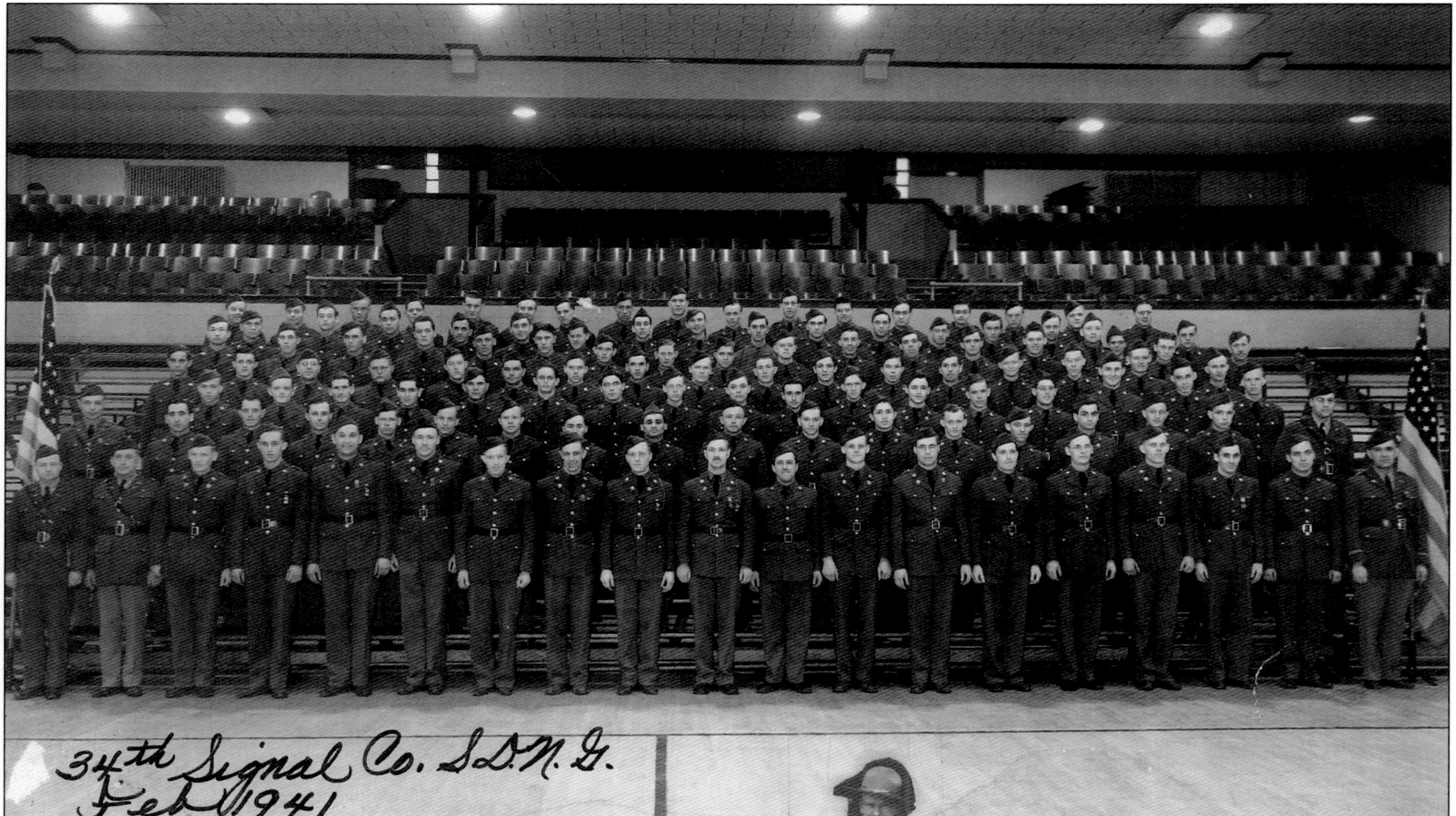

The 34th Signal Company gathered for this photo in the Watertown City Auditorium in February 1941. The company was part of the first American division sent overseas in World War II. It was organized in Watertown as a National Guard unit in 1929, and was called into federal service with the 34th Red Bull Infantry Division in February 1941. The 34th Infantry Division saw more than 500 days of combat in Algeria, Tunisia, and Italy—more than any other division during World War II.

Three

SCHOOLS AND CHURCHES

Schools and churches provide people with more than just education and religion; they supply guidance and spiritual fulfillment. In Codington County, one-room country schools existed until 1970. Today they remain on the landscape as township meeting halls or grain storage bins. The first school in the county was Kranzburg School District Number 5. Built in 1879, it was one of the earliest rural one-room schools in South Dakota. Watertown currently supports eight elementary schools, one middle school, and two high schools. Kranzburg, Waverly, South Shore, Florence, and Henry each have their own school district.

Most country churches in the county have disappeared as well. The few that remain either still function as churches or are simply abandoned. Codington County attracted many hearty and pious German Catholic settlers. One of the oldest churches in the county is the Holy Rosary Catholic Church also in Kranzburg. Organized in 1879, the parish built the current church in 1898.

Even though Catholicism is the dominant denomination in Codington County, the religious choices of area residents has become more diverse over the years. Two early Protestant denominations founded by Yankee settlers primarily from the East Coast and Wisconsin that are still strong in Watertown are the Methodist and Congregational Churches. There are now more than 40 churches in Watertown and Codington County.

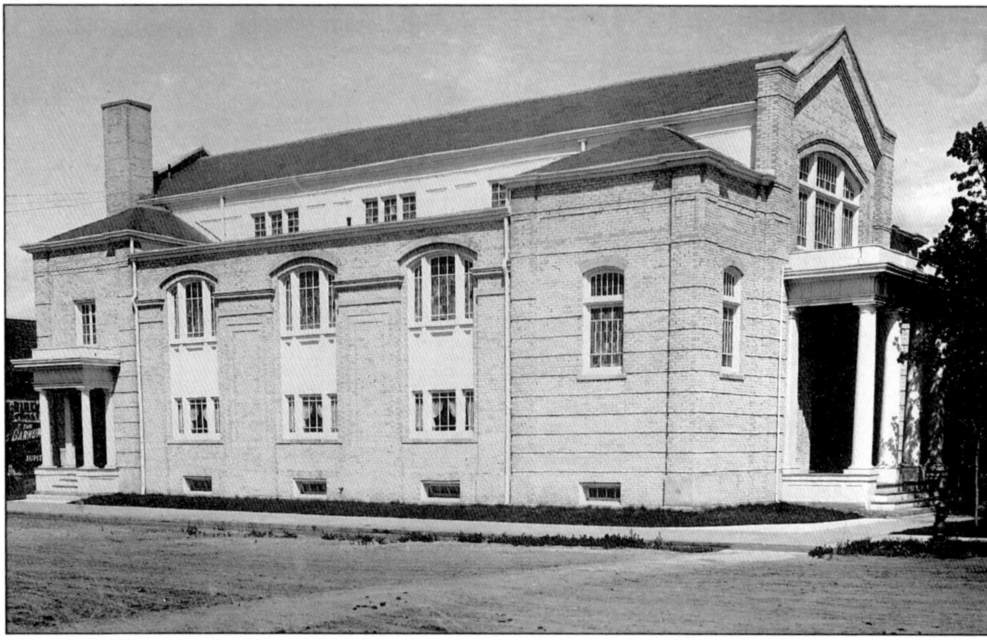

The First Church of Christ Scientist was designed by local architect Maurice Hockman, and constructed on the northeast corner of the intersection of Maple Street and First Avenue South about 1910. The current Marquette bank building replaced the church in 1979. (Courtesy Ken and Lyn Sheldon.)

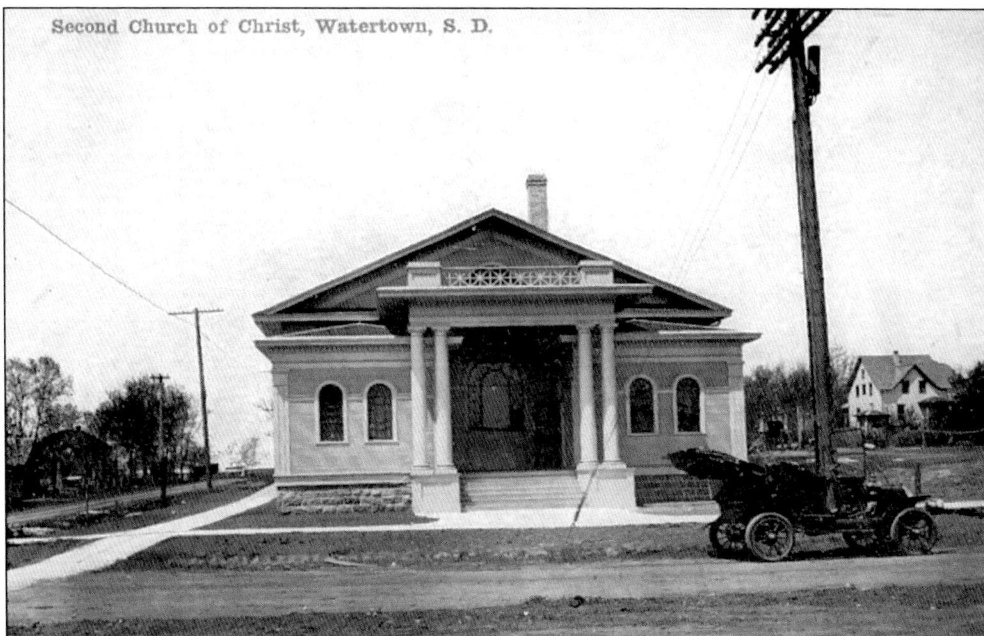

Maurice Hockman also designed a second church for the Watertown Christian Scientists, constructed on the northwest corner of the intersection of Broadway and Third Avenue North, also about 1910. Two stories were added to the structure in the 1920s to form the current Temple Apartments.

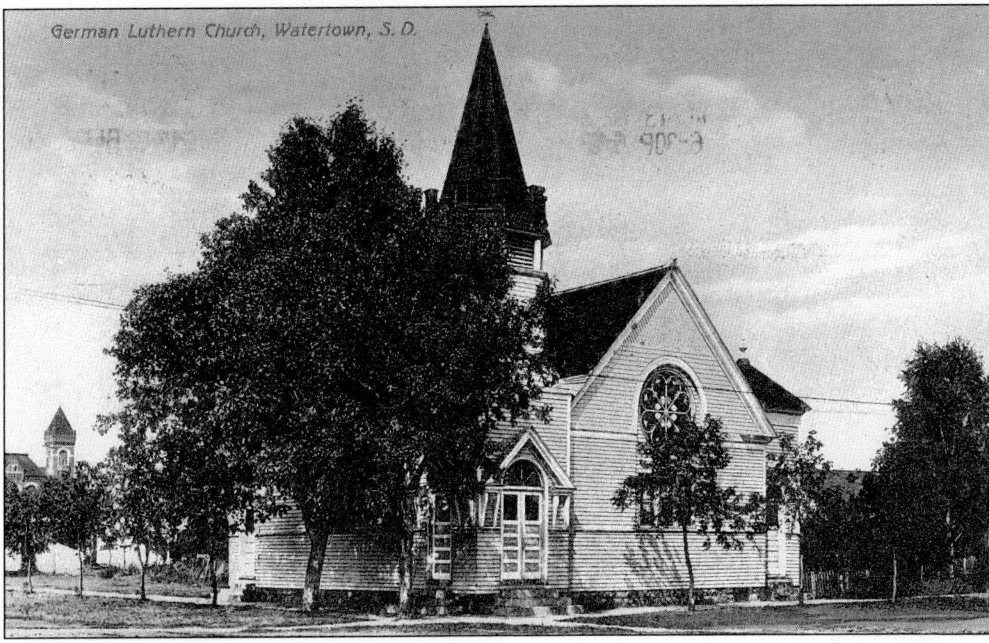

The German Lutheran Church pictured on this postcard postmarked August 13, 1909, was constructed 1902, on the northwest corner of the intersection of Second Street East and Second Avenue South. The congregation had previously shared a church with the Scandinavian Lutherans, which was built in 1886 on the southeast corner of the intersection of Maple Street and First Avenue North. (Courtesy Bud and Arleen Larson.)

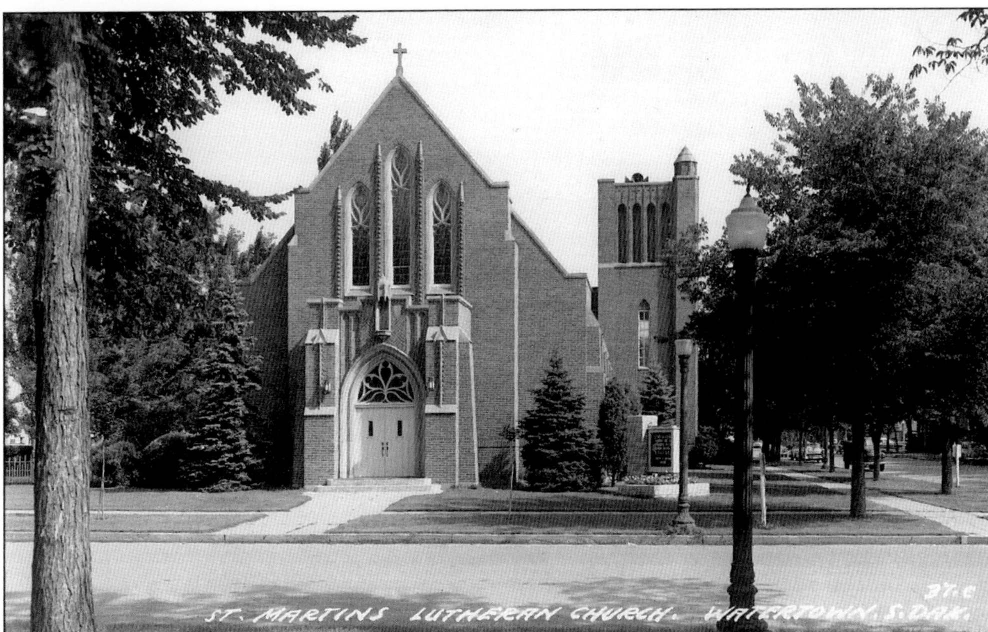

The new brick and stone St. Martin's Evangelical Lutheran Church replaced the congregation's wood church on the same site in 1939. A larger church was needed by 2000, however, and the congregation constructed a new church with an attached elementary school in north Watertown.

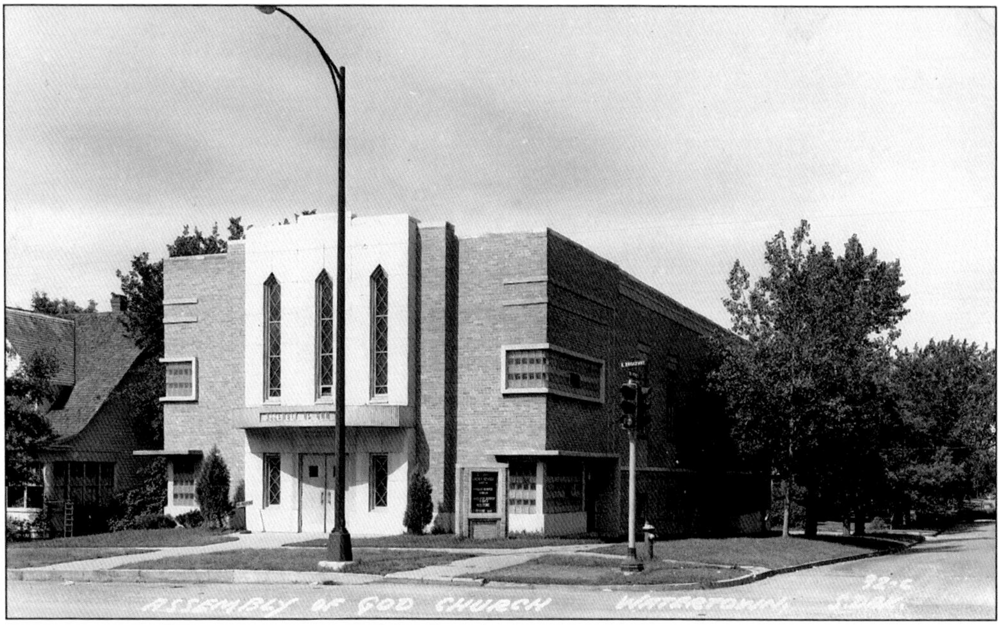

Construction of Watertown's Assembly of God Church at 201 South Broadway began in October 1948, but the church was not dedicated until April 1950. The church was organized about 1933, and previously held services in a building on the northwest corner of the intersection of Second Street West and Fourth Avenue South, called the Watertown Gospel Tabernacle.

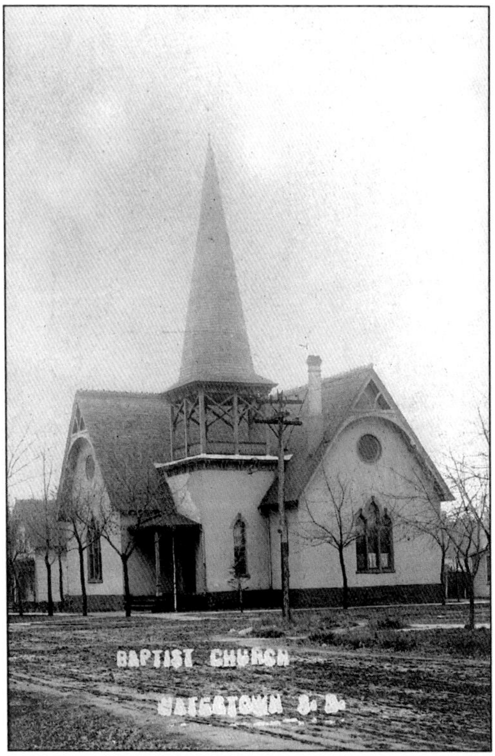

Watertown's Baptist congregation was organized in 1879, and constructed a beautiful frame church on the southeast corner of the intersection of Second Street East and First Avenue South in 1883. The Salvation Army began using the church in 1976, but it was eventually razed in 1992 for the construction of a Habitat for Humanity house. (Courtesy Ken and Lyn Sheldon.)

The Methodist Episcopal Church on this postcard postmarked July 8, 1908, was the congregation's second church, and was built about 1890 on the southeast corner of the intersection of Broadway and Second Avenue South. It was replaced about 1915 with the current stone church still in use, pictured below.

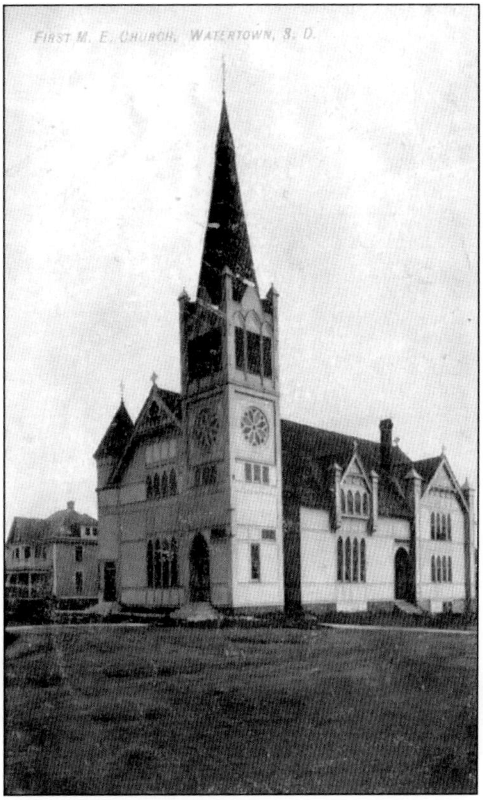

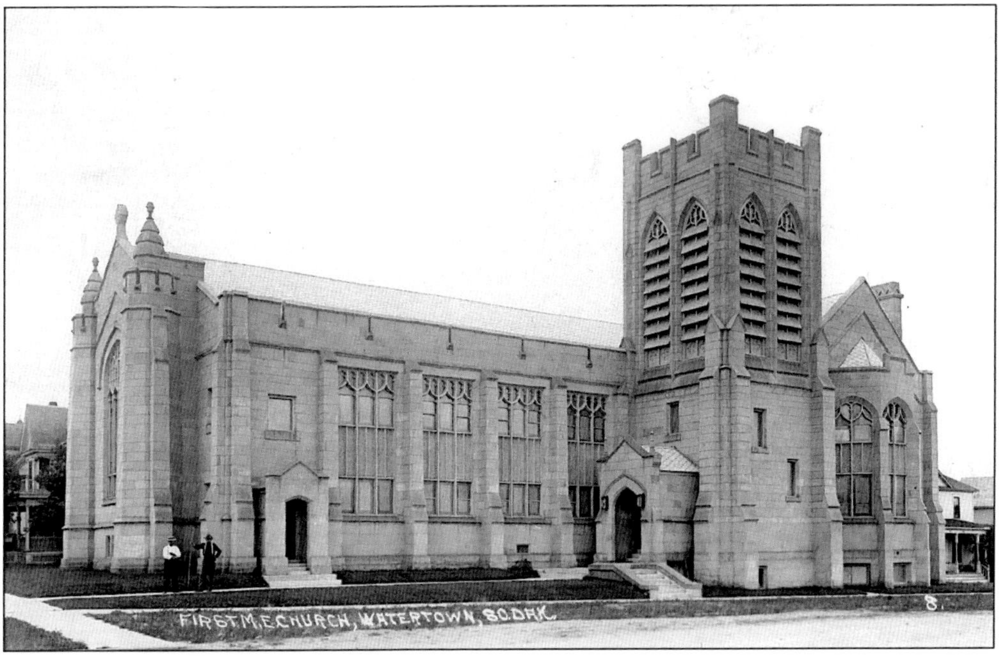

(Courtesy Bud and Arleen Larson.)

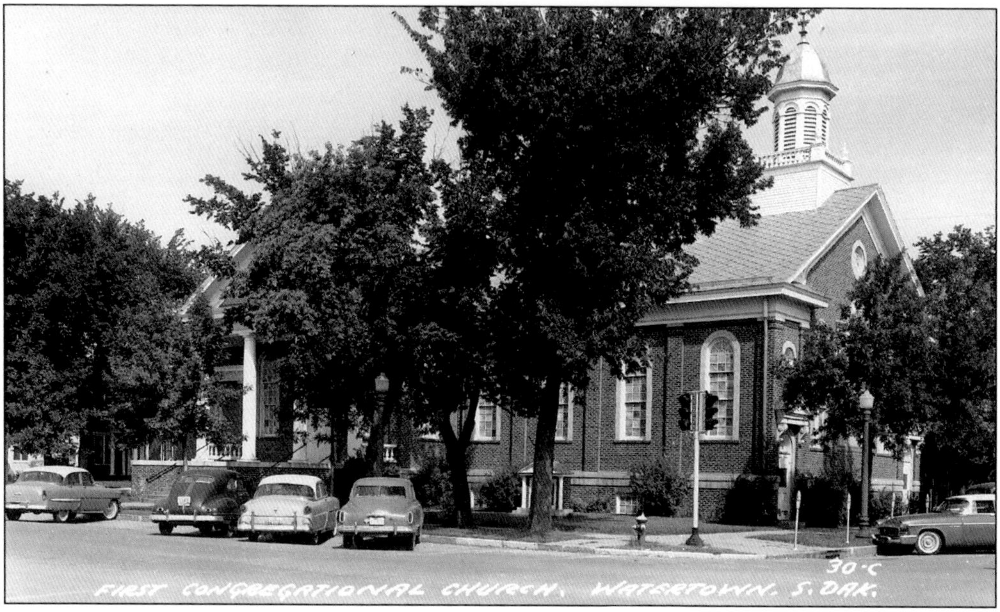

The Congregational denomination was the first to organize in what is now Codington County, and held its first service in C.C. Wiley's hotel building at the original site of Watertown near Lake Kampeska. The first Congregational Church was constructed in 1881, on the same site as the present church that replaced it in 1917, at the northwest corner of the intersection of Second Street East and First Avenue South. A fire in 1963 gutted the interior of the church, but it was rebuilt, and rededicated in 1964.

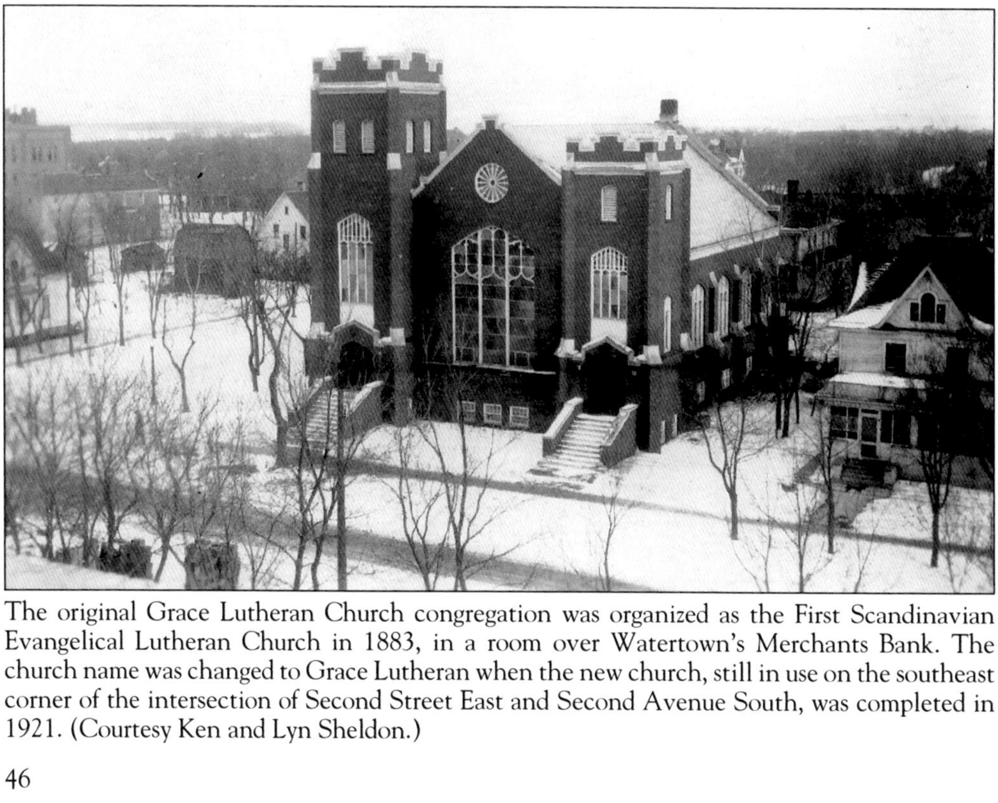

The original Grace Lutheran Church congregation was organized as the First Scandinavian Evangelical Lutheran Church in 1883, in a room over Watertown's Merchants Bank. The church name was changed to Grace Lutheran when the new church, still in use on the southeast corner of the intersection of Second Street East and Second Avenue South, was completed in 1921. (Courtesy Ken and Lyn Sheldon.)

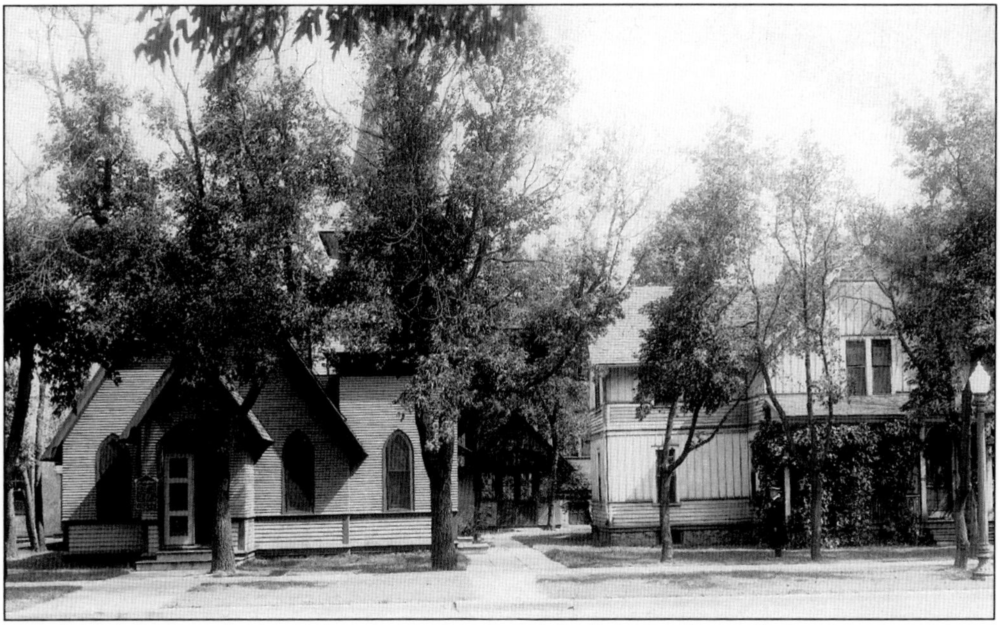

The Trinity Episcopal Church, pictured with its guildhall on South Maple Street in an undated photo by W.C. Gowin, was the first church in Watertown to have a pipe organ, acquired in 1886. This first church building was constructed in 1882 and served the parish until 1963, when the old church was razed. The congregation held services in the Masonic Temple on North Broadway until its new church on Fourteenth Avenue Northwest was finished in 1966. (Courtesy Ken and Lyn Sheldon.)

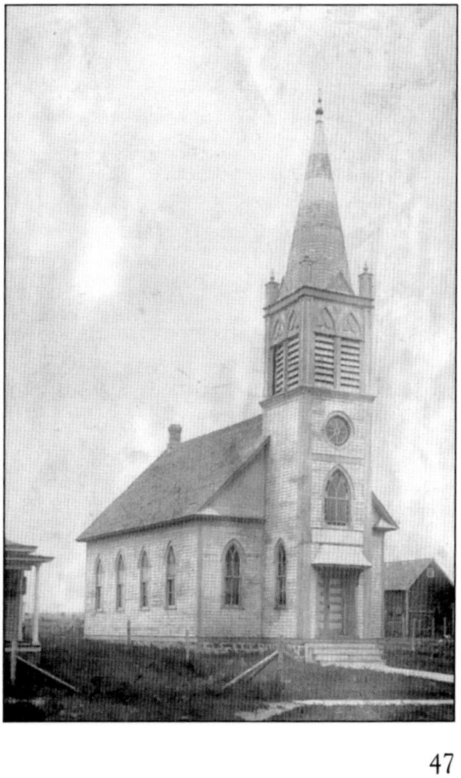

The German Lutheran Church in South Shore on this postcard postmarked November 7, 1911, was constructed in 1905, and was named Immanuel Evangelical Lutheran Church. It was replaced in 1968, when the South Shore congregation merged with the Lutheran congregation from Germantown Township and decided to build a new church.

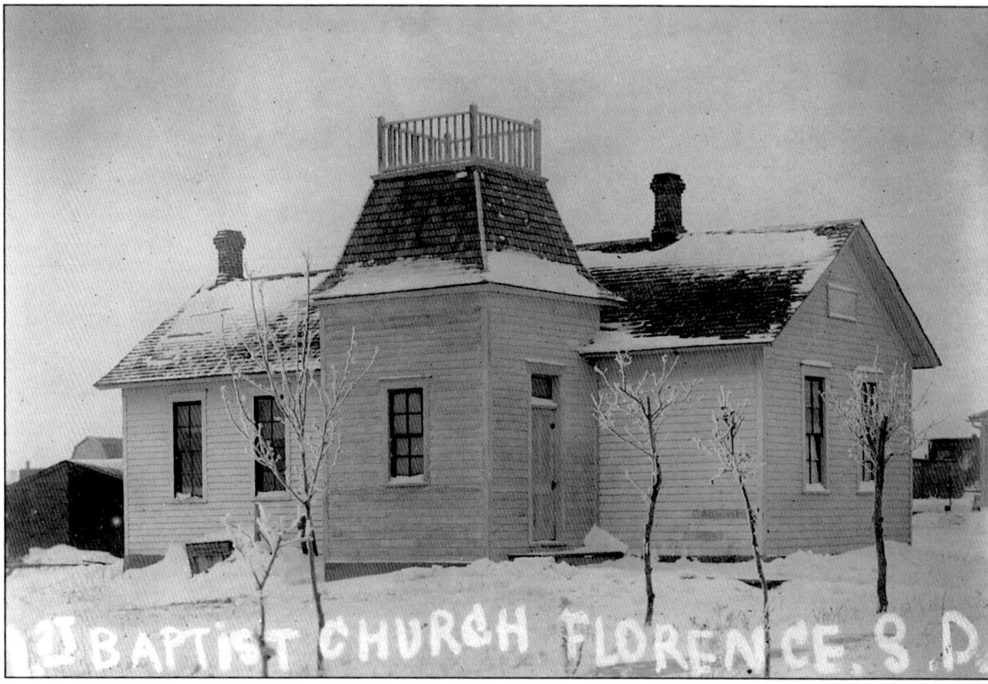

The First Baptist Church congregation in Florence, in this undated photo of the church, included the Jostad, Huppler, Mallgren, Nelsen, and Wilbur families, among others. The church closed because of a dwindling congregation, and was moved to the Ed Maag property for use as a garage.

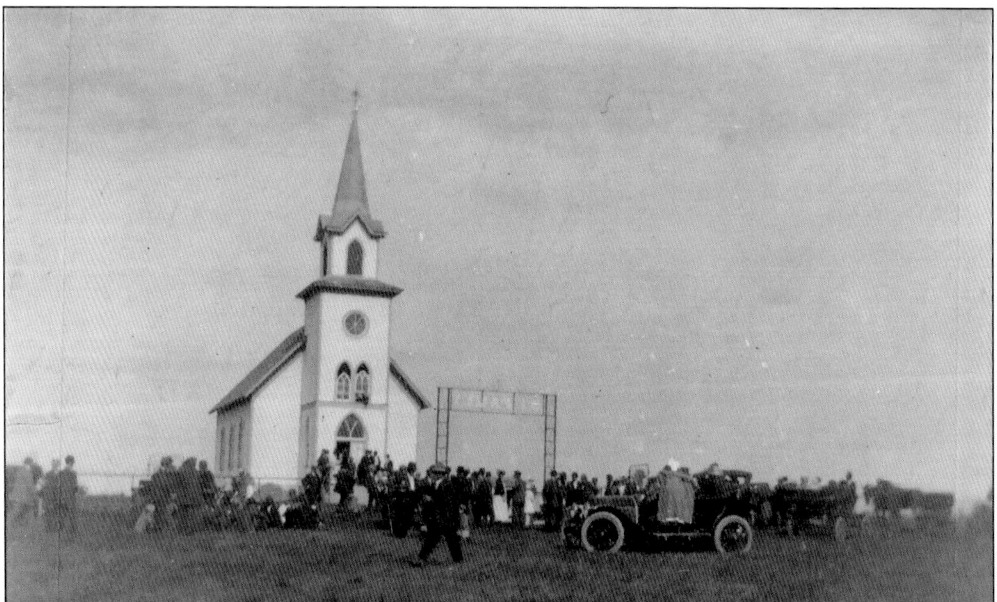

The St. Pauli Lutheran congregation was organized in Eden Township in 1883. The church and cemetery, in this undated photo, are still cared for by the St. Pauli Cemetery Association, though the congregation disbanded in 1976.

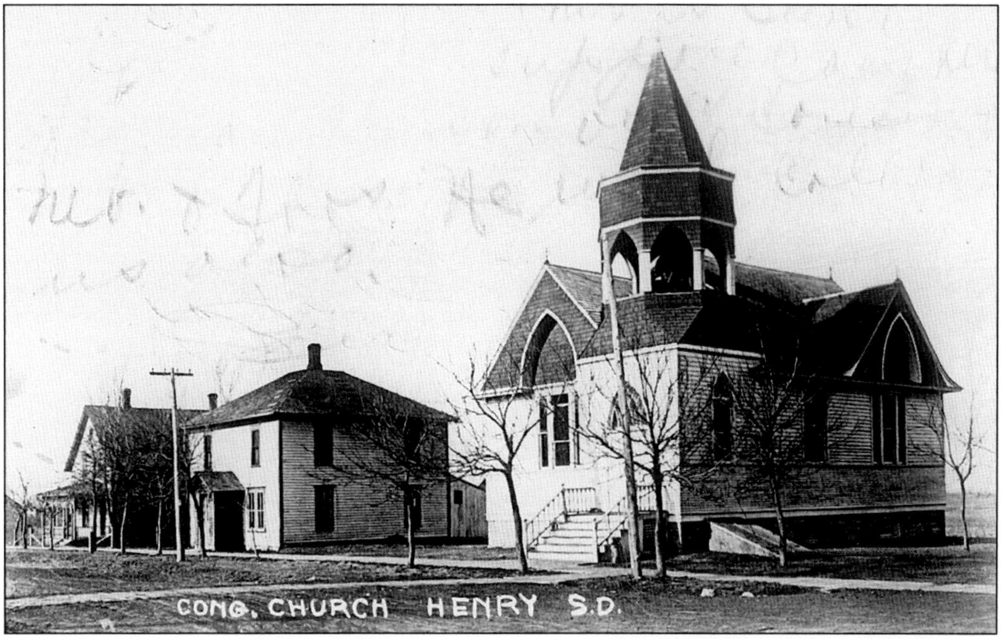

The Congregational Church in Henry, South Dakota was built in 1886, on the northwest corner of the intersection of Third and Oak streets. The church is still standing, but is abandoned.

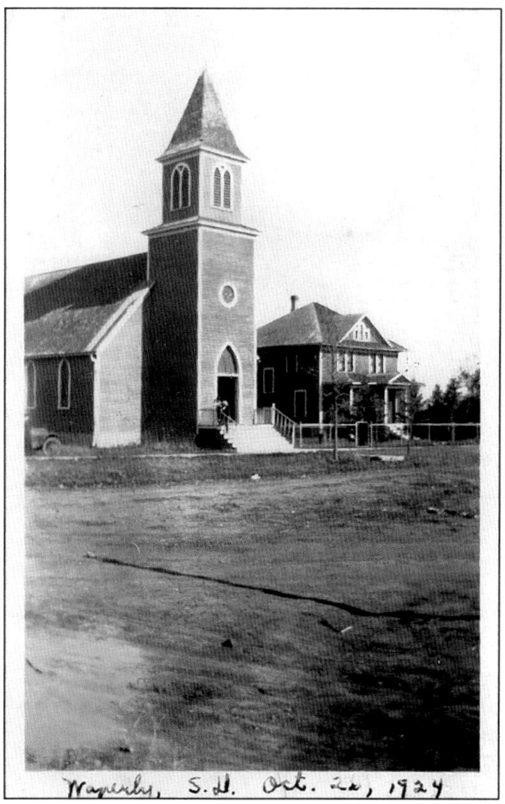

Waverly parishioners hired a contractor by the name of Kuhn, from Kranzburg, to construct their St. Joseph's Church, in 1896. Parishioners, such as Peter Bauer, also helped with construction of the church. St. Joseph's is pictured next to the parish house built in 1912, in this snapshot dated October 26, 1924.

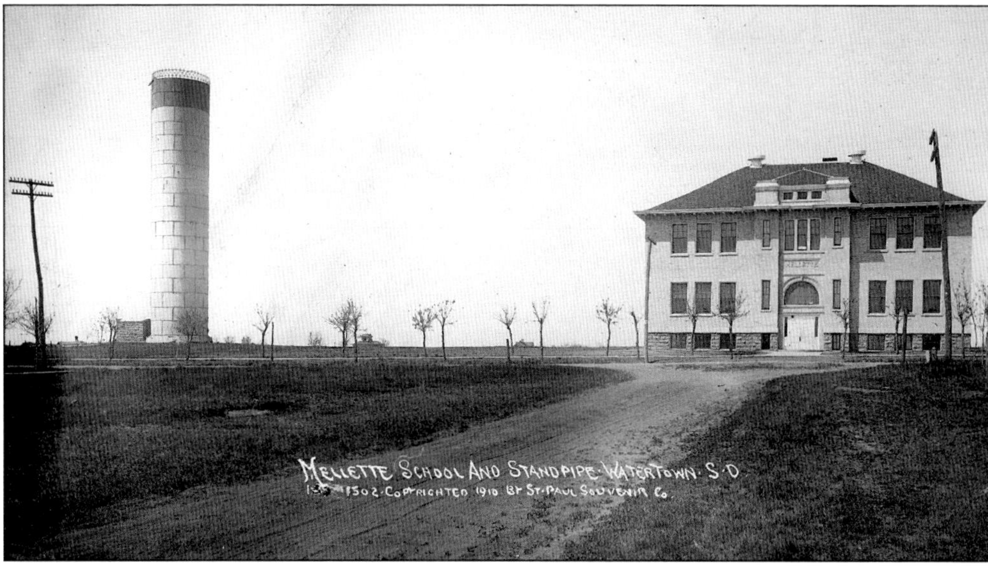

The Mellette Elementary School was constructed atop the hill in northwest Watertown in 1908, on the block between Sixth and Seventh Avenues North and Second and Third Streets West. The school bears the name of the first governor of South Dakota, Arthur Mellette, whose home was located just a few blocks from the school. The old school was recently replaced with a modern one on the same site. The standpipe in this view facing west, was built in 1888, and dates to the beginning of the city waterworks. (Courtesy Ken and Lyn Sheldon.)

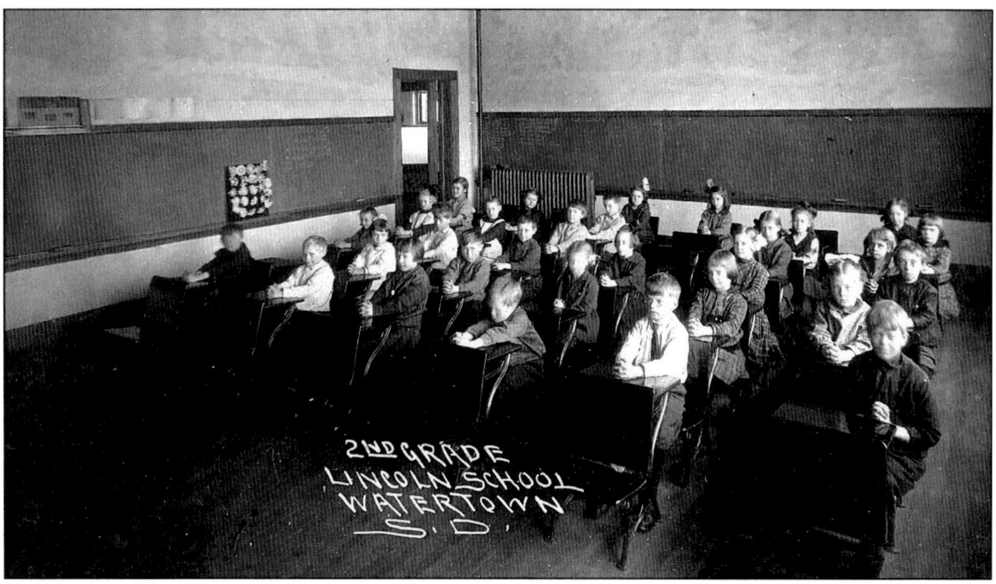

The second grade students in this undated photo are seated in a classroom in the old Lincoln School, which was originally Watertown's first school building on Second Avenue Southeast, and was moved to its location in this photo on Third Street West in the early 1890s. The new Lincoln School was constructed on Thirteenth Street Northeast in 1986, in a rapidly growing residential development. The old Lincoln School was moved to the southwest corner of the intersection of Third Street West and First Avenue South, and is today used as an apartment building. (Courtesy Bud and Arleen Larson.)

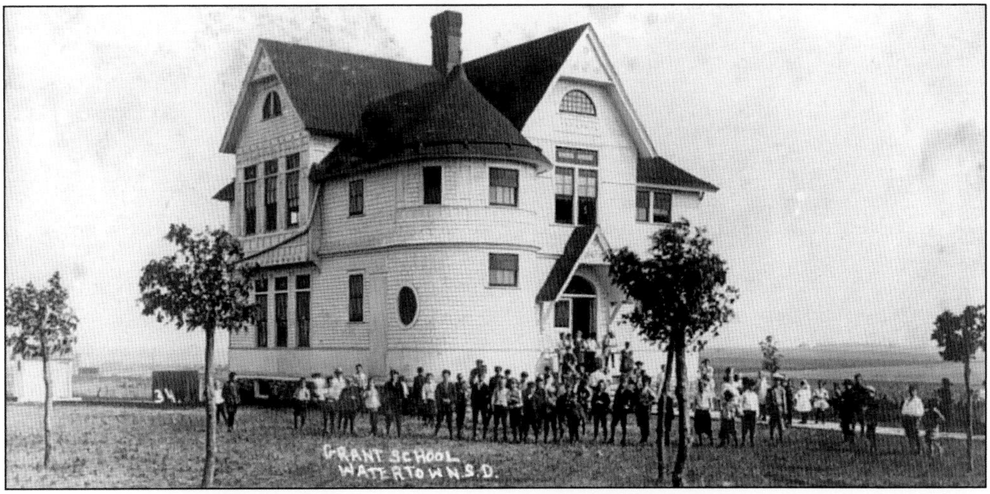

The Grant and Garfield Schools were constructed in 1886 to handle the increasing enrollment at the First Ward School located on the south side of Second Avenue South, between Maple and Second Street East. The Grant School, pictured on this postcard dated 1909, was constructed in northeast Watertown, on Third Street East, between Sixth and Seventh Avenues North. By 1914 the old Grant School facilities were outdated, so it was moved several blocks south for use as a house, and a modern brick and stone school was constructed. The new brick building also outlived its use as a school, and its demolition was slated by the school board for the summer of 2001. (Courtesy Ken and Lyn Sheldon.)

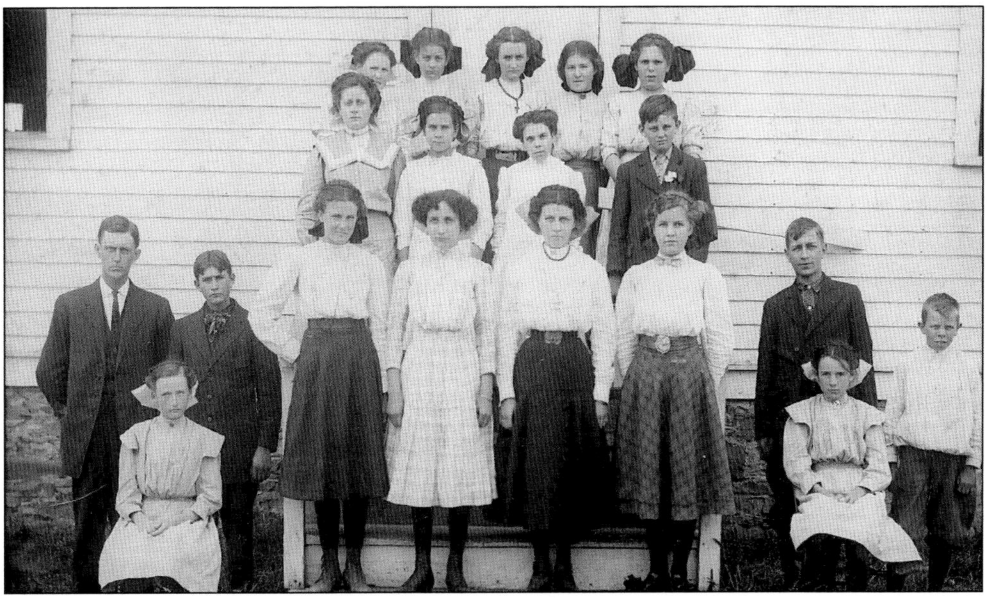

These students were photographed in front of the Garfield School in southeast Watertown. They are not all identified, but the Sieverts sisters are seated on either side. Pictured, from left to right, are as follows: (front row) Professor Soder, H. Burns, Fay Crawford, Grace Franklin, Marg McKugh, Dorothy Duffner, Art Rau, and Howard Gross; (middle row) Ellison, Beth Coffin, unidentified, and Ellison. Ruth Miller and Marie Hanten are the only girls identified in the back row, standing on the right. The first Garfield school was moved to Fifth Street Southeast, and was replaced in 1915 with a new brick school, which is now slated for demolition in the summer of 2002.

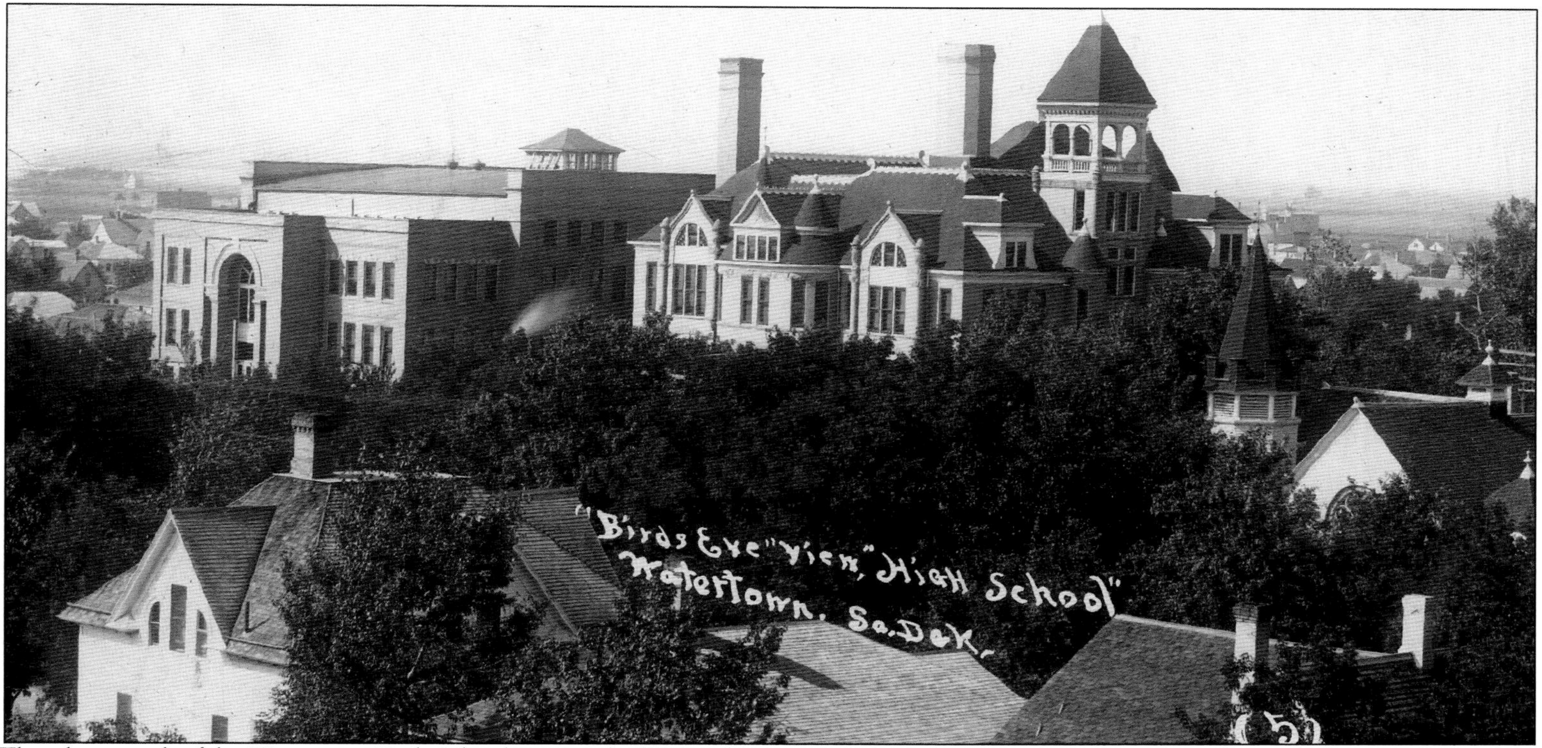

This photograph of the Watertown High School, postmarked December 12, 1913, was taken facing southwest from the top of the new Immaculate Conception School on First Avenue South. The old school building in front was constructed in 1889. In 1910, an addition was constructed on the south side of the old school. When another new high school was constructed in 1920, the 1889 school was rotated to the east side of the 1910 building. The 1889 and 1910 buildings were both demolished in 1964 when the new high school was opened in northeast Watertown. The middle school continued to use the 1920 building until the current middle school was opened north of the 1964 high school in 1975. The 1920 high school building was then also razed, and the Maple Place senior apartments and Jenkins Town View Apartments were constructed on the old high school block. The steeple visible in the trees to the right of the school belongs to the German Lutheran Church, on the current site of the old St. Martin's Lutheran Church. (Courtesy Ken and Lyn Sheldon.)

This unidentified group of students, pictured with their teacher, seated center, is probably an eighth grade graduating class. Flowers in the background are arranged to indicate they are the "Class of [19]04."

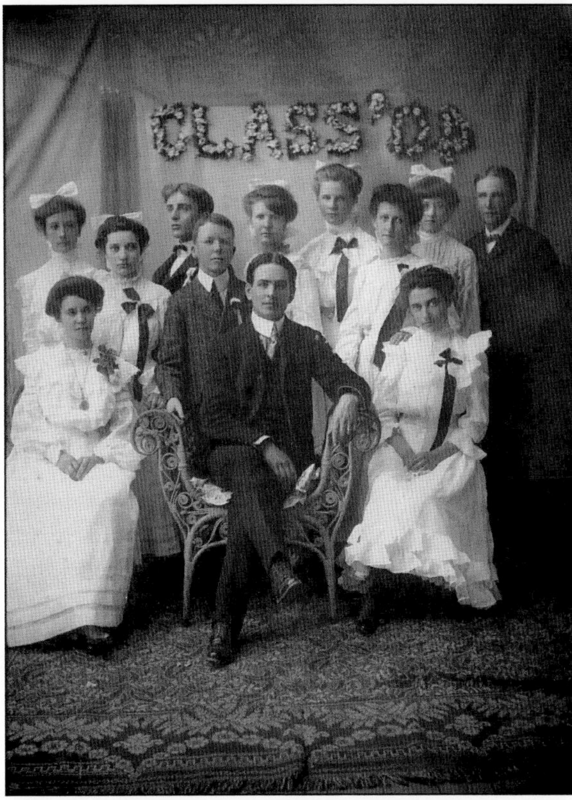

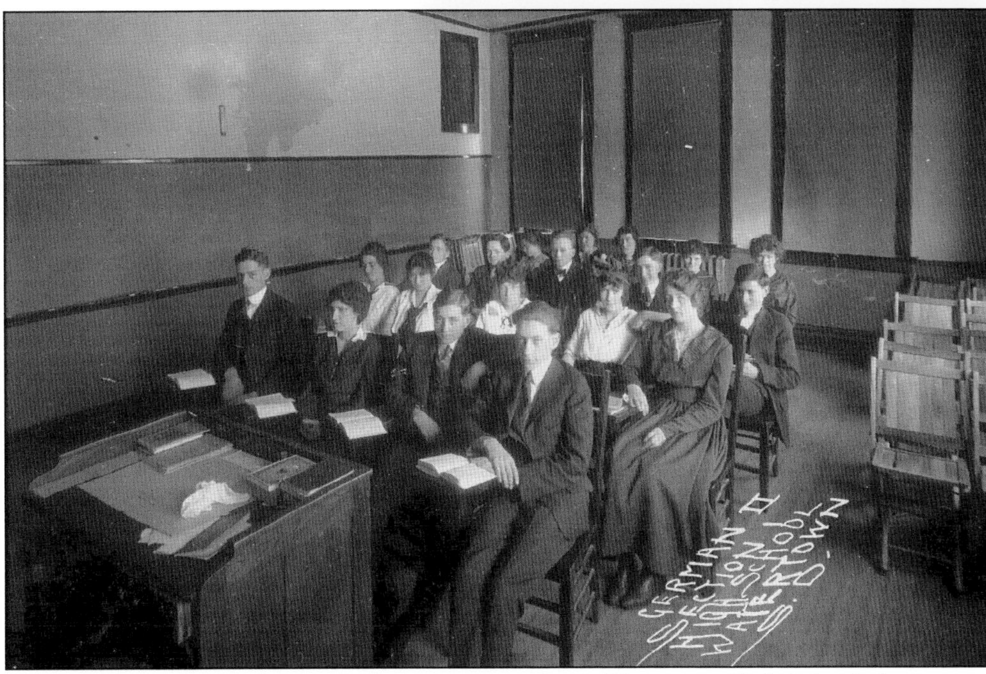

A second-level German language class was captured in a Watertown High School classroom in this undated photo postcard from the late 1910s. (Courtesy Ken and Lyn Sheldon.)

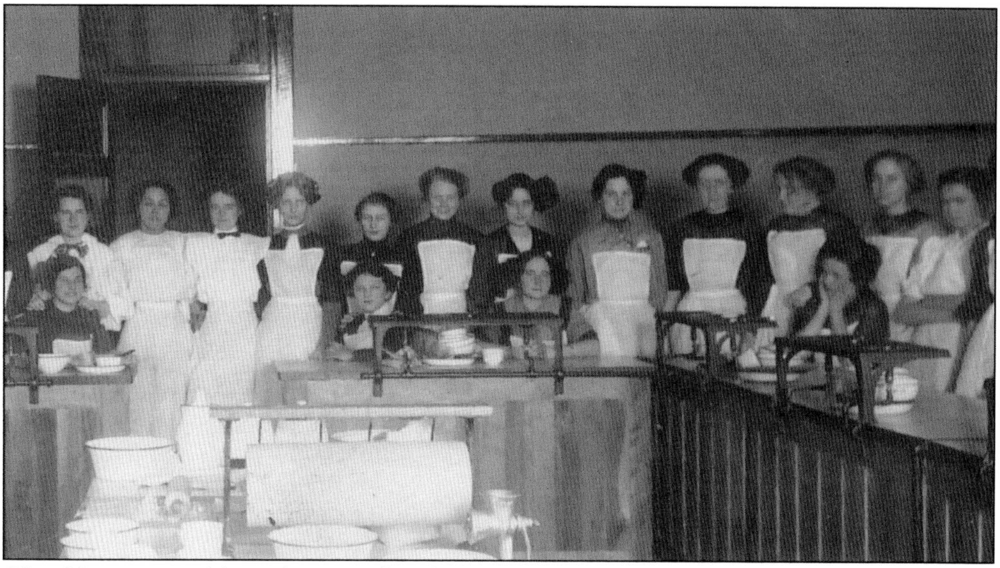

Olga Olson is one of the girls pictured in this 1911 or 1912 Domestic Science class at Watertown High School. Mrs. Fred Schreiber was the Domestic Science teacher.

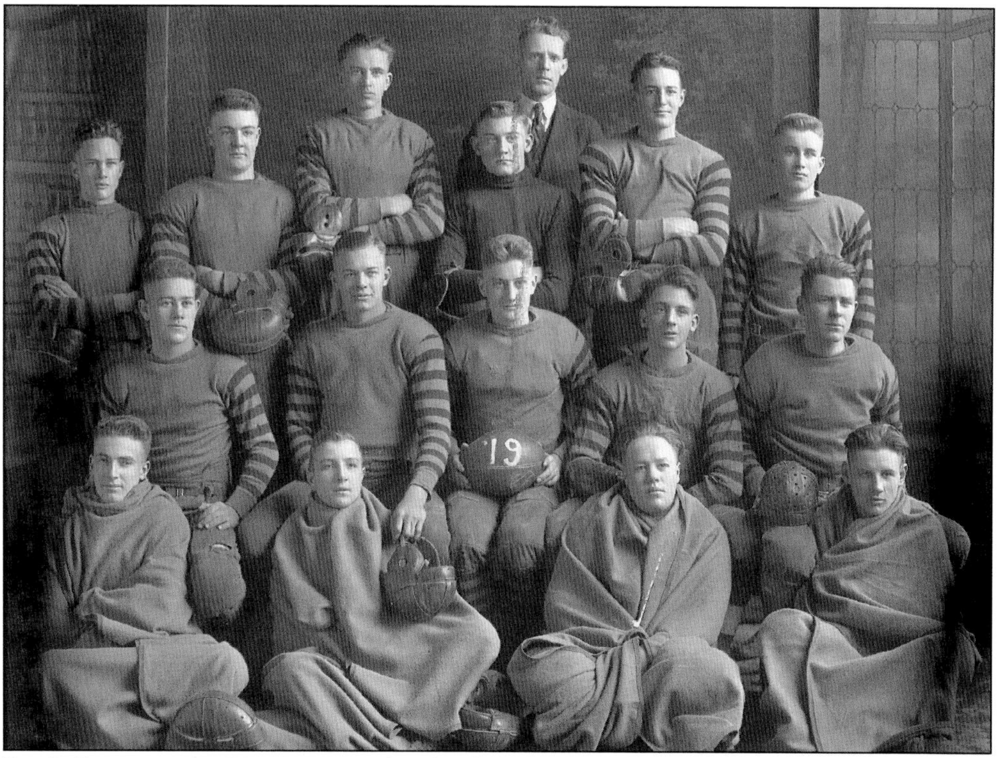

Football teams at the Watertown High School were organized as early as the 1890s, but the team did not begin interscholastic competition until 1906, the first year the team went undefeated. The unidentified students in this photo were members of the 1919 WHS team. Evidently, there were not enough uniforms to go around that year, so the young lads seated in front wrapped themselves in warm blankets.

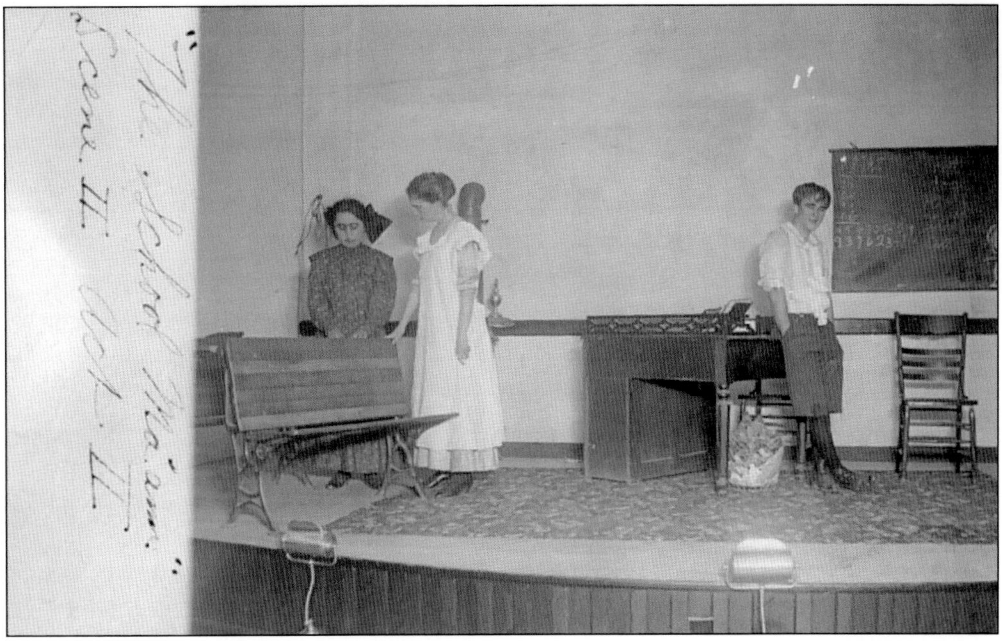

Glad Kosier, Marion George, and Sydney McMullen participated in the Watertown High School production of *The School Ma'am*, in the above undated photo of Act II, Scene 2, from the early 1910s. McMullen was later first tenor in the Watertown High School Quartet, pictured below, third from left, with John Foley, first bass, Theodore Lamm, second bass, and Stowe Elliott, second tenor, about 1916.

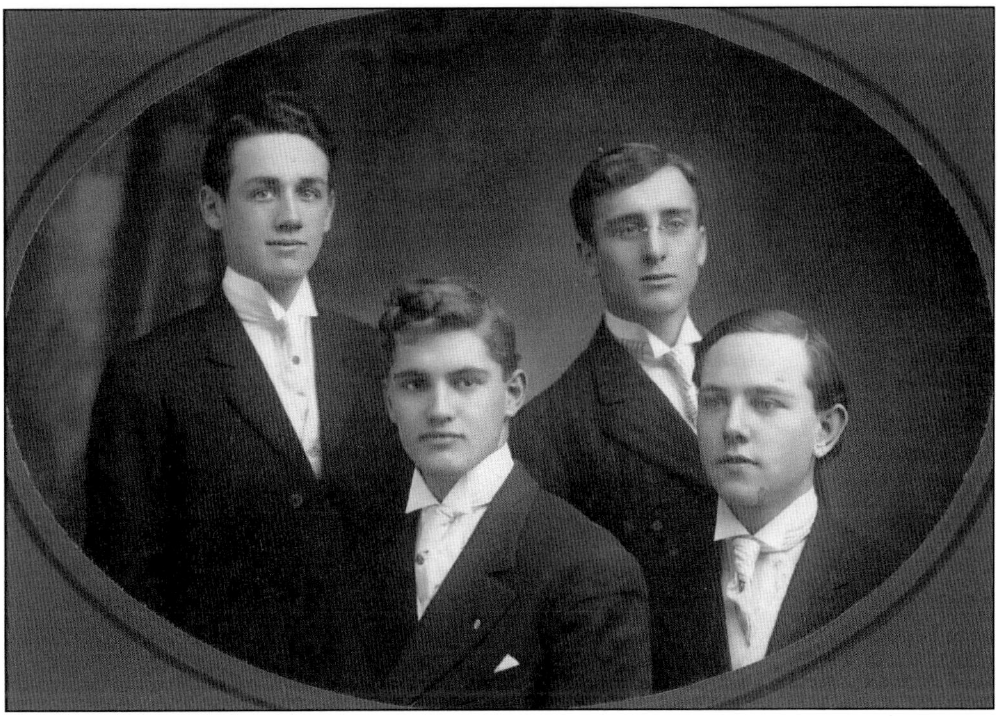

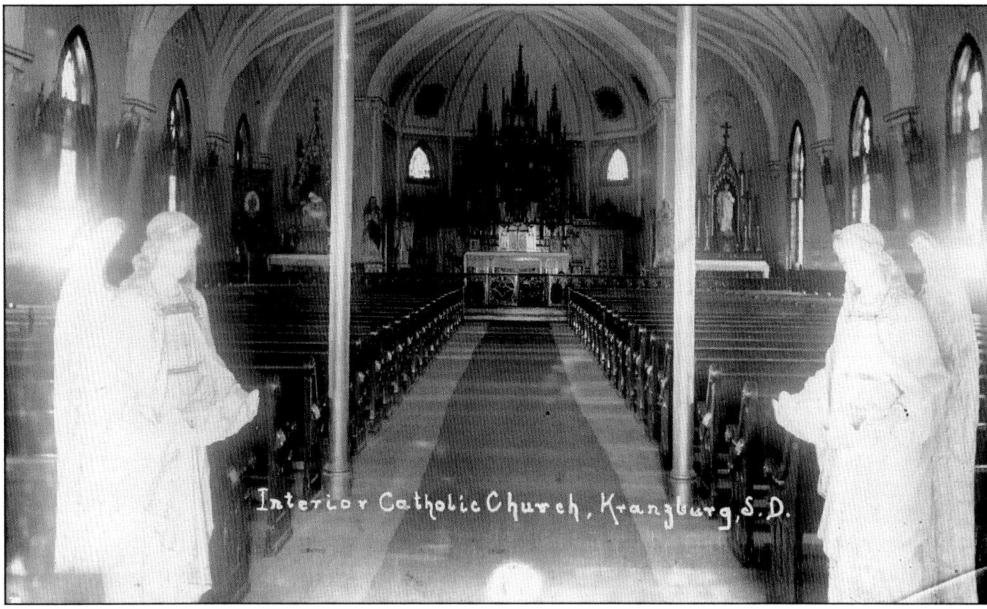

This photograph of the interior of the Holy Rosary Church in Kranzburg could be called ethereal. The first parish church—a $600, 20-foot-by-2-foot frame structure—was constructed immediately in 1879, the same year the town was founded. The present gothic brick church, the interior of which is pictured on this undated photo postcard, was constructed in 1898 during the pastorate of the Rev. H. Victor.

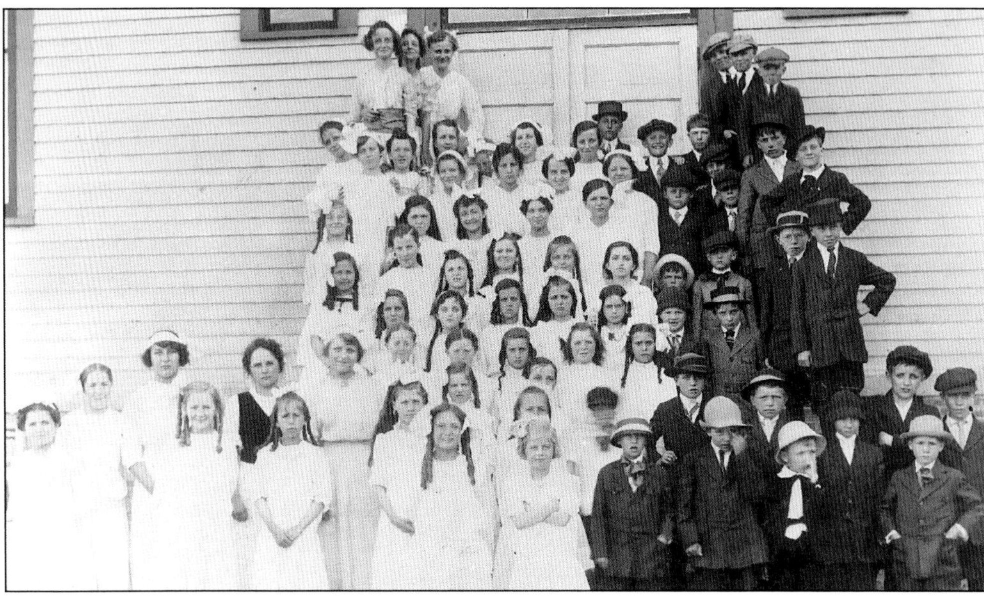

The first school building for the Holy Rosary Parochial School in Kranzburg was constructed in 1906 next to the church. In 1914, the school was moved across the street to make room for a new rectory. The school and Sisters' living quarters were completely destroyed by a fire of unknown origin on Christmas Eve 1945. Temporary quarters were found for classes until the new school, approved December 30, was opened on February 27, 1950. Parochial school students are pictured here on the steps of the school about 1916.

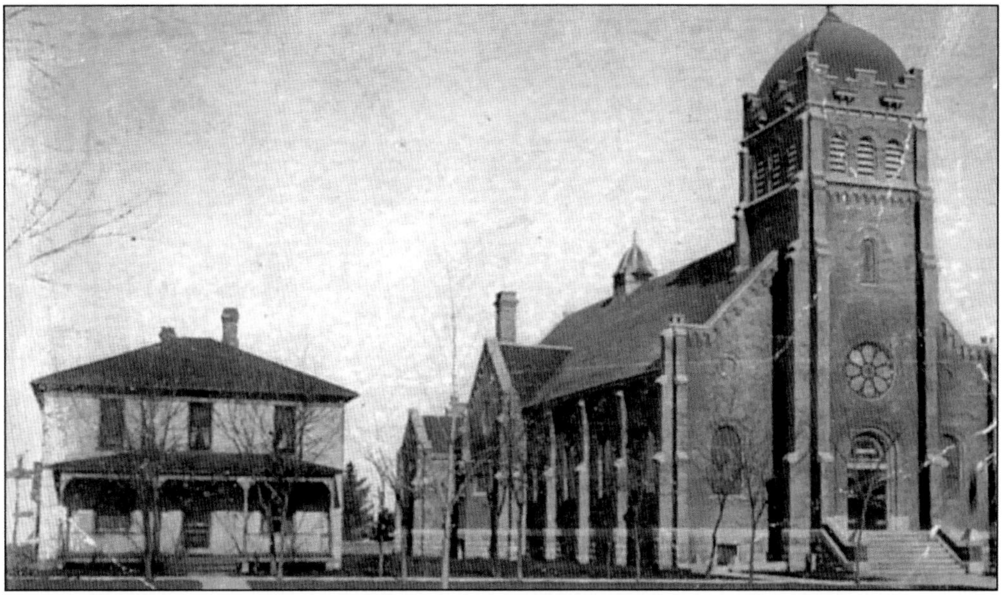

The Immaculate Conception parish's first permanent church was the old church of the Christian Church congregation. Watertown residents of Irish and German descent, including John B. Hanten, Andrew Foley, and Ed Lamm, were instrumental in building the beautiful, new brick and stone church, completed on East Kemp Avenue in 1906. This postcard, postmarked January 8, 1908, shows the new church and neighboring duplex. The church slowly deteriorated, however, and the congregation built a new church building on First Avenue Southeast. The old Immaculate Conception Church was demolished in 1996, and the empty property became a parking lot for the neighboring buildings.

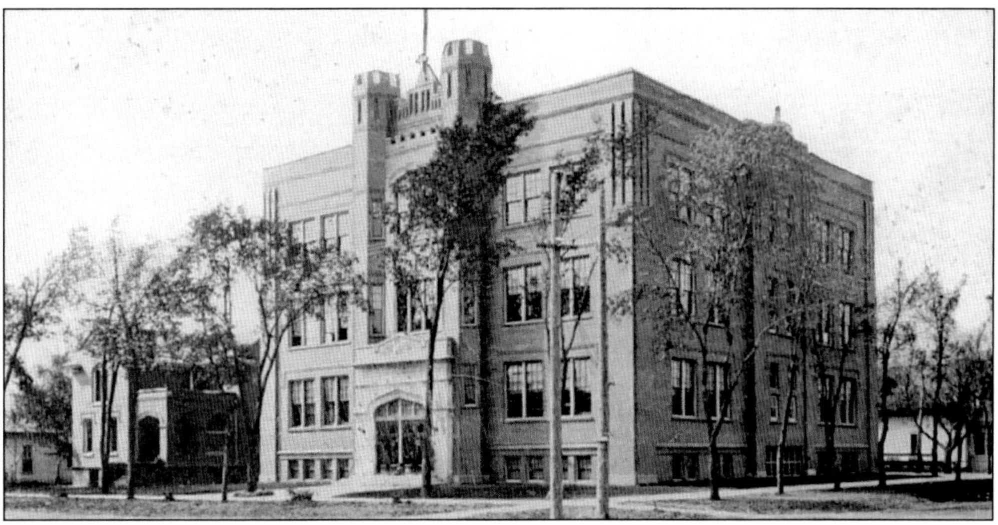

The Immaculate Conception Catholic School began in 1910 in the basement of the church with six grades, and plans to begin construction of a new school building on Third Street East between First and Second Avenues South. The new $80,000 school, on this undated postcard, opened in 1913 with eight grades and the same number of classrooms. An addition to the school was dedicated in August of 1964. The old 1913 school was razed in 1989 to make room for a parking lot. (Courtesy Ken and Lyn Sheldon.)

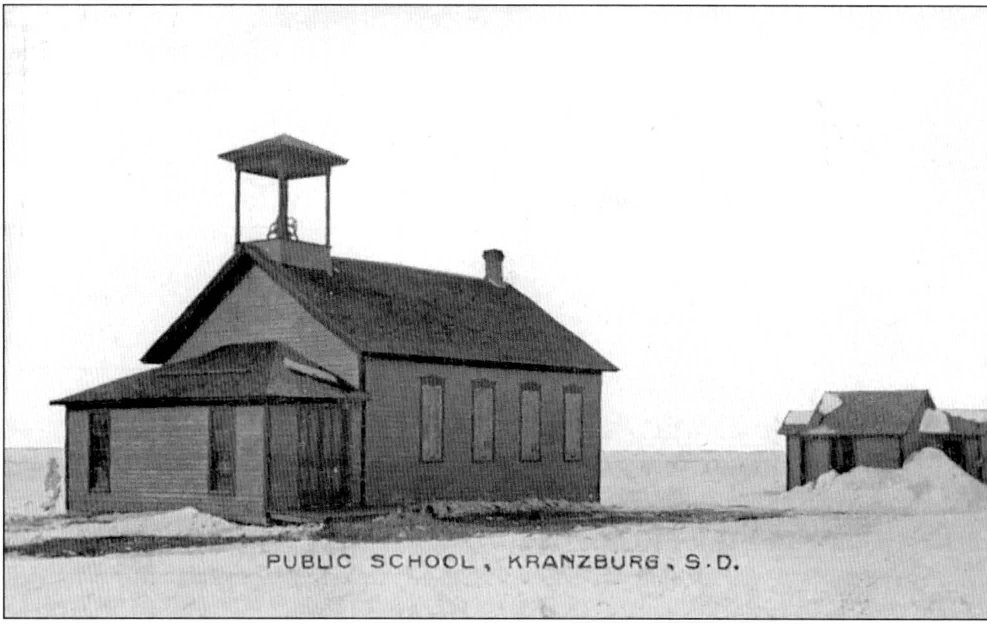

The Kranzburg School of District 5, still preserved on its original site in the town of Kranzburg, was organized and built in 1879, and is one of the oldest one-room schools still standing in Codington County. The first school term was conducted from December 1879 to March 1880. The school was still in operation in 1968 when school districts in Codington County and across the state were reorganized.

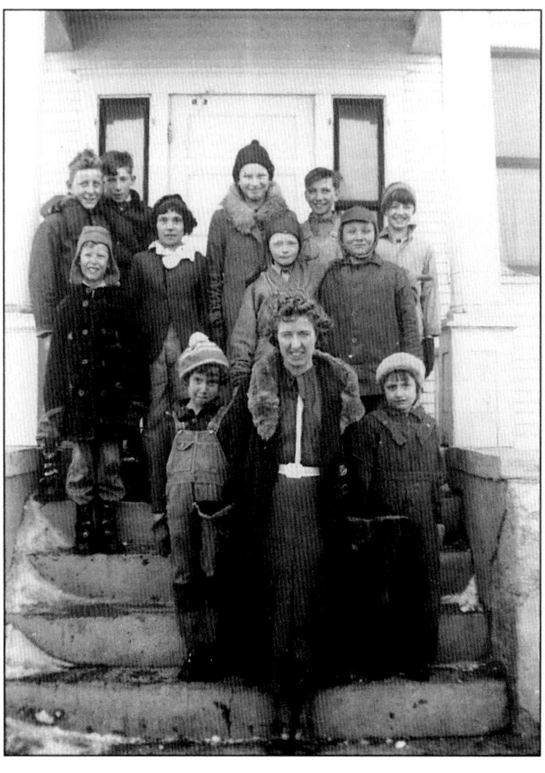

The Fuller School in District 10 was organized and constructed about 1879. This snapshot from about 1936 pictures teacher Mary O'Toole with her pupils during the 1936-1937 school term.

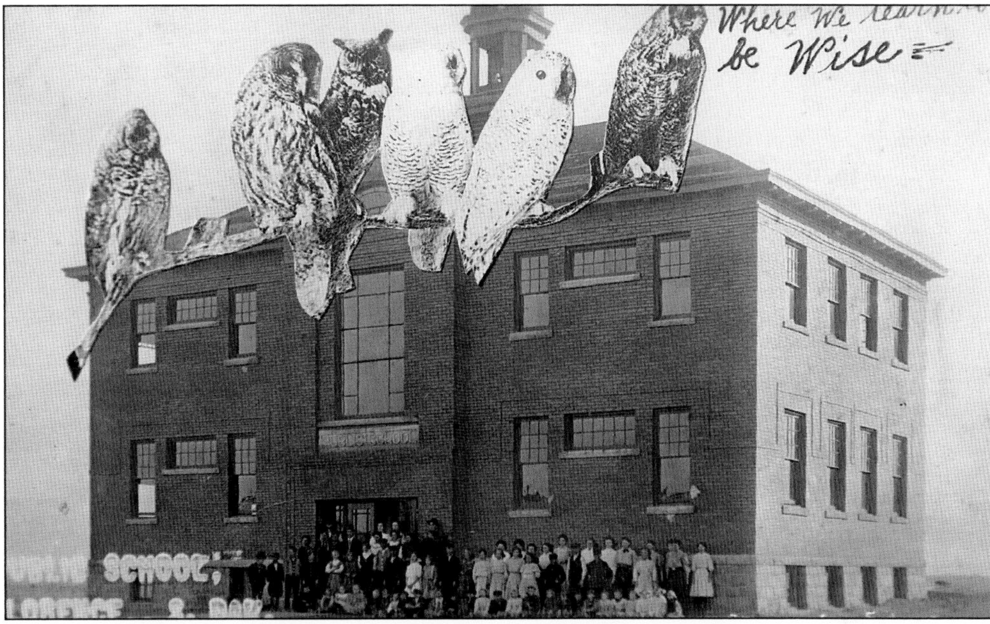

The Florence School of Fuller Township School District 28 was completed in 1907. An attempt at humor was made on this undated postcard, with pictures of owls pasted on the roof of the school building, and the phrase, "Where we learn to be wise," written in the upper right hand corner. Eight grades and a two-year high school were operated in the school. A combination auditorium and classroom building added in 1925 was destroyed by fire in 1955, but was replaced immediately.

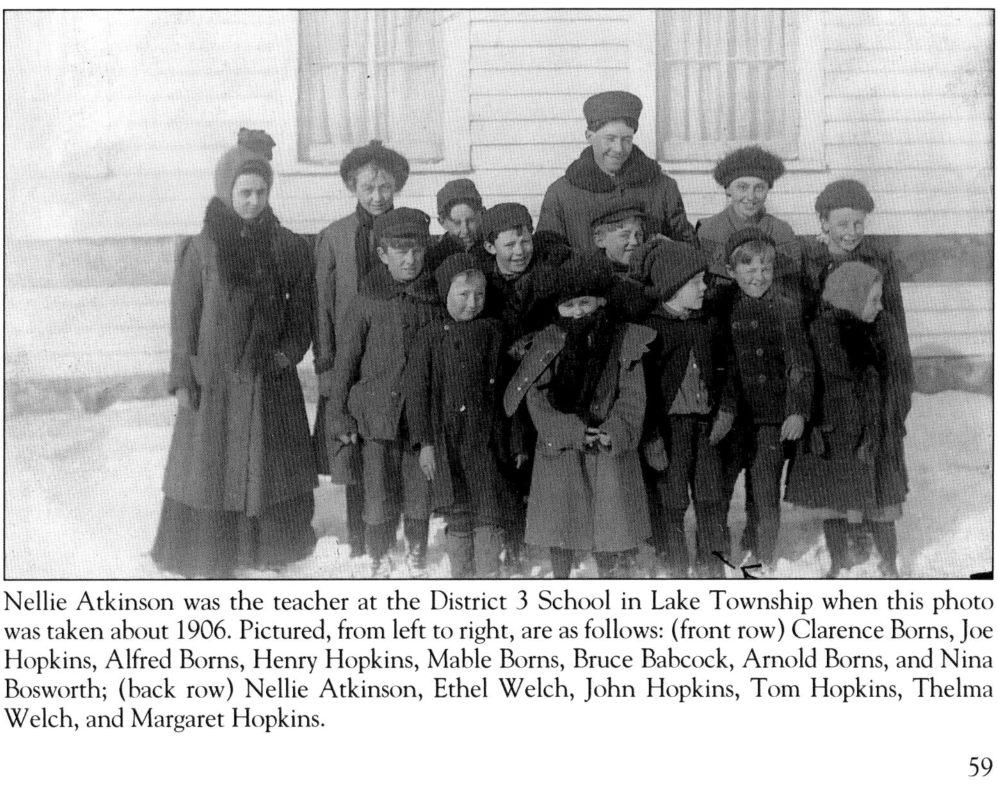

Nellie Atkinson was the teacher at the District 3 School in Lake Township when this photo was taken about 1906. Pictured, from left to right, are as follows: (front row) Clarence Borns, Joe Hopkins, Alfred Borns, Henry Hopkins, Mable Borns, Bruce Babcock, Arnold Borns, and Nina Bosworth; (back row) Nellie Atkinson, Ethel Welch, John Hopkins, Tom Hopkins, Thelma Welch, and Margaret Hopkins.

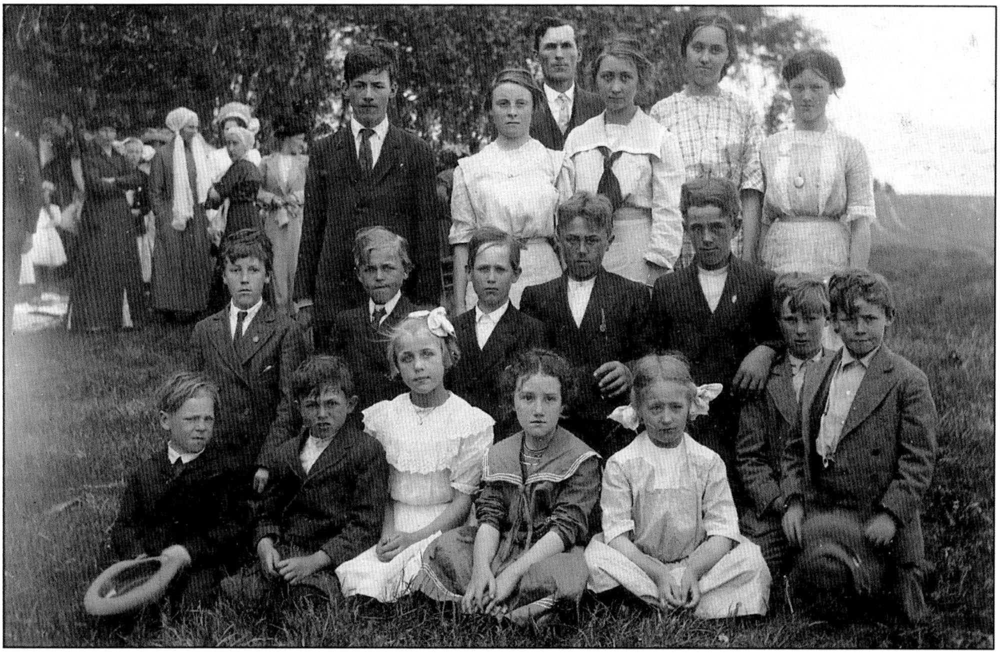

Several years later, in 1911 or 1912, many of the same students from District 3, in the previous photo, gathered at Warner's Grove on the west end of Lake Kampeska for a school picnic. The students, from left to right, are as follows: (front row) Orville Nelson, Charlie Oaks, Mabel Borns, Doris Babcock, and Ruby Welch; (middle row) Bruce Babcock, Herb Welch, Alfred Borns, Henry Hopkins, Arnold Borns, Clarence Borns, and Aloyius Hopkins; (back row) Joe Hopkins, Margaret Hopkins, J.W. Carroll (teacher), Ethel Welch, Thelma Welch, and Edna Saer.

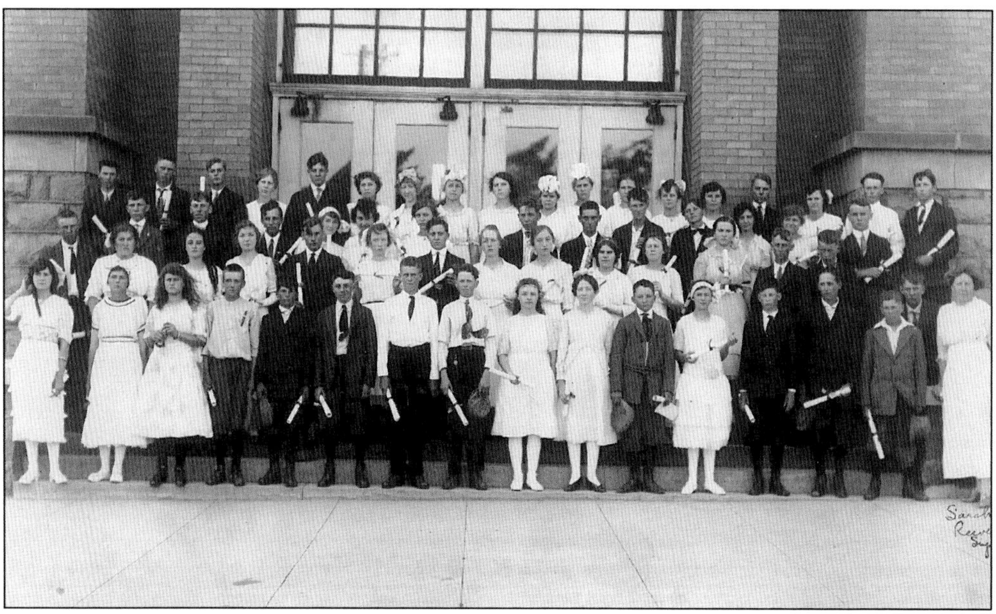

The 1915 Codington County eighth grade graduates pictured here are gathered on the steps of the Watertown High School. Doris Babcock, is identified third from left in the second row, and Sarah Reeve, the County Superintendent of Schools is the first on the right in the first row.

Four

Around the Neighborhood

Watertown was formed as a typical railroad "T" town. The main business streets ran perpendicular to the railroad tracks. Because the tracks did not run exactly east and west, townspeople built streets that ran at an angle from the northwest to the southeast, but perpendicular to the tracks. Land platted and added to the city after the original city plat was laid out remedied the mistake and created streets running north and south, and avenues running east and west. Most early industry was located south of the main railroad tracks and early housing was on the north and south side. House styles in Watertown reflected styles in similar communities across the Midwest. Many of Watertown's historic houses reflect styles from the Victorian period: Italianate, Queen Anne, and Second Empire.

Codington County is fortunate to have more than 30 houses and farms listed on the National Register of Historic Places. The Commercial Historic District in Uptown Watertown includes 115 buildings, 67 of which contribute to the National Register of Historic Places.

Photos in this chapter represent a gamut of people and homes: prominent and plain, city and rural, young and old, and man, woman, and child. All had an important contribution to the history of Watertown and Codington County.

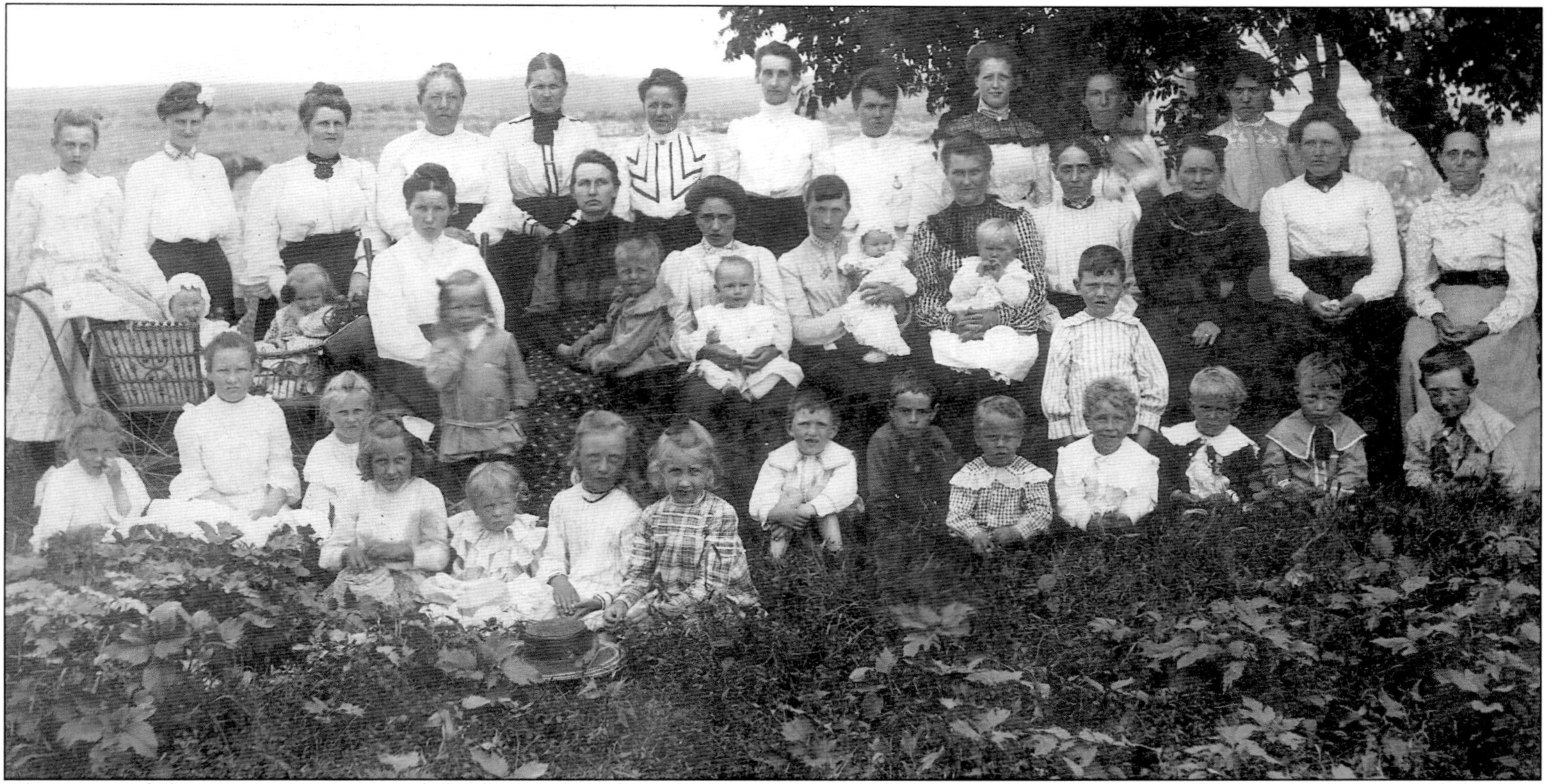

This group of Florence area women and children gathered, in 1905, at the home of Ed Shorts, five miles north of Florence. The town of Florence was not established until a year later. Pictured, from left to right, are the following: (front row) Lizzie Halse, Mary (Drake) Johnson, Cecil (Halse) Drake, Ella Short, Florence Thorson, Pearl (Maxwell) Thorson, Ida Short, unidentified, Carl Putnam, unidentified, Clarence Drake, Dell Drake, unidentified, unidentified, and Reuben Halse; (middle row) unidentified, Mrs. Ed. Short, unidentified, Mrs. Effie Thorson, Mrs. Francis Drake holding Howard in lap, Mrs. Christ Strobel, Mrs. Frank Painter, Mrs. William Drake, and Mrs. Emma Halse; (back row) Lulu Putnam, unidentified, Mary Foldager and daughter Myrtle in baby carriage, Lucy Halse, Eliza Drake, Mrs. Jim Brooke, Mrs. Ernest Putnam, Mrs. George Thompson, Flora Drake, Mrs. Robert Halse, and Libby Neville.

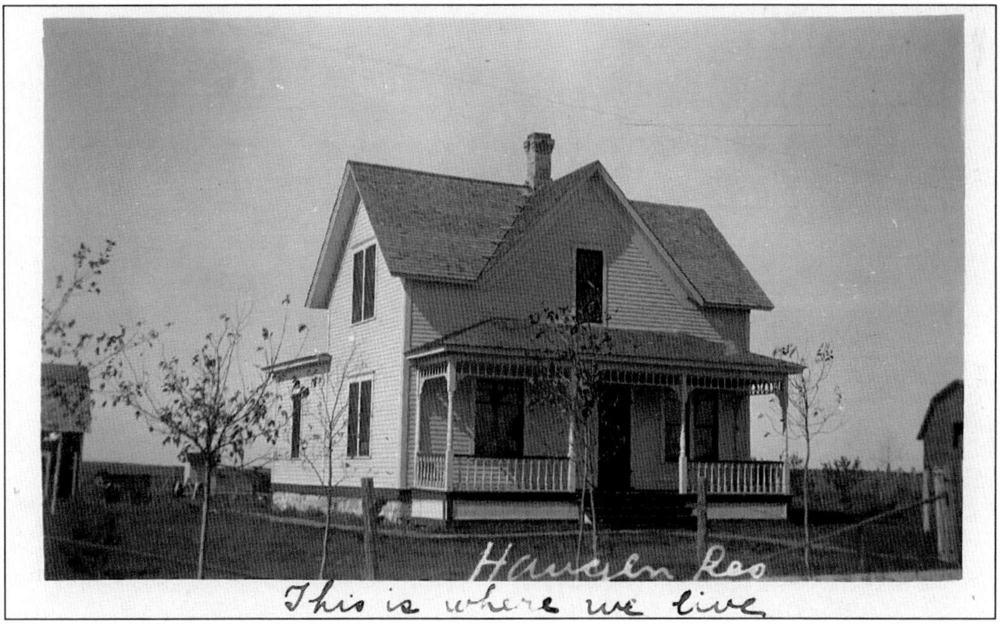

Pictured here in this *c.* 1911 image is the A.T. Haugen residence, located north of Wallace, near the Ustrud School, District 34. Bessie Haugen sent this postcard to her friend, Magdalena Rau, when Lena was working at the St. Joseph Hospital in St. Paul, Minnesota.

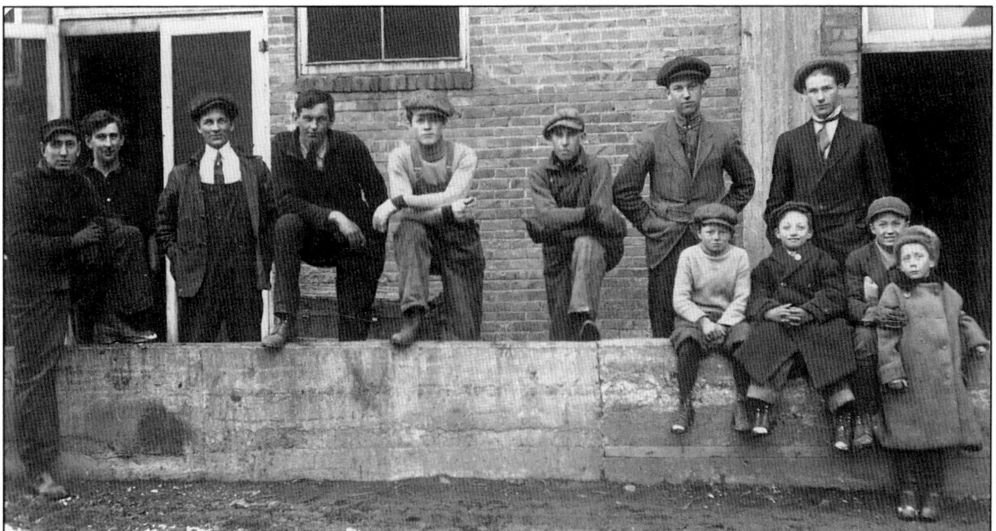

These young men and the building behind them on this undated postcard are unidentified. If you can positively identify any of them, please contact the Codington County Historical Society. The photo was probably taken between 1910 and 1919.

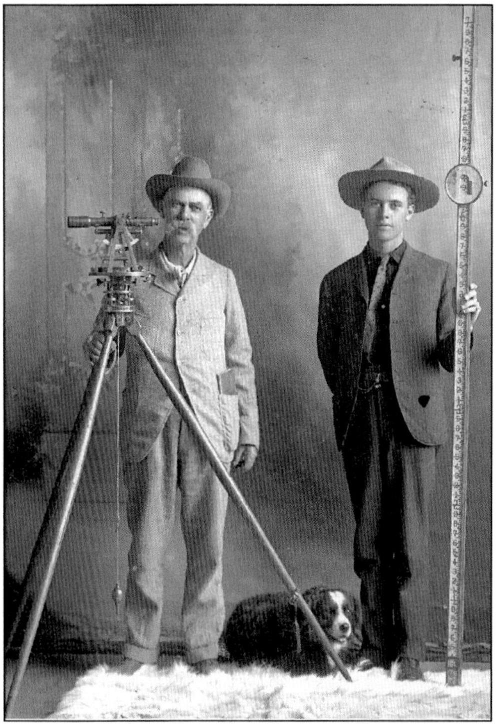

George Carpenter and his son, J.C., are pictured in this portrait from about 1901. Carpenter was a Civil War veteran who settled in Codington County in 1878, and was elected county surveyor soon after. He helped layout the town of Watertown and other towns in the state and also surveyed the Great Northern Railroad. Harmony Hill, over which Highway 81 runs south of Watertown, was previously named Carpenter Hill, to honor George Carpenter.

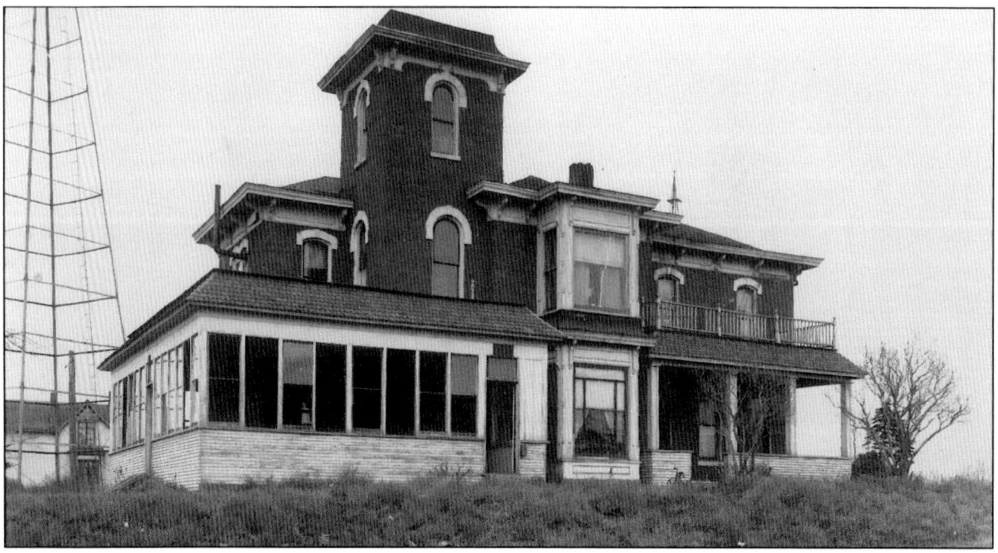

Construction of Arthur Mellette's new brick home in northwest Watertown was completed in 1885, though the Mellettes lived there only nine years. Mellette, a bondsman for the state treasurer, W.W. Taylor, was forced to surrender his entire personal fortune when Taylor fled the country with $367,000. The house was home to Watertown's first radio station, KGCR, for a short time in the late 1920s, but when the station left in 1932, it soon fell back into its former state of disrepair. Many children believed it to be haunted, though none of the home's residents ever died there. The house was condemned in the 1940s, but a group of concerned women and men successfully saved it from demolition, restored it, and opened it as a historic house museum about the Mellette family.

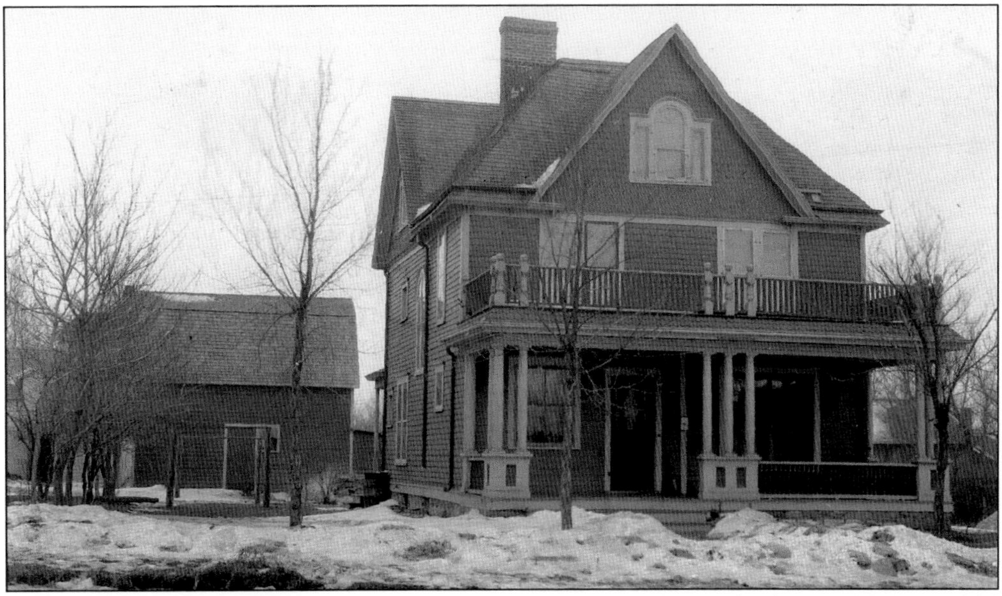

This residence, at 314 Second Street Northwest in Watertown, was the home of E.O. Lerdahl from the time of this photo, about 1914, until the 1940s. Lerdahl was a traveling salesman at the time of this photo, and later became an agent for the Hamm Brewing Company, which had an office in Watertown. The house still stands, though the columned porch was removed.

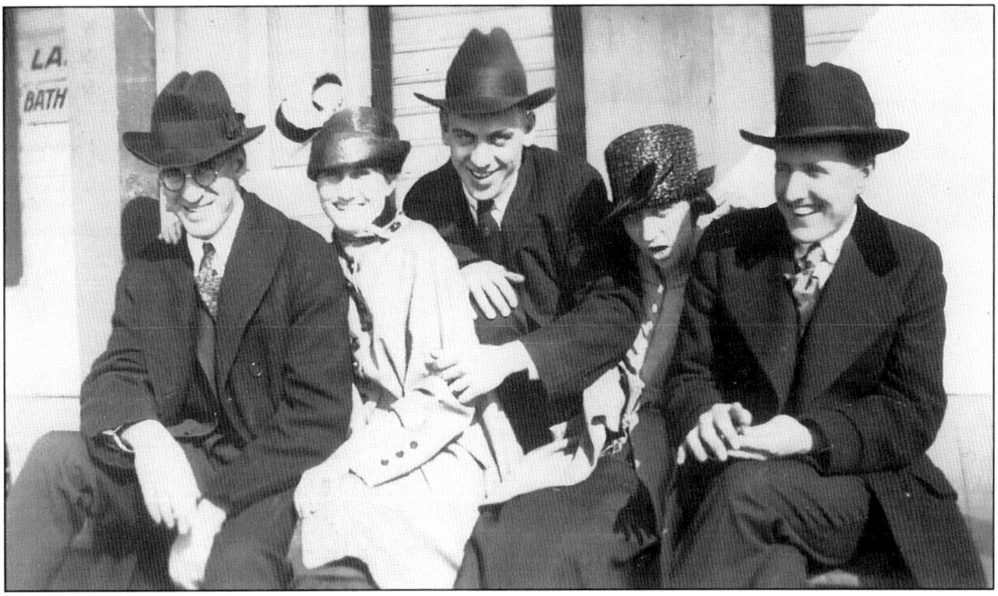

Included in this undated photo of friends are Audrae and Lloyd Dayton, at right. Audrae Lerdahl and Lloyd Dayton were married June 25, 1919, in the Scandinavian Lutheran Church at the present location of Grace Lutheran, at the southeast corner of the intersection of Second Street East and Second Avenue South. Lloyd and his son Ed were employees of the Sperling shoe store on South Broadway for many years.

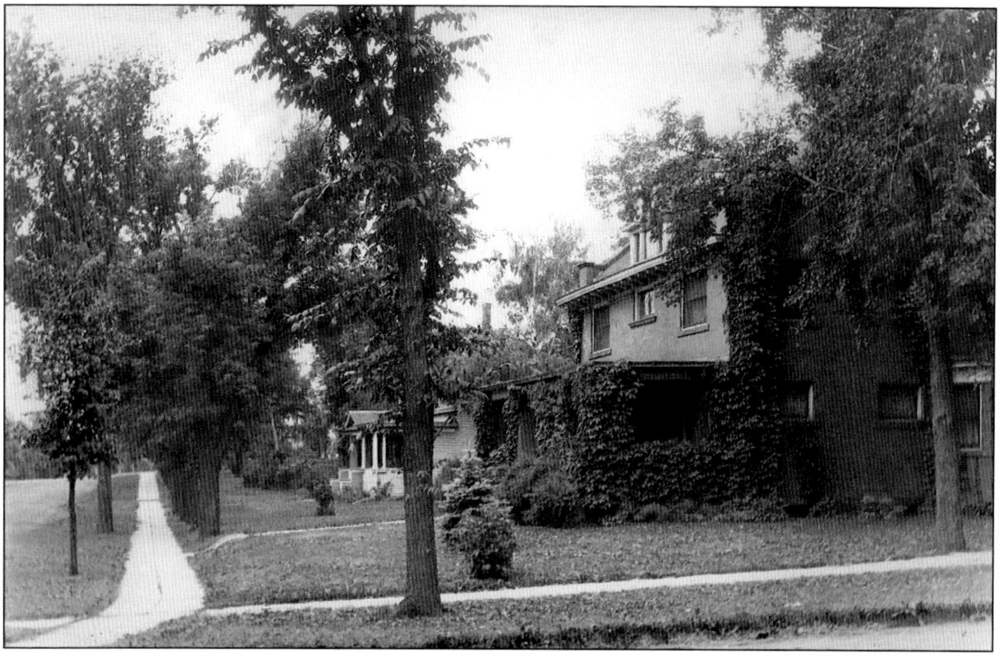

The David Jones home, at right, and Herb Sheldon home are pictured in this undated view of Park Street, looking south from Fifth Avenue North. The Jones' home was designed by Maurice Hockman, and was built in 1909. Jones was a pharmacist and owner of Jones Drug, and vice-president of Midland National Life Insurance. Sheldon, cashier of the Citizens National Bank, built his home in 1886.

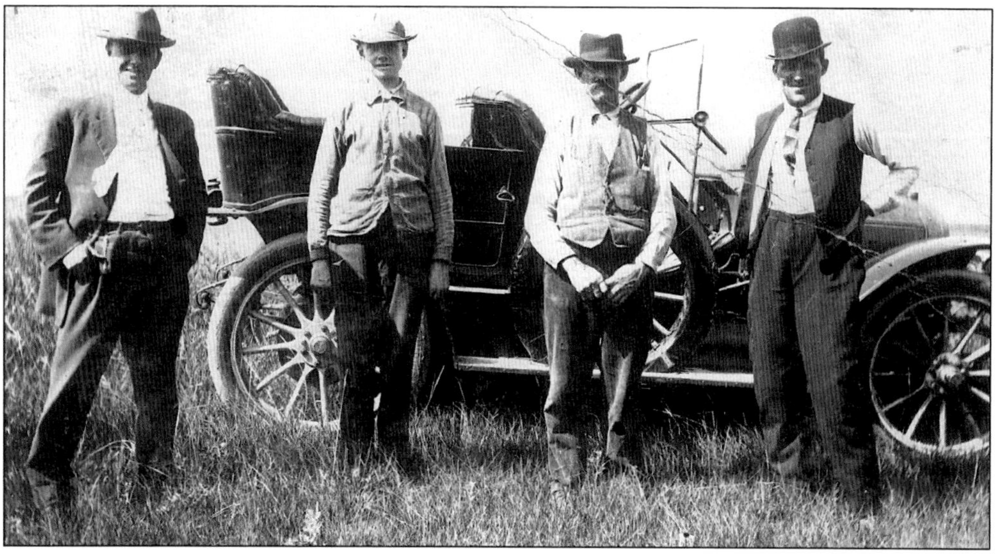

Andrew Palm of Lake Norden, South Dakota, was hired as the superintendent of the Codington County Better Farming Association on April 1, 1913, and became quickly successful and popular, organizing farmers and homemakers clubs across the county. He helped organize the Lakeview Farmers club near Yahota in 1914. On July 19, 1913, Palm sent this postcard of H. Rice, H. Almsted, F. Almsted, and H. Rogers to Rogers, and identified them as "Some of the Codington Co. Good Farmers."

Brothers Clement and Isadore Mondloch began their careers in construction by helping their carpenter father John when they were just in grade school. The brothers worked together in shipyards in California and Washington, later returning to the Henry area to build some the most beautiful homes in the surrounding towns. This photo of the brothers is from about 1907.

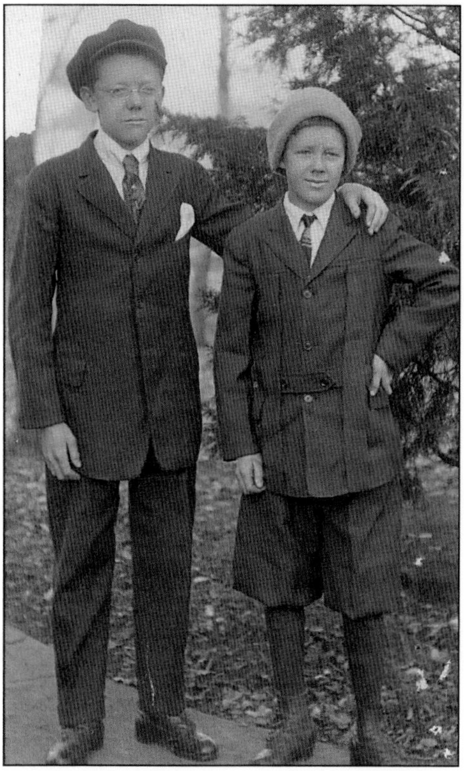

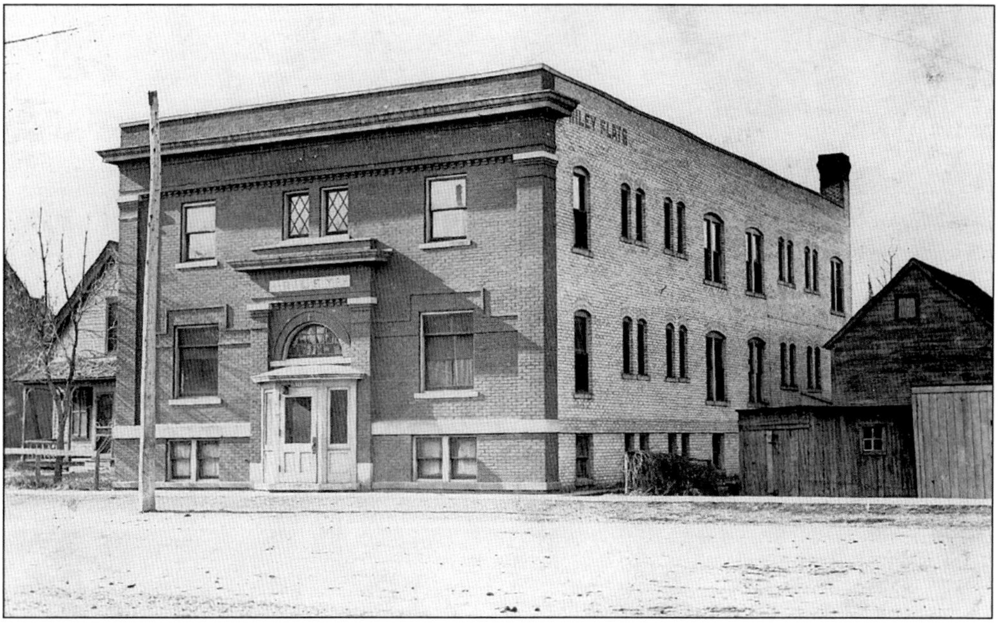

When the Riley Flats apartment building was constructed in 1914 at 15 Third Street Southeast, it was the largest of its kind in the city of Watertown at that time. The building was promoted as "modern," the apartments having a large living room, a kitchenette, a bathroom and closet, and each apartment having an independent meter for gas lighting, the halls being lit with electricity. The name of the building changed to Ritz by 1919.

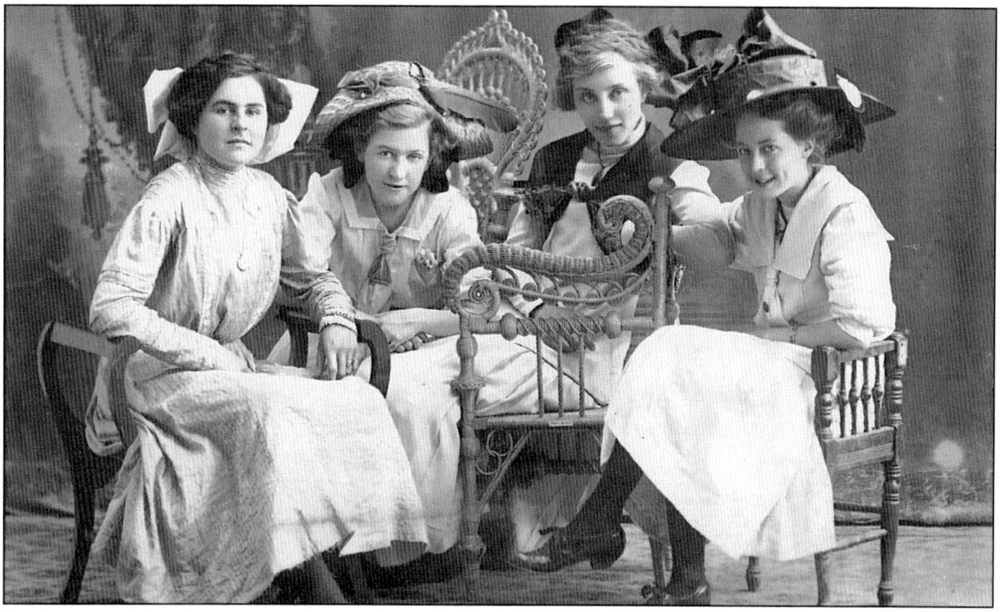

Big hats and hair bows were the style when this picture postcard was made of Audrae Lerdahl, right, and three of her friends, about 1915.

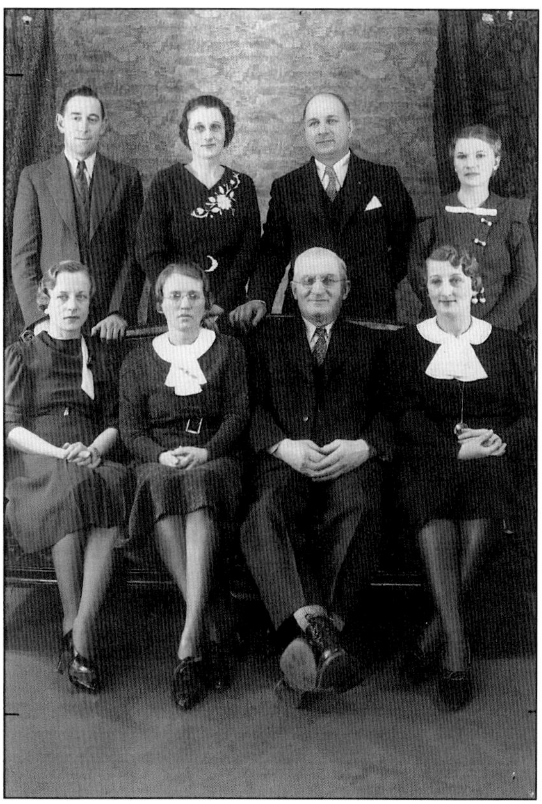

The Lincoln Hotel staff is pictured in this photograph from about 1930. The only person in the photo who was not a member of the Rau family is Jerry Drake, at left in the back. A Lincoln Hotel menu from about that time names Ethel Rau as housekeeper, Ida as cashier, Mabel as hostess, Hilda in the office, Alice at the front desk, Jerry Drake as assistant manager, and Arthur Rau as manager. Albert Rau, the head of the Rau household and owner of the hotel, is seated in the front.

Five

Industry and Agriculture

Codington County has always been anchored by an agricultural economy. Agriculture is responsible for influencing many aspects of the local economy, from elevators and the railroad, to chemical and seed companies.

Even though the farm economy is reasonably strong, Codington County has not escaped the nationwide trend of decreasing numbers of farms and increasing size of farms. Another trend that Codington County is not immune to is migration of rural residents to cities. This trend has occurred nationwide since the 1930s and is most severe in agricultural states. A brief example: From 1964 to 1997, the number of farms in South Dakota decreased from 49,703 to 31,284, a reduction of 18,419 farms. That is a 37 percent decrease in the number of farms in 33 years. Conversely, the average farm size in 1964 was 917 acres and in 1997 it was 1,418. That represents an increase of 501 acres per farm, a 35 percent increase in size in 33 years.

Watertown had historically and currently has several other major employers. The Watertown School District is the largest current employer in Watertown followed by Prairie Lakes Hospital, Midcom, Premier Bankcard, Terex-Telelect, Angus-Palm, Oak Valley Farms, CoEv, Minnesota Rubber, Jenkins Living Center, Persona, Dakota Tube, and Smith Equipment. Together, these businesses employ 4,398 of the 15,305 people between the ages of 18 and 65 in Watertown; 28.7 percent of people in that age group work at one of those 13 businesses.

The following photos in this chapter exhibit agricultural and industrial scenes in Codington County and Watertown.

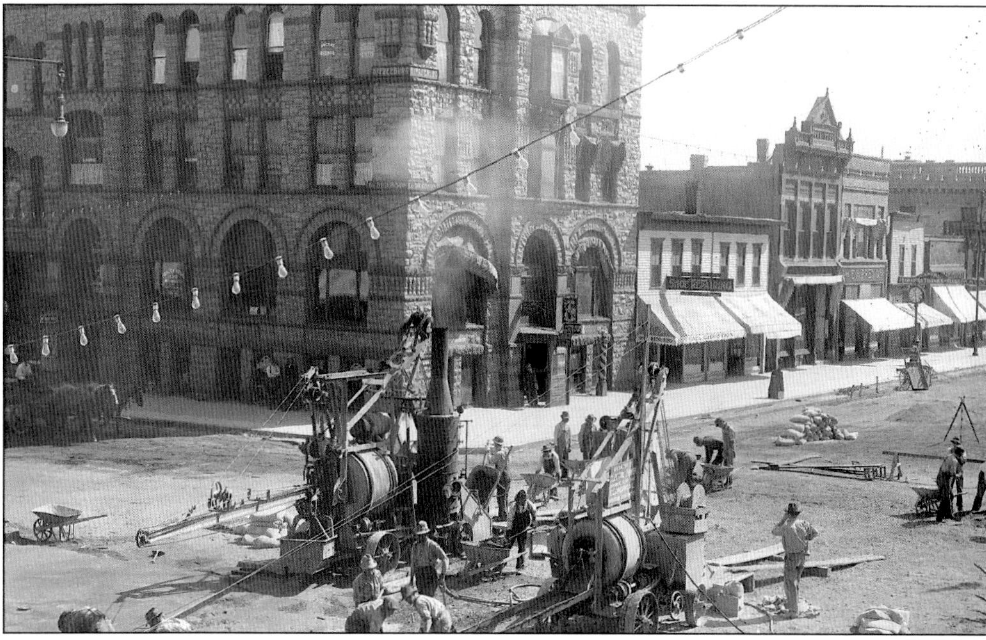

The City of Watertown made preparations to begin paving the Uptown streets in 1912, and the paving, done by the Charles Atkinson paving company, was completed in the summer of 1913. The City Council set aside November 7, 1913, as a "gala" day to celebrate the paving completion. This view of paving at the intersection of Kemp Avenue and Broadway faces southeast, toward the Granite Block. The other businesses, on the east side of South Broadway, starting next to the Granite Block, are George Christion Shoe Repairing; Nelson & Reed hardware; E.H. Prey jeweler; C.A. Neill Harness, Trunks, and Bags; and the last two are unidentified.

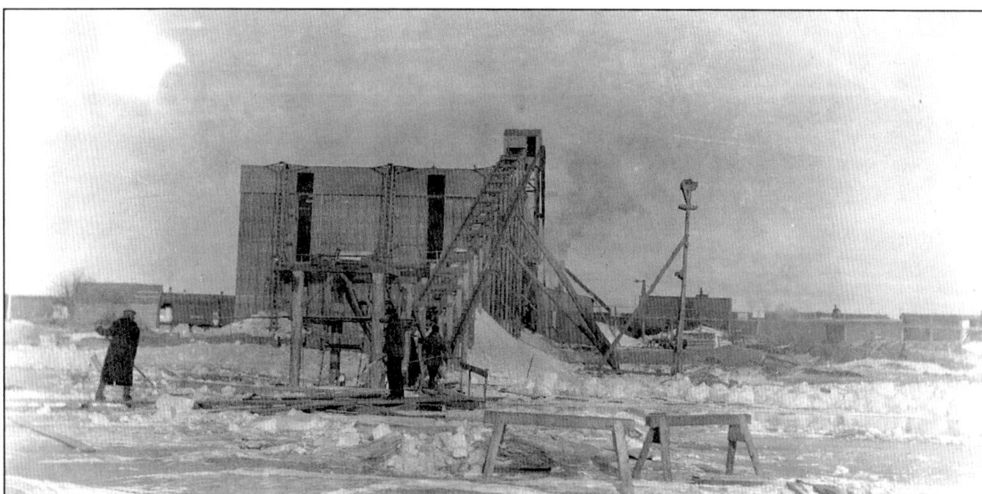

The Kampeska Materials Company operated this ice plant at Lake Kampeska from 1898 until the 1940s. Crews harvested thousands of tons of ice every year, usually beginning after Christmas. Once a large space was cleaned, ready for cutting, any new snow severely hampered the harvesting process. The Swift & Company plant was one of the biggest consumers of ice from Lake Kampeska, requiring several full railroad carloads daily. The ice buildings at Lake Kampeska were razed about 1960. (Courtesy Ken and Lyn Sheldon.)

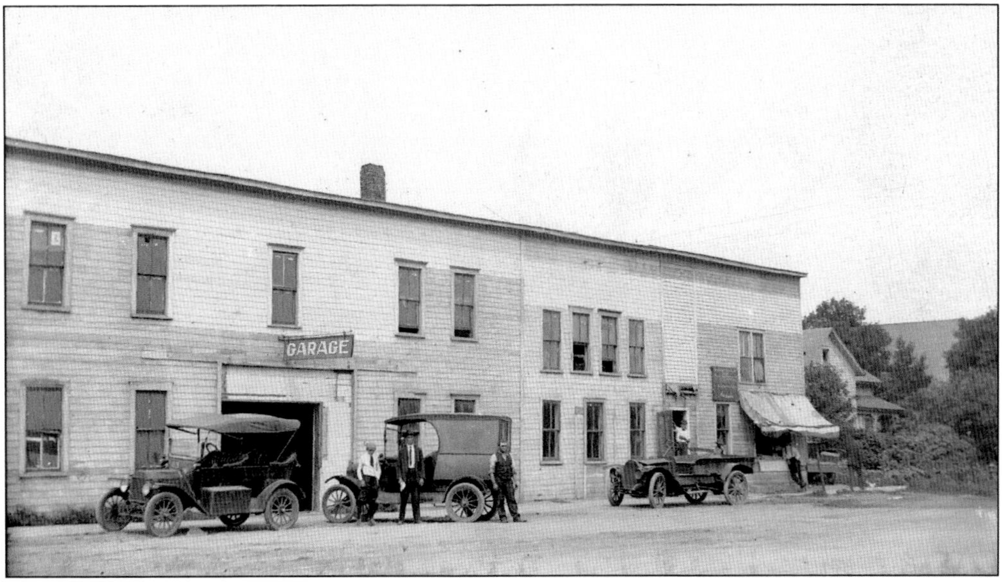

By 1903, John Pum was running his tanning and harness making business in this structure on West Kemp Avenue. The tannery bought all kinds of hides, and made hats, mittens, and coats in addition to harnesses. When he retired about 1914, the business became the Watertown Hide & Fur Co., and moved to North Broadway about 1919. The building was then a junk shop and a grocery store, before it was turned into apartments. It was demolished about 1955.

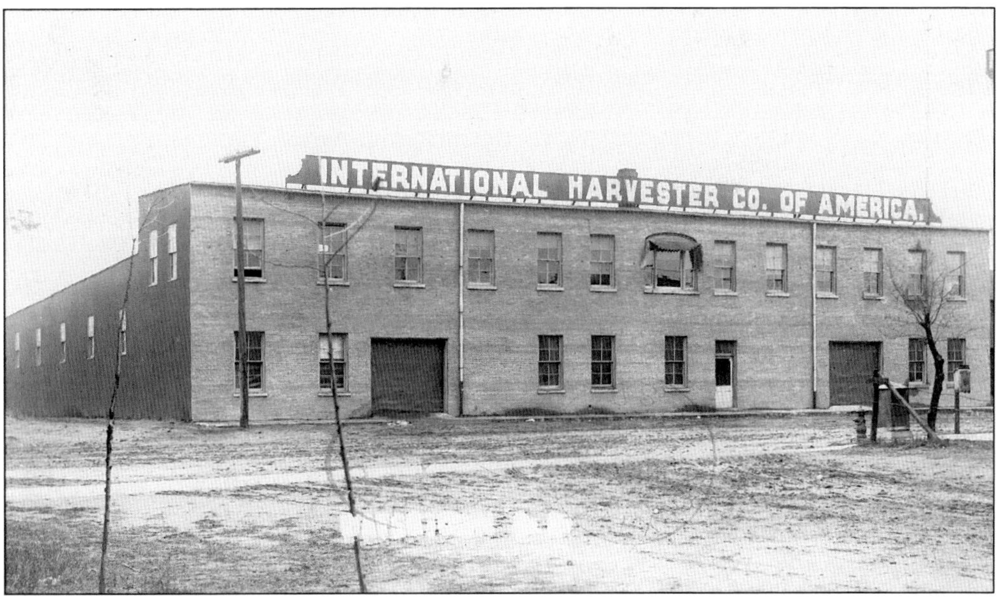

After having just an agent located in the Granite Block for several years, the International Harvester Company constructed a 125 feet by 130 feet warehouse and sales building on First Avenue Northwest, just north of where First Street West runs south from First Avenue North. An addition was built in 1909, to form the building on this undated photo postcard. Increased sales compelled the company to construct the four-story brick and reinforced concrete building across from Watertown's current fire station on First Avenue in 1918, which they used until about 1950. (Courtesy Ken and Lyn Sheldon.)

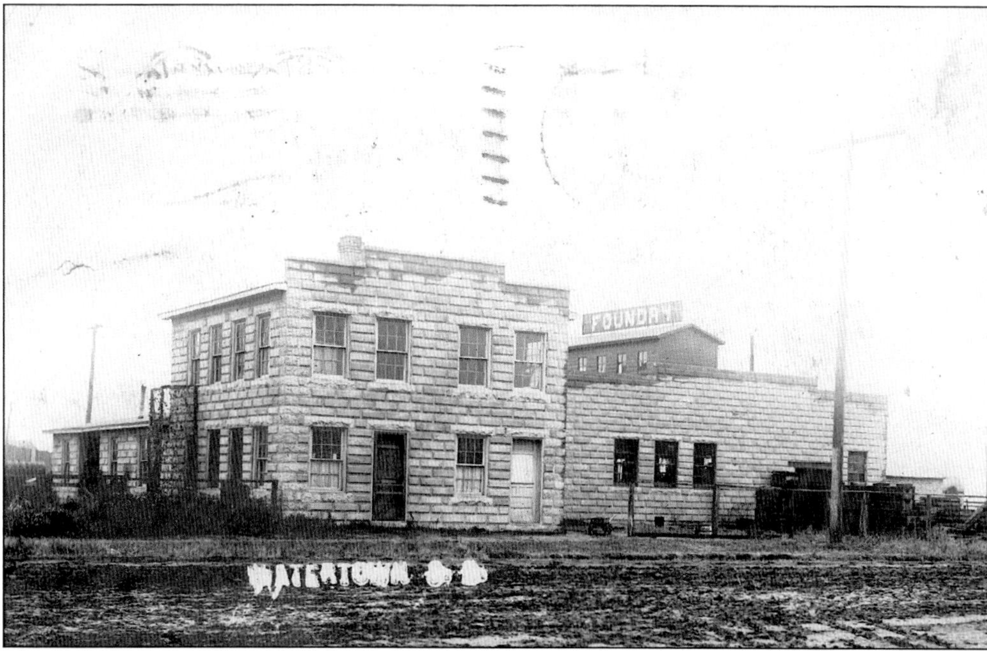

J.H. Bruns started the foundry on this postcard postmarked September 14, 1908, at First Avenue North, between Fourth and Fifth streets East, about 1906. He operated it until it became the Watertown Foundry in the 1940s. Schull Construction located here in 1960. (Courtesy Ken and Lyn Sheldon.)

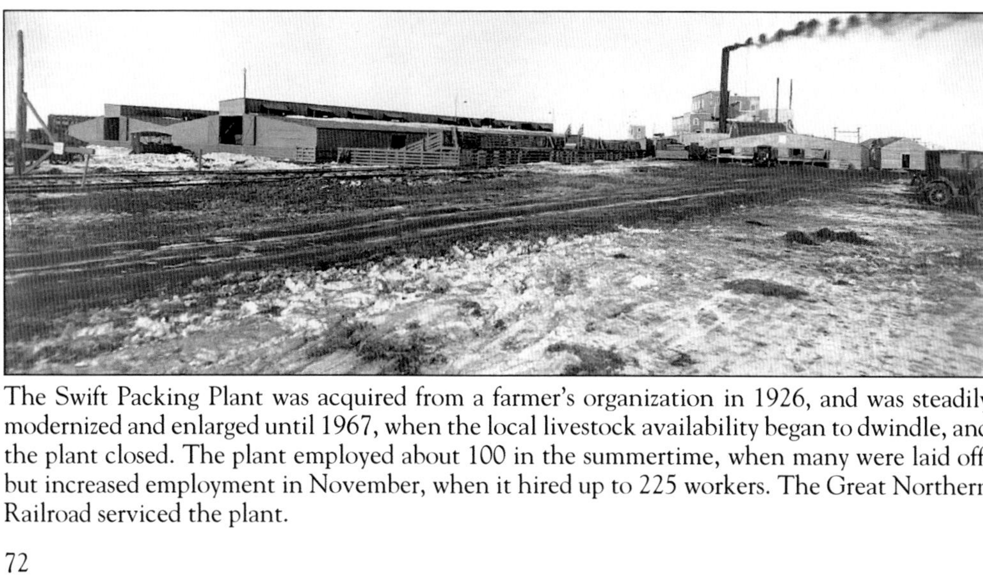

The Swift Packing Plant was acquired from a farmer's organization in 1926, and was steadily modernized and enlarged until 1967, when the local livestock availability began to dwindle, and the plant closed. The plant employed about 100 in the summertime, when many were laid off, but increased employment in November, when it hired up to 225 workers. The Great Northern Railroad serviced the plant.

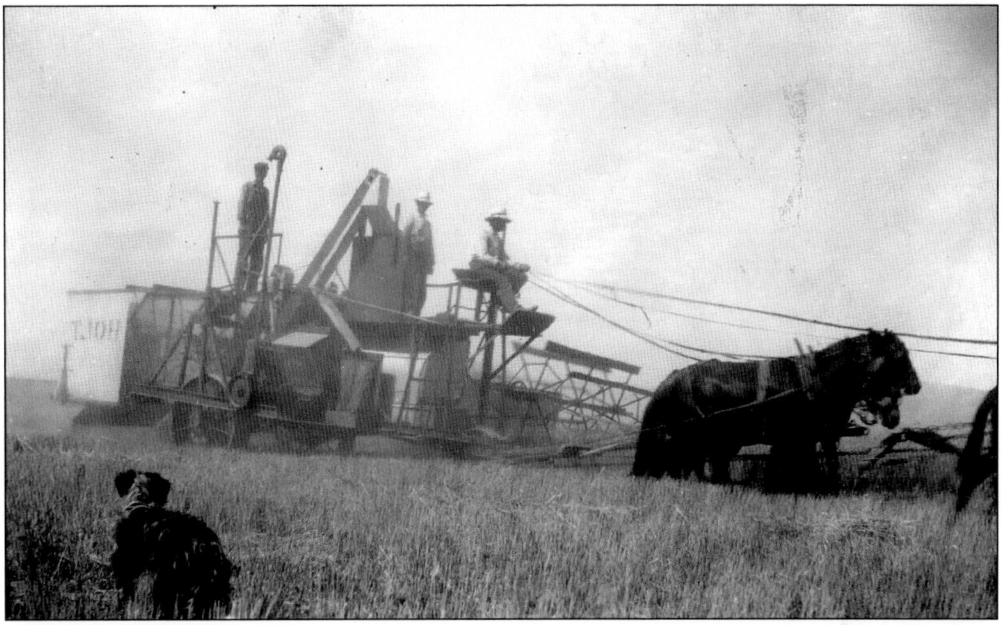

When creating this photo postcard, the maker reversed the negative. The letters on the threshing machine should spell HOLT. This Holt machine is an early type of combine harvester, on which the teamster sat on a long perch over the top of the team, and levelers worked racks to keep the separator level. The workers and location in this photo are unidentified. The photo was donated to the historical society by Dick Lantsberger.

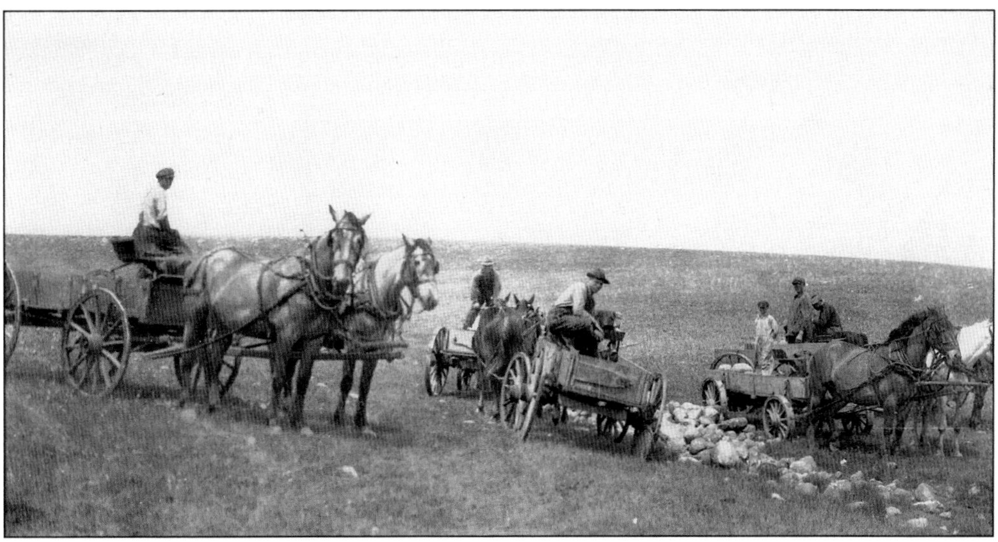

Some of the men and boys in this photograph, capturing the rock-picking process near South Shore, may be from the family of Otto and Bertha Korth.

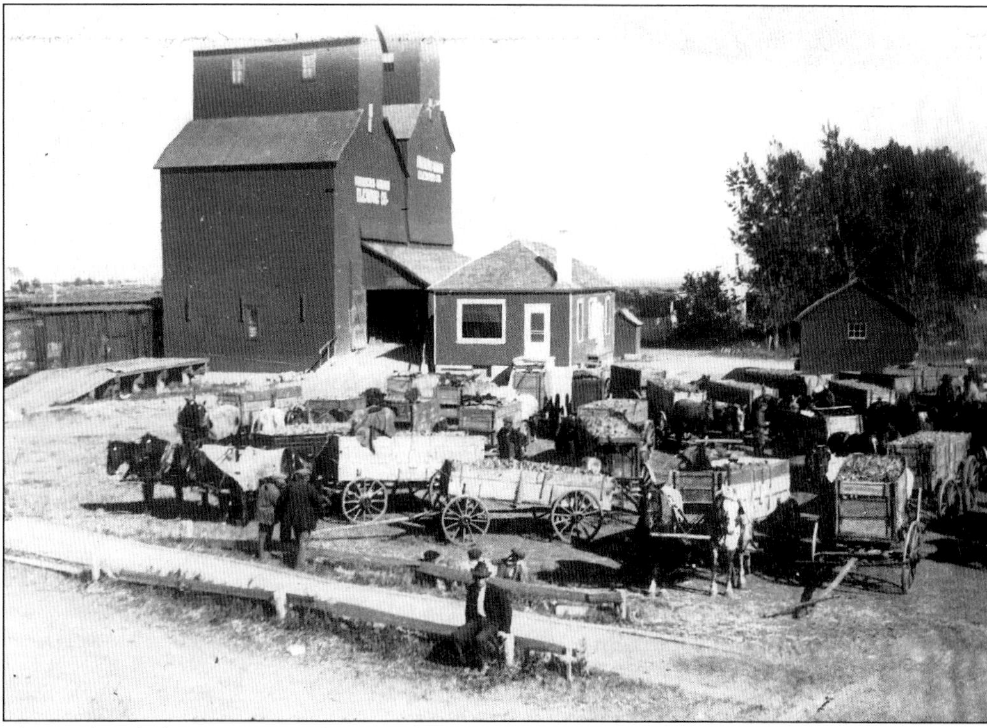

This undated photo captures dozens of wagonloads of potatoes lined up at the Henry, South Dakota elevator, sometime in the early 1900s.

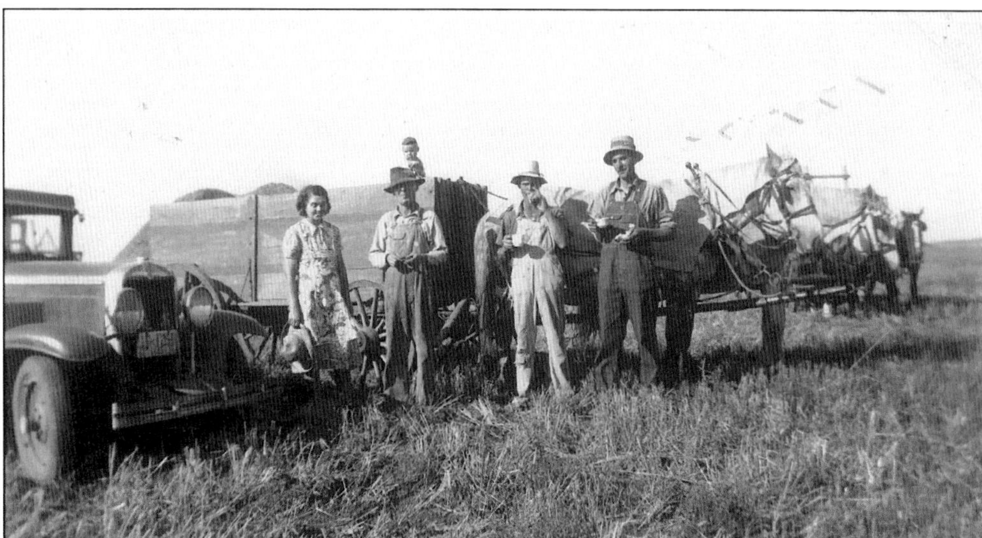

This snapshot captured members of the Chandler, Reichling, and Reddy families on a lunch break from threshing in Sheridan Township in 1938.

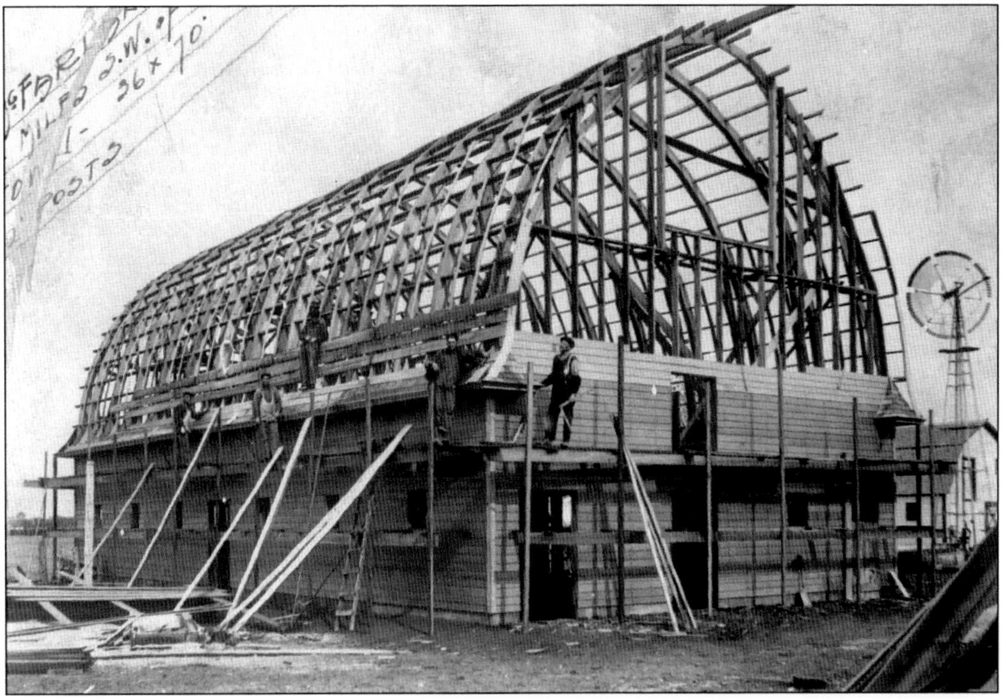

The Majerus Construction Company of Watertown built this barn in the 1920s for William McFarland, whose land was four miles southwest of Watertown, in Pelican Township. McFarland's wife Ellen died in 1922, the same year they built a new house.

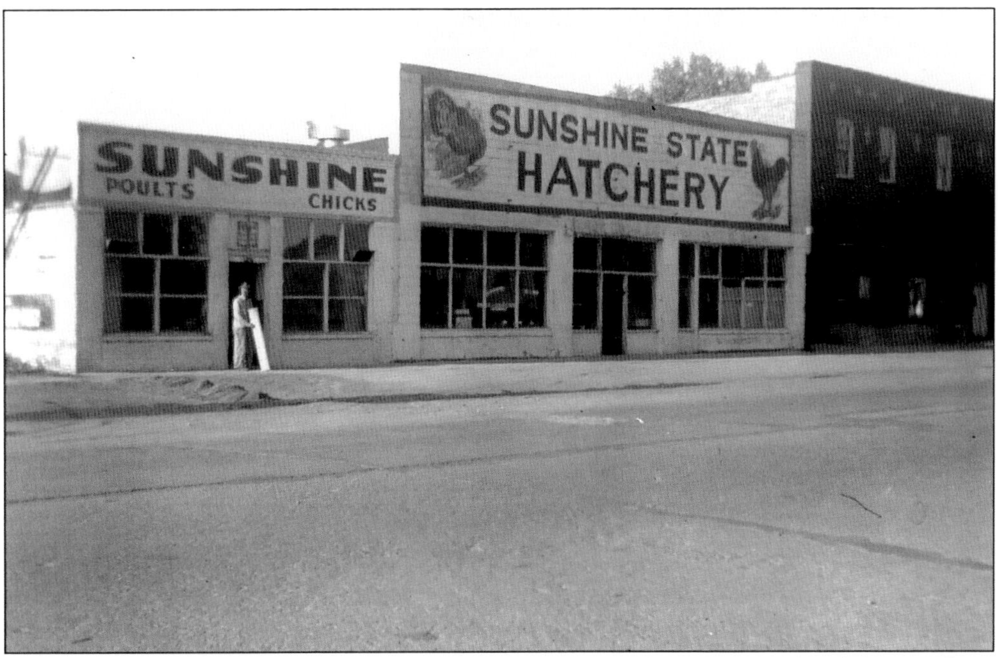

By 1939, the Gallisath Garage at 314 First Avenue Northeast was replaced by Sunshine Hatcheries, in this photo dated "before September 1949." Panatorium Dry Cleaning now occupies the building.

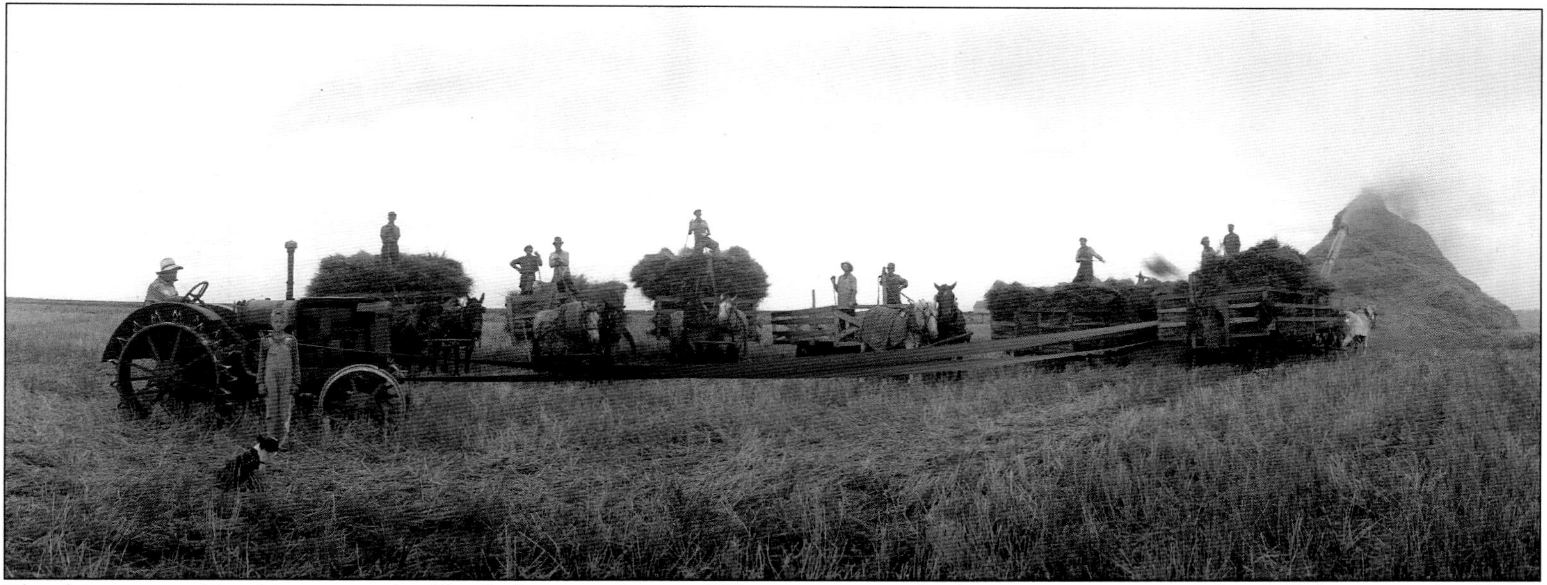

Threshing scenes like this one on the Kirsch farm, northeast of Watertown, near Gardner, were common in South Dakota into the 1940s. Photographers, like Carl Gray and his son Harold, packed their equipment in the threshing season and headed to the fields to take panoramic photos of the threshing rigs and their crews.

Six

Getting Around

As in most western cities, the first form of transportation in Codington County other than horse power was the railroad. The first railroad to come to Watertown was the Winona & St. Peter in 1873. A grasshopper plague and prairie fires that burned railroad bridges discouraged many settlers from coming to the area until the late 1870s. Watertown eventually became the railroad hub of northeastern South Dakota with five depots and lines going through the town. The railroad was primarily responsible for the growth of Watertown; it brought people and freight in, and took out grain to markets elsewhere.

Another reason why Watertown is still growing is because of the interstate. When Interstate 29 was being built, town leaders convinced the federal government to bend the highway to the west so that it was within a few miles of Watertown. That slight change in direction was one of the most significant things to happen to the city. It was a boon for businesses and helped keep Watertown growing instead of shrinking, especially in the last 20 years.

Thanks to forward-thinking citizens in the 1920s, Watertown was not left out of the air travel industry. The current airport was formerly a military airbase used to train airmen in World War II. For that reason, the runways are extremely long and can accommodate any size aircraft in the world currently flying.

Photos in this chapter show some of the structures and machines used for travel by denizens of Watertown and Codington County.

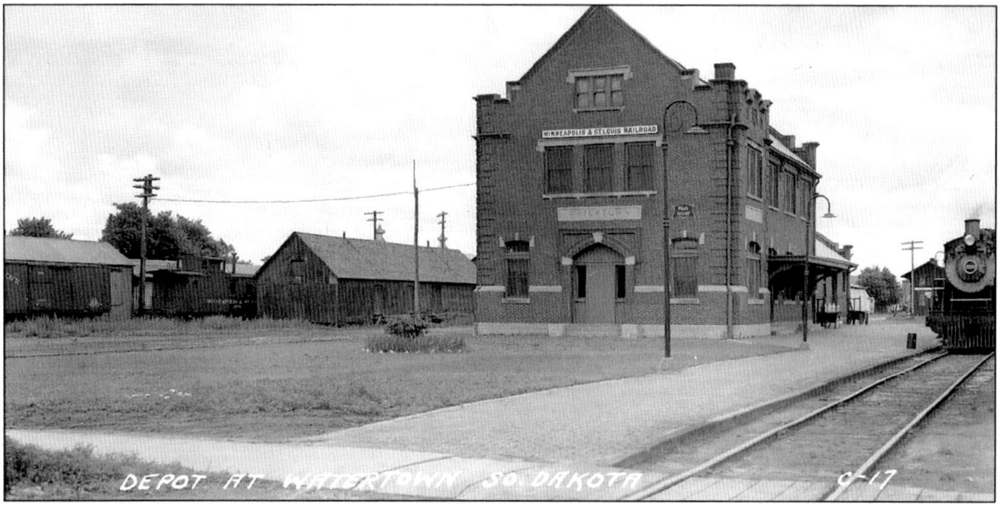

Construction of the Rock Island and Minneapolis & St. Louis depot on North Broadway, in this photo about 1940, was completed in 1912, and is the last passenger depot still standing in Watertown. It is well-remembered by many area residents, because the M. & St. L. had the only passenger service to Minneapolis from northeast South Dakota, until it was discontinued and the final departure was made on July 21, 1960. The Codington County Historical Society owned and operated the depot as a railroad museum from 1986 to 1996, but overhead costs forced its sale, and it now stands vacant. (Courtesy Ken and Lyn Sheldon.)

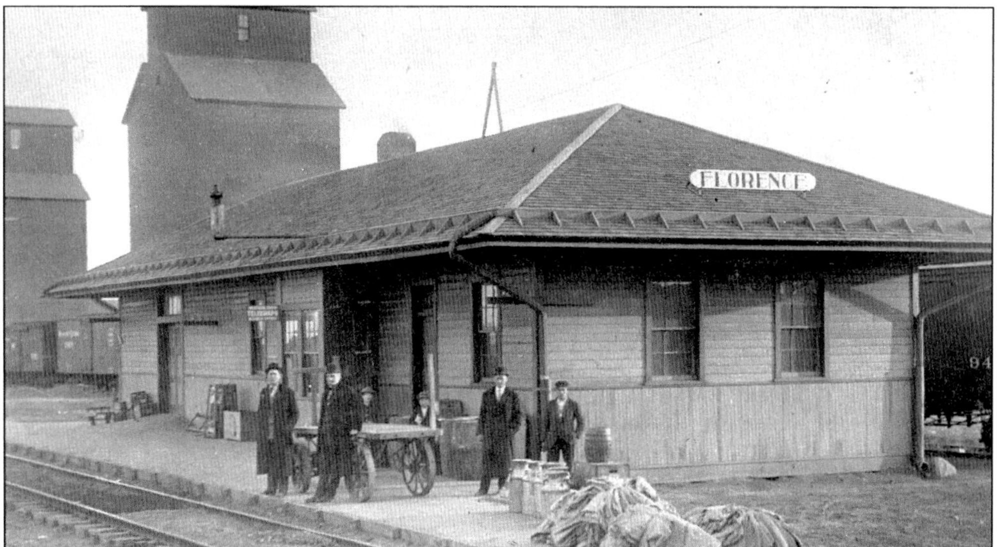

The town of Florence, northwest of Watertown, was served by the Minneapolis & St. Louis Railroad, which began extension of its track west of Watertown in 1905. The official plat of the town was filed with the Codington County Register of Deeds on June 19, 1906, and from then on, construction of frame and brick buildings was unremitting. The first issue of the town's newspaper, *The Florence Forum*, was published a month later on July 20, 1906, and reported almost sixty businesses established in the new community. Judging from the clean appearance of the depot and the new look of the railroad track, which is barely covered with ballast, this photo of the Florence depot dates to about 1906.

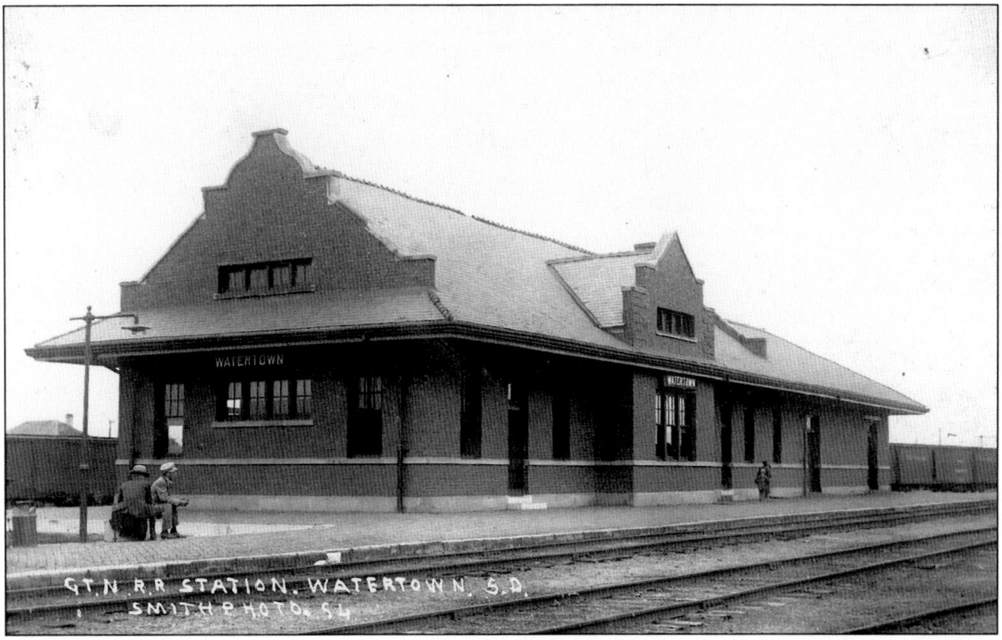

The Great Northern Railway constructed a new brick and stone depot on Fifth Street West, at the terminus of Second Avenue South in Watertown, in 1909. The depot was an aesthetic and sound structure, but was razed in 1992. (Courtesy Ken and Lyn Sheldon.)

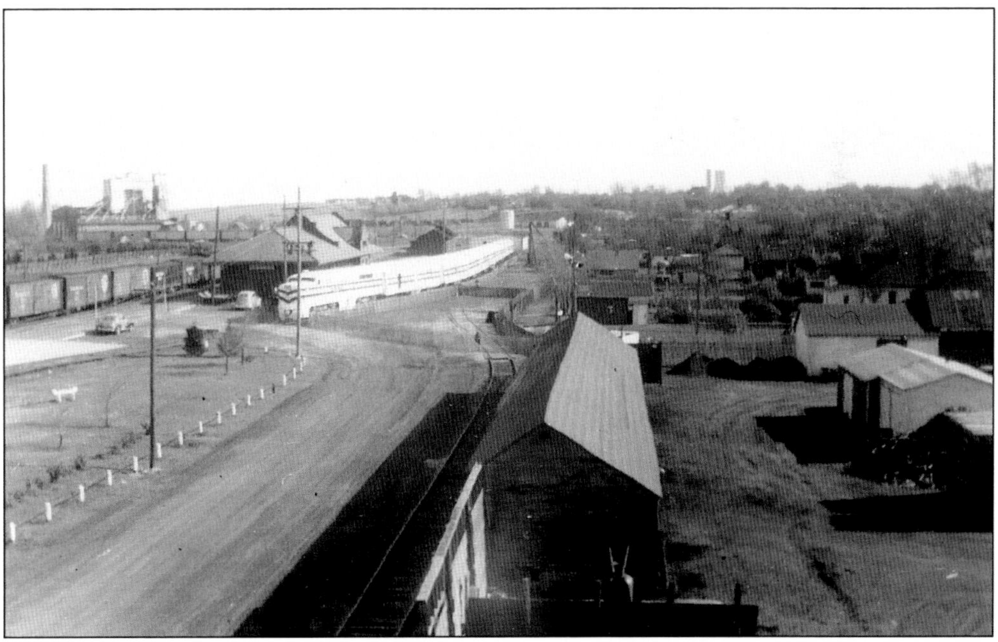

A Great Northern passenger train is stopped at the railroad's depot on Fifth Street West, in this snapshot from about 1950. The Great Northern discontinued its passenger service to Watertown about 1952, according to local veteran Great Northern employee Leo Huston.

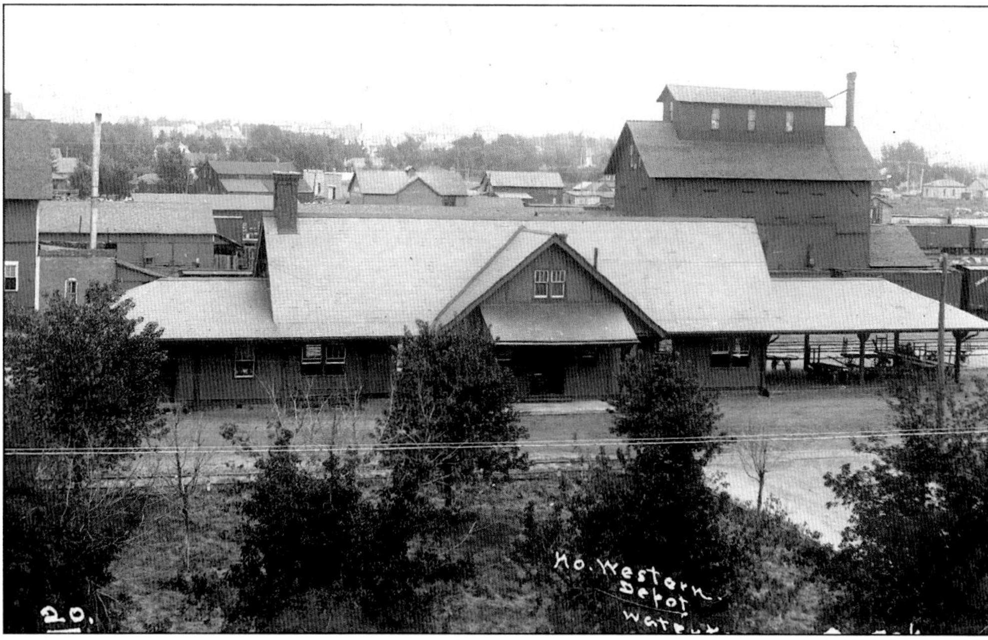

Watertown's Chicago & Northwestern Railroad depot was located just north of First Avenue North and the terminus of Second Street East, about where Lakeland Nurseries is today. The depot was constructed in the early 1880s, when the C&NW reached Watertown. The C&NW eventually took over the Minneapolis & St. Louis Railroad depot on North Broadway, and the old depot was sold to Melvin Schmieding in 1965, and moved to his farm southeast of Watertown.

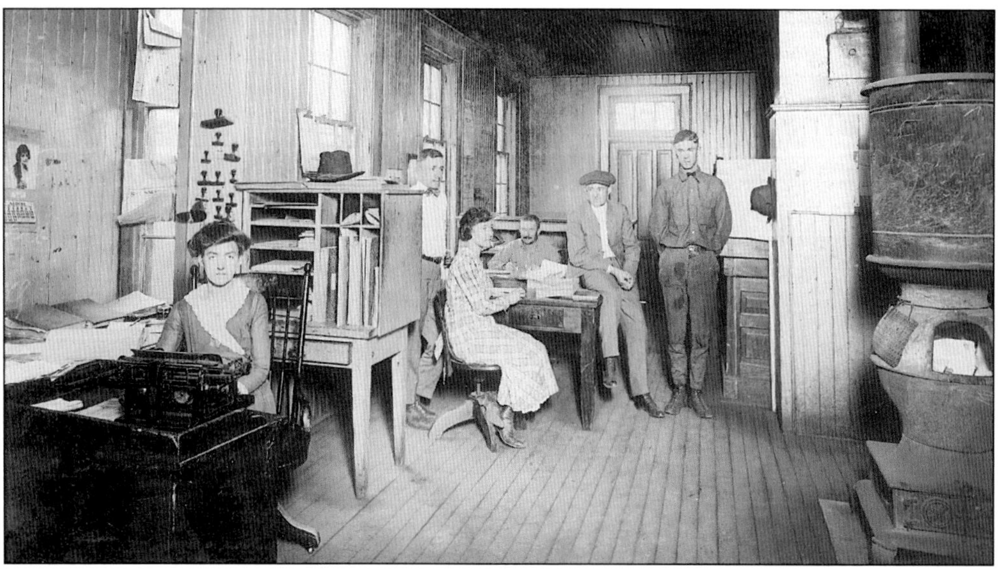

The employees in this photo of the Chicago & Northwestern freight depot from about 1926, are, from left to right, the following: Rema Sours, Robert Peller, Gena Strombotne, Pete Burnston, Mr. Prescot from Winona, Minnesota, and Carl Nevenheim. Gena (Strombotne) Arnsdorf wrote an essay about the working conditions at the freight depot for the Codington County Historical Society in 1987. She said that the depot was updated with electricity, storm windows, and an adding machine, after she wrote a letter to the superintendent in Winona, Minnesota.

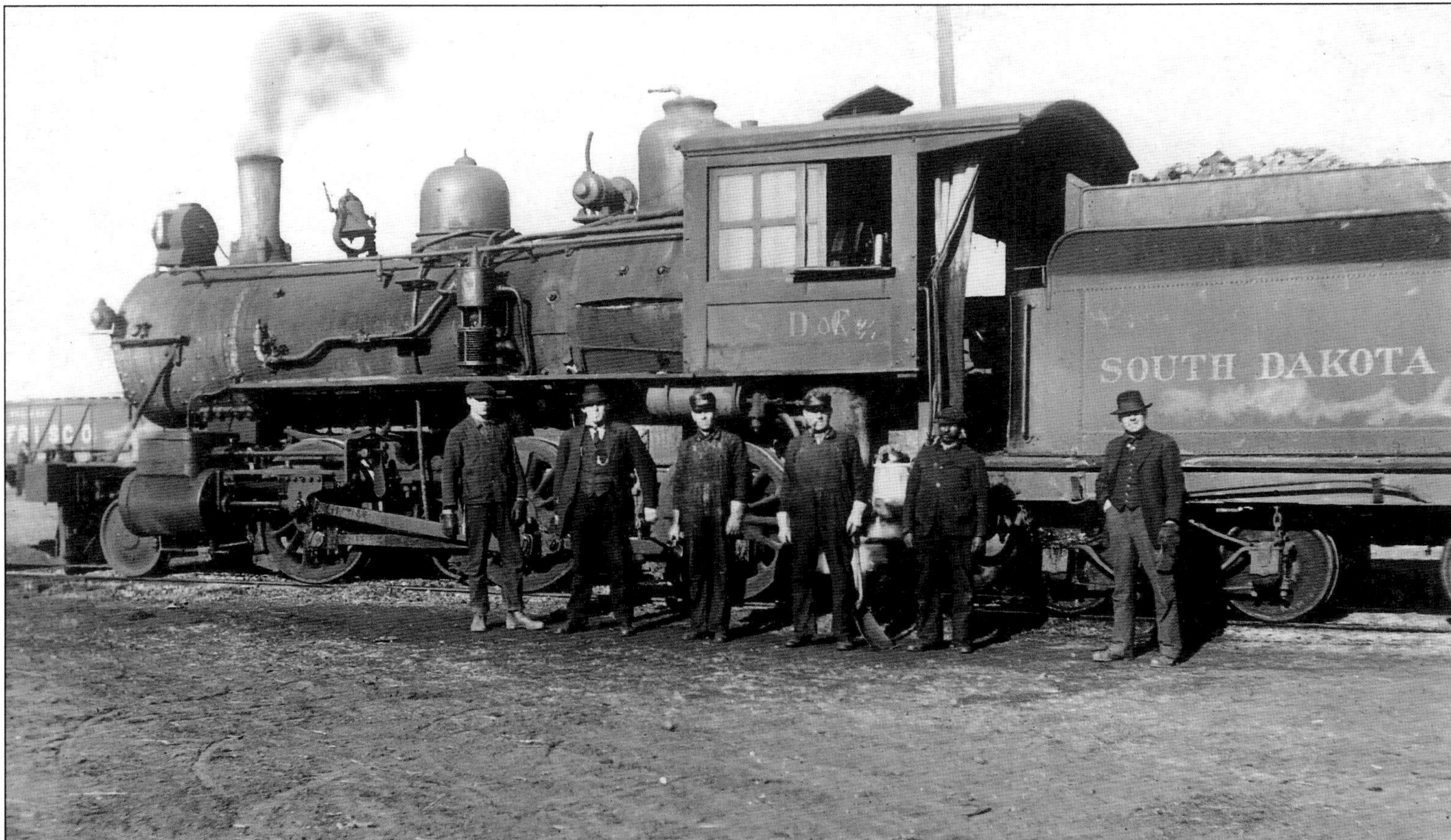

A South Dakota Central Railroad crew took a minute to pose with their engine for this undated photo postcard. The South Dakota Central Railway, a subsidiary of the Chicago & Northwestern, opened its line from Brookings to Watertown in 1882. This line became the only railroad line between Watertown and Sioux Falls.

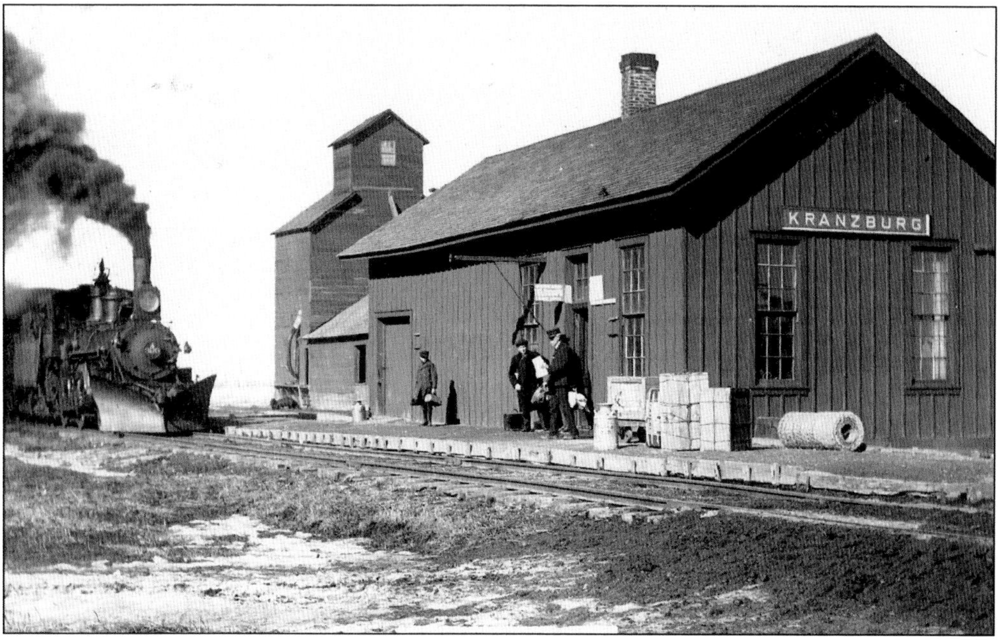

The town of Kranzburg was established in 1878 as a station on the Winona & St. Peter Railroad, a division of the Chicago & Northwestern Railway, when the rail line was built to Watertown that year. This photo postcard, postmarked March 19, 1909, shows several passengers waiting for the westbound train pulling up to the platform, with a seasonal snow plow still attached to the front.

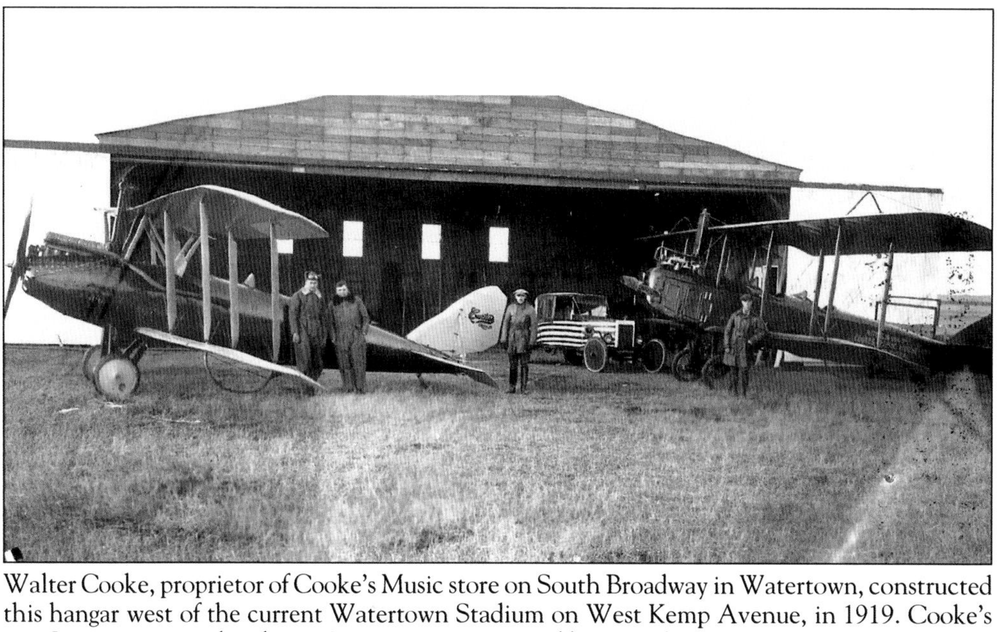

Walter Cooke, proprietor of Cooke's Music store on South Broadway in Watertown, constructed this hangar west of the current Watertown Stadium on West Kemp Avenue, in 1919. Cooke's son, Lavonne, an early pilot in Watertown, is pictured here on the far left, in front of the Curtis airplane. Cooke also started the Watertown School of Flying in 1919, and took the first aerial photos of Watertown in June of that year. Ralph Hubbard started a small airport in the area in 1929.

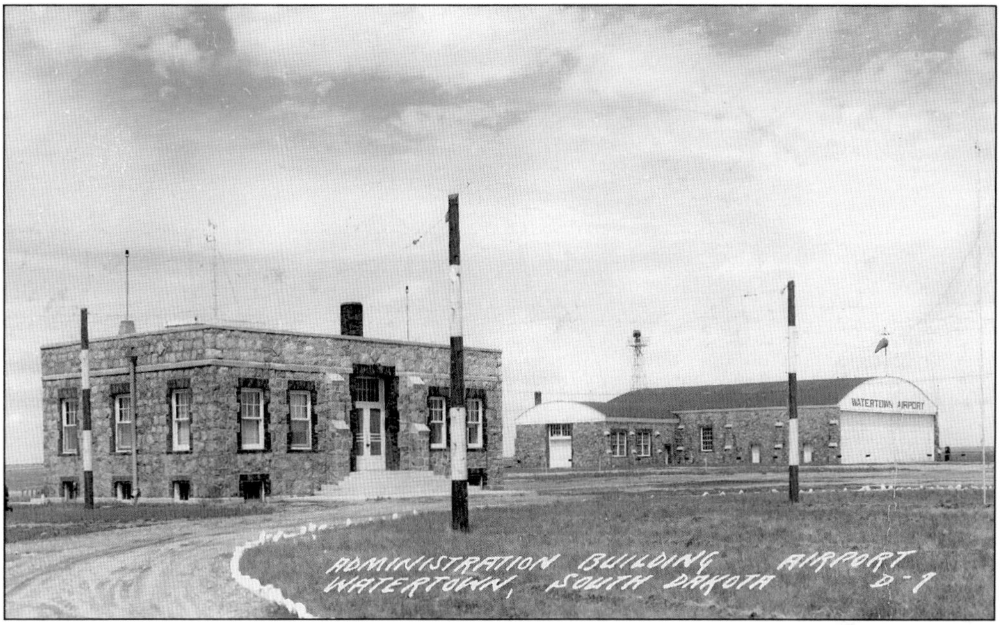

The Watertown Chamber of Commerce took on the responsibility of pursuing the possibility of centralized airport facilities for the city in 1930. The Majerus Construction Company of Watertown and men employed through the federal Works Progress Administration began construction of the hangar at the Watertown Airport, the building on the right, January 1, 1934. Construction of the airport administration building, pictured below and at left in the top photo, occurred in 1936, also by the WPA. The Army Air Corps took over the city airport facilities for use as a satellite for its air base in Sioux City, Iowa, during World War II, and constructed more buildings for barracks, offices, and other uses. The base closed December 1943, but the facilities were still used by the military until the end of the war. The airport and all the buildings were then returned to the city.

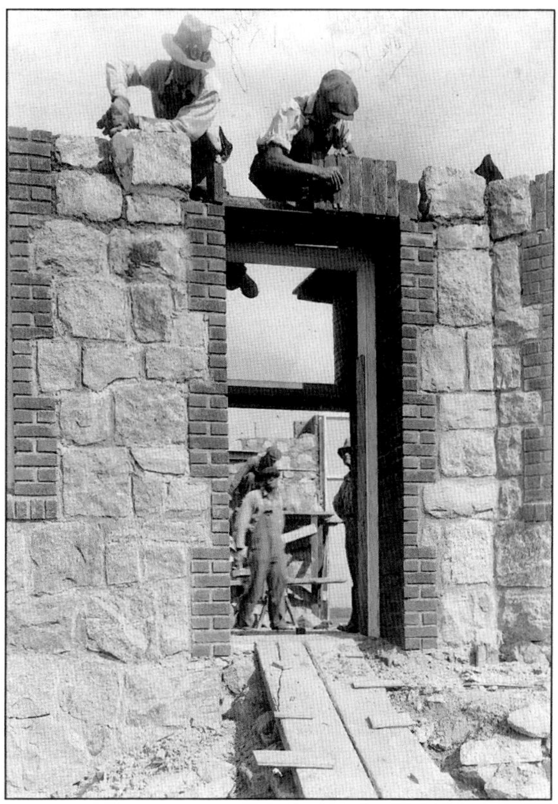

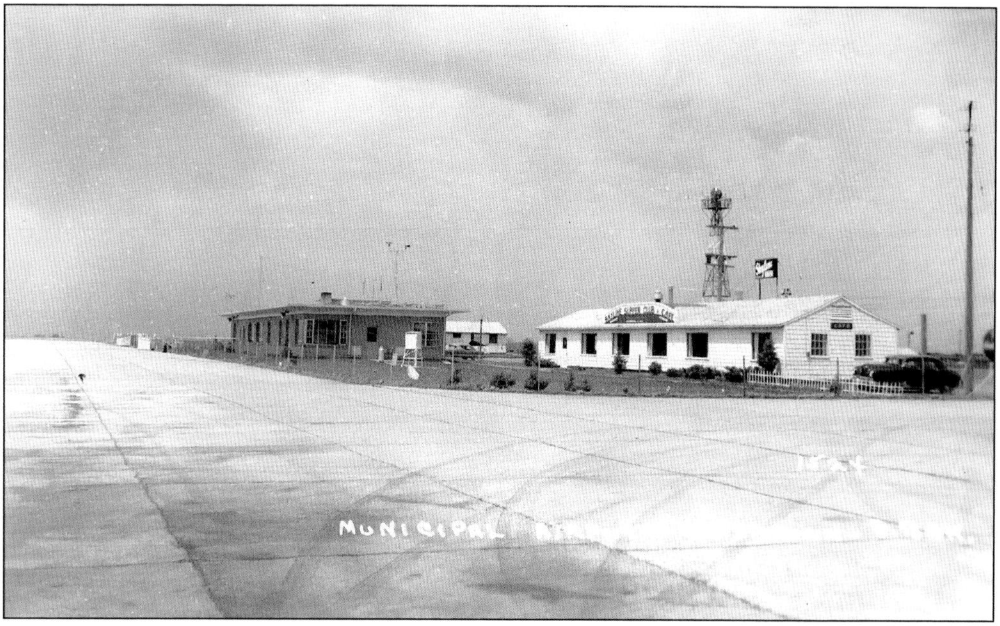

The Skyline Supper Club, the white building in this photo of the Watertown Airport from about 1950, was started about 1948. The café was moved into the terminal building in 1956, and many improvements continued to be made on the airport buildings, equipment, and runway. The airport continues to be an asset to the city. (Courtesy Ken and Lyn Sheldon.)

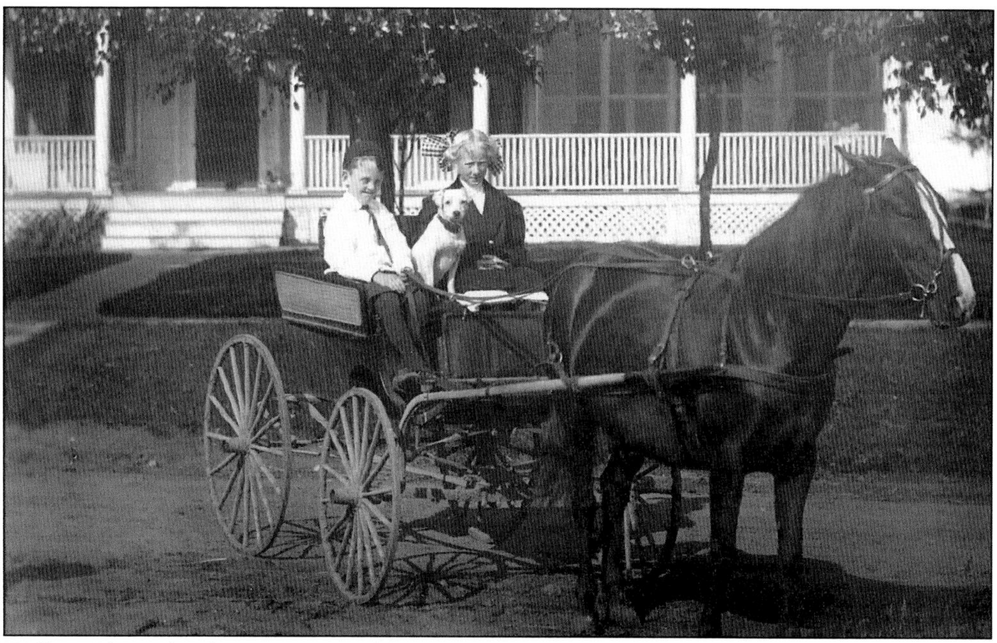

Wilbur Glass' daughter Louise and her cousin are pictured in a pony cart on this undated photo postcard, probably taken in front of the Glass home in Watertown, on Second Street Northwest. Glass was an attorney whose offices were in the Granite Block. Pony carts were a useful form of transportation for short distances and for rural children attending one-room country schools.

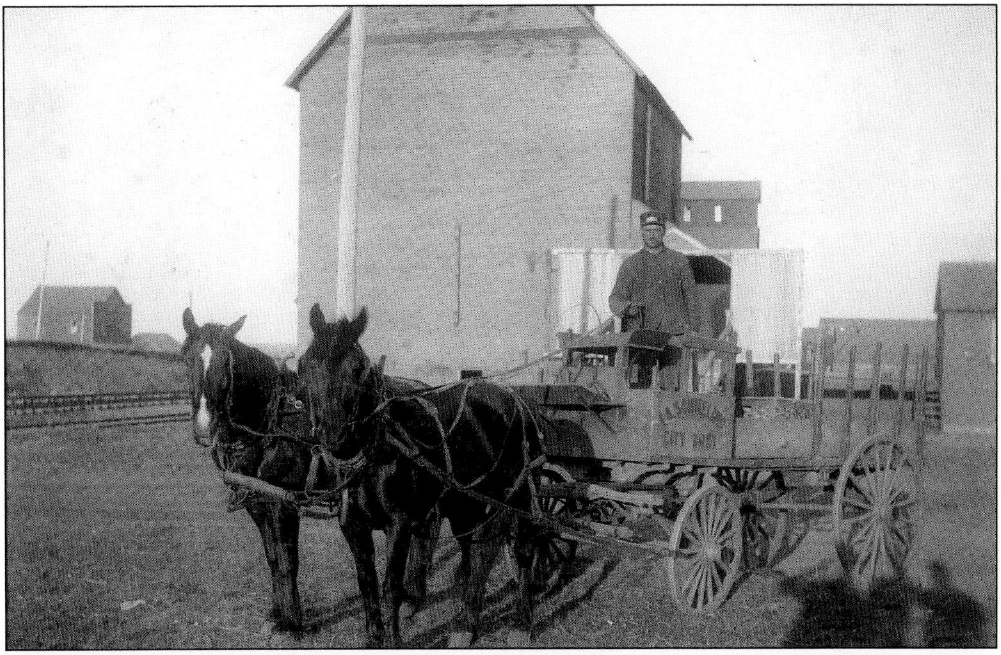

A South Shore man stands in this F.A. Schmeling City Dray wagon near the South Shore elevators in this photo dated 1907. In addition to his dray business, Frank Schmeling was also a carpenter and farmer. Note the shadow of the two photographers, with the camera standing between them, in the lower right hand corner.

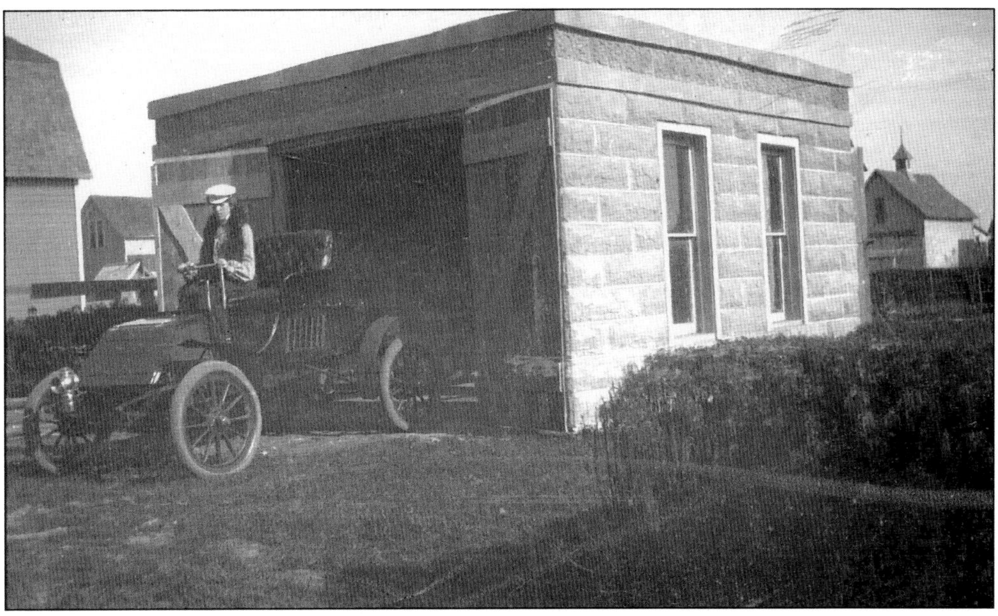

The location and owner of the garage in this photograph are unidentified, but writing on the back dates it to 1904, and claims it as the "first 'garage' in Watertown." The garage may have belonged to A.C. Gilruth, owner of the Gilruth Department Store, who had the first "horseless carriage" in Watertown, but H.D. Rice donated the photograph to the historical society, so it also could have been his garage.

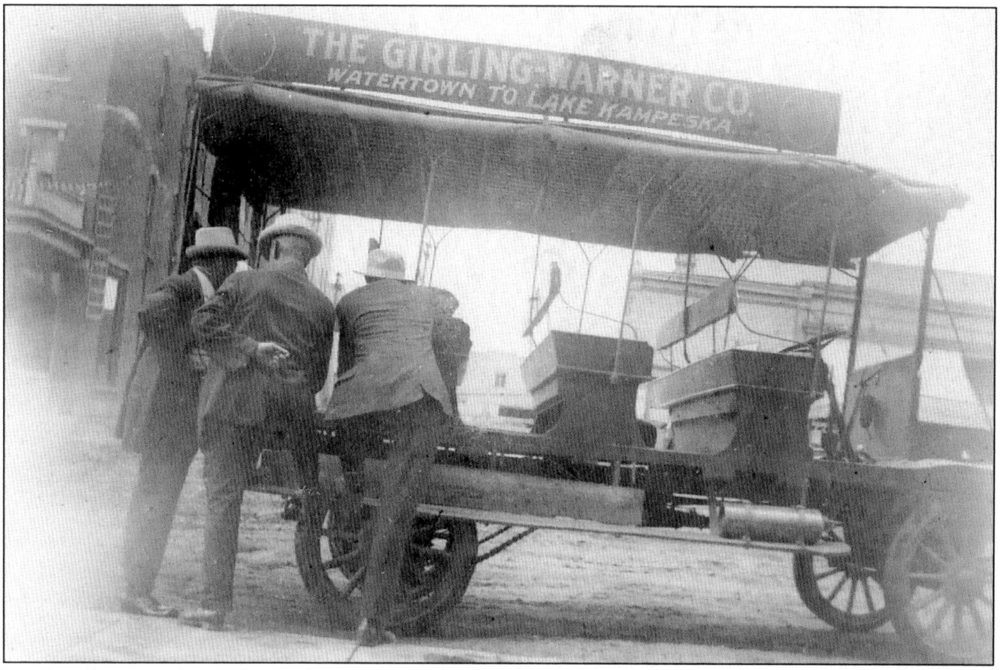

Little is known about the Girling-Warner Company motorized shuttle service from Watertown to Lake Kampeska, but this undated photo was taken on North Maple Street, close to the Lincoln Hotel. The corner of the Grand Central Hotel at 15 North Maple is visible on the left side of the photo.

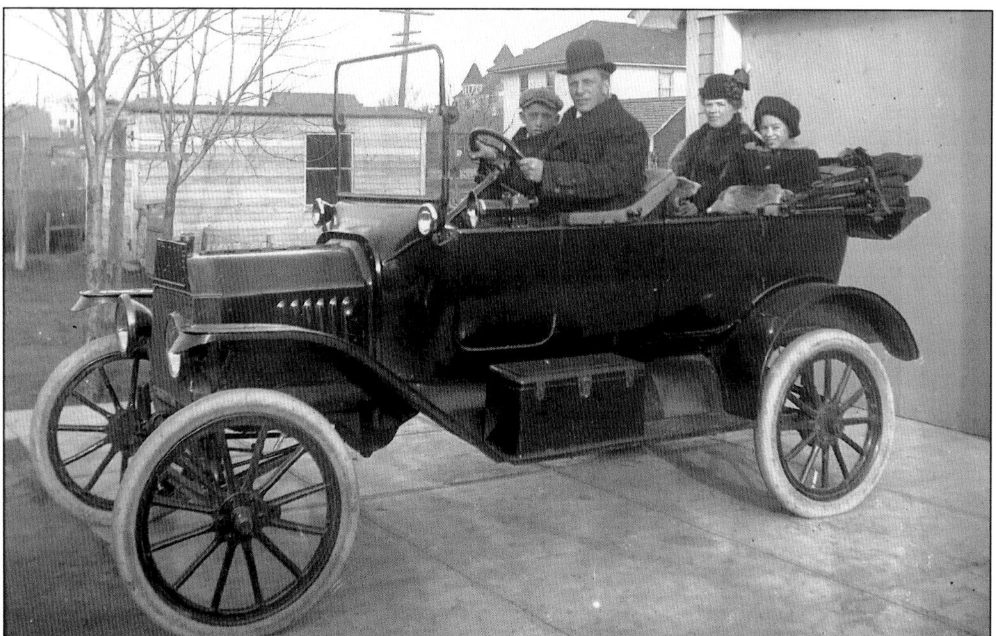

A.C. Nelson, part owner of the Nelson-Reed Hardware store once located on South Broadway, is shown in this undated photo with his family in their Model T Ford. They are, from left to right, Lyle, A.C., Myrtle, and Agnes. The Nelson home was located at 414 South Broadway.

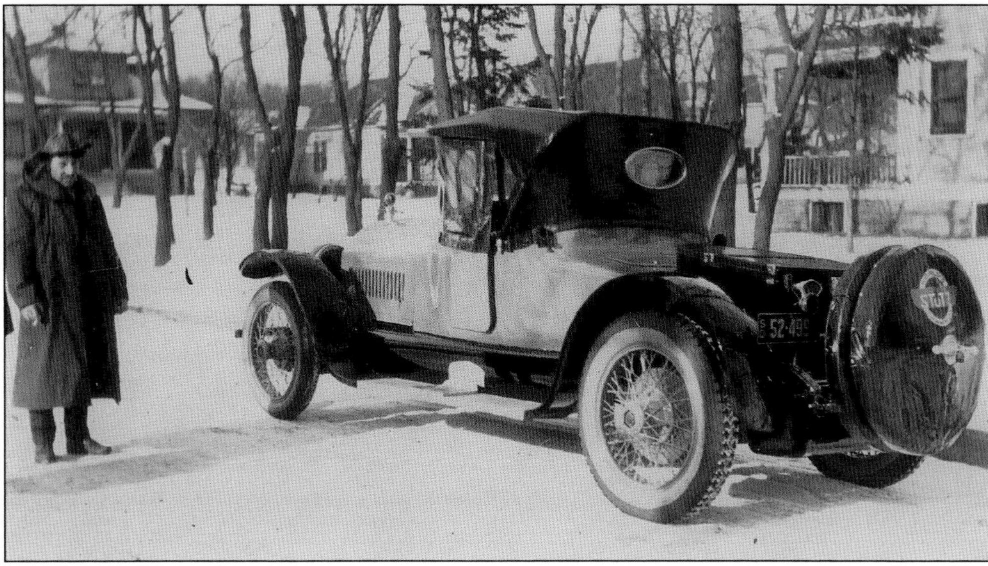

The Stutz Bearcat in this photo is possibly parked on Third Avenue North in Watertown. No other identifying information is listed on the photo. The Stutz Bearcat was advertised in the early 1900s as the "Car That Made Good in a Day." The famous Bearcat sports car appeared in 1912.

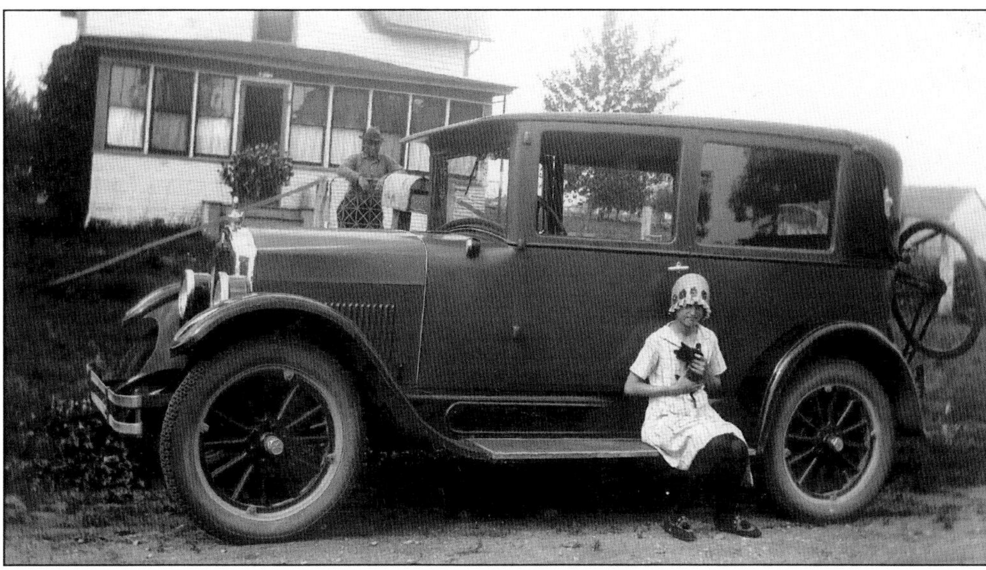

Rosella Schroeder is pictured on the running board of her father, William's, Star Car, possibly on the John Schroeder farm near Watertown, in the mid-1920s. H.S. Brink named Earl Hollenbeck as a dealer of the Star automobile in Watertown in the mid-1920s, in a caption for the "Picture of the Week" series in the January 3, 1986 edition of the *Watertown Public Opinion*, and commented, "...the Star was a short life car, but its 4-cylinder Red Seal Continental motor could out-demonstrate anything."

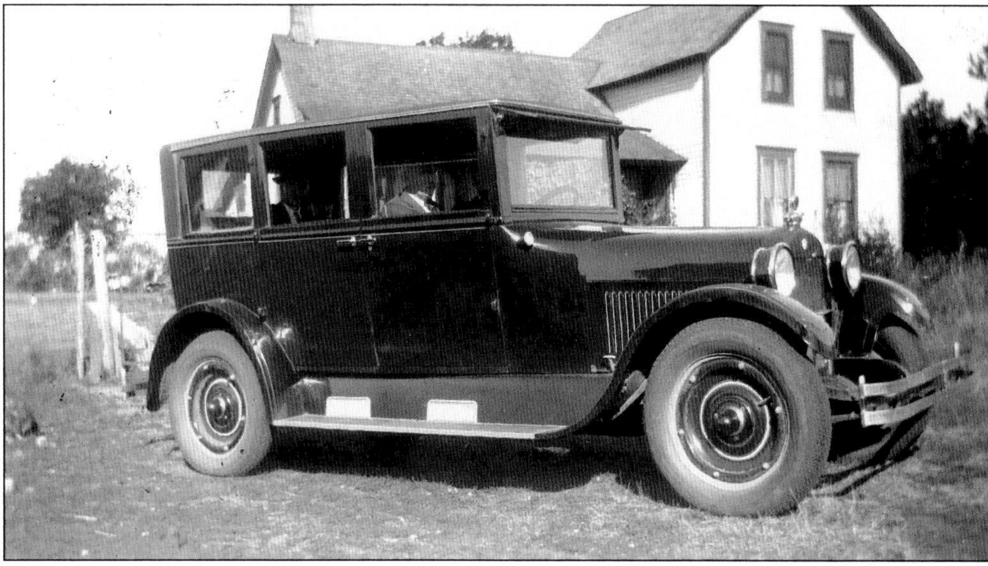

This early automobile was photographed in front of the Mathias Fleming family home near Still Lake, east of Florence, probably in the late 1920s.

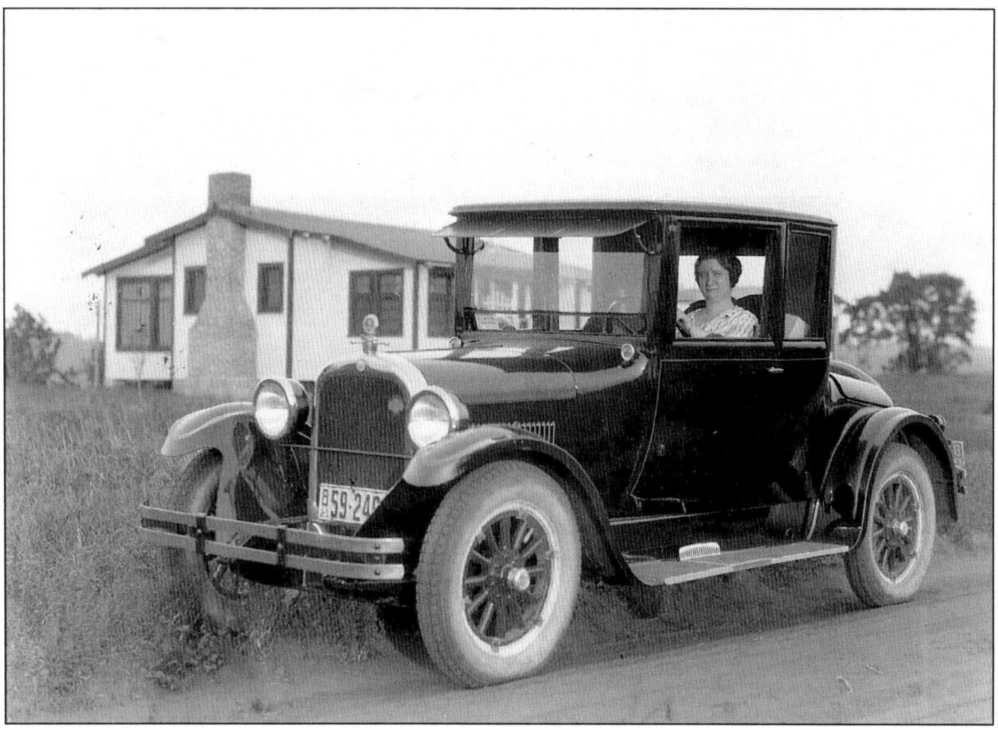

Magdalena Rau is pictured in a Dodge car, probably in front of the Rau family cabin at Lake Kampeska, in this snapshot dated 1925.

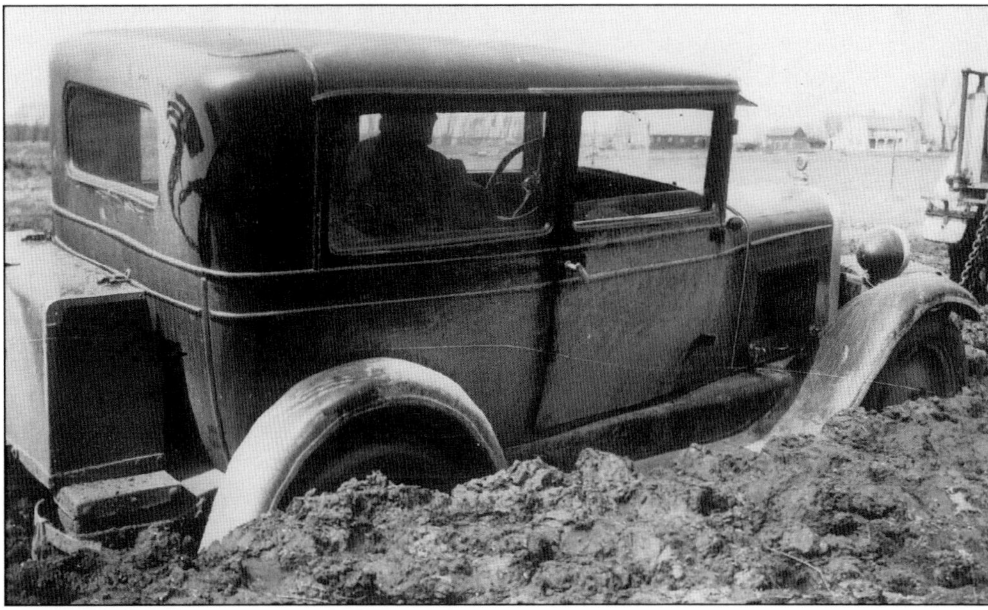

An unidentified car is pictured in this snapshot, stuck in a "mudhole on gravel six miles south of Watertown," on what is now Highway 81, in the spring of 1929, according to writing on the back of the photo. The 24-mile stretch of the Meridian Highway, as U.S. Highway 81 was first known, through Codington County, was constructed, in an incredible feat, in one day, June 25, 1912, with 24 crews simultaneously constructing one mile of the road each.

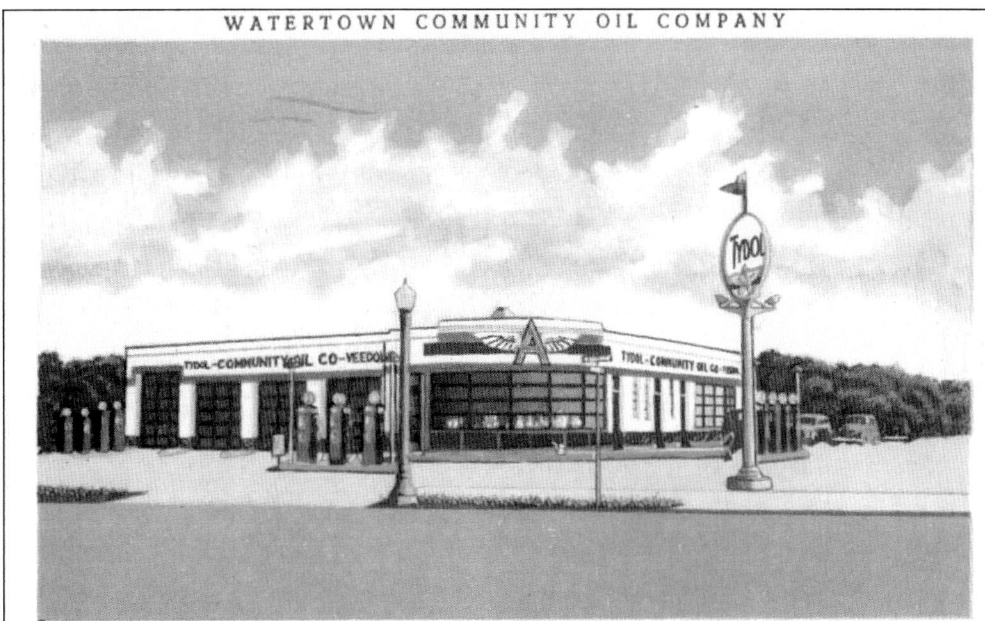

The Watertown Community Oil Company is claimed as "South Dakota's Largest, Finest Super Service Station" on this postcard, postmarked June 12, 1942. The company was founded in 1926, on the northeast corner of the intersection of Broadway and First Avenue North, and now runs under the Ampride brand at the same location. (Courtesy Ken and Lyn Sheldon.)

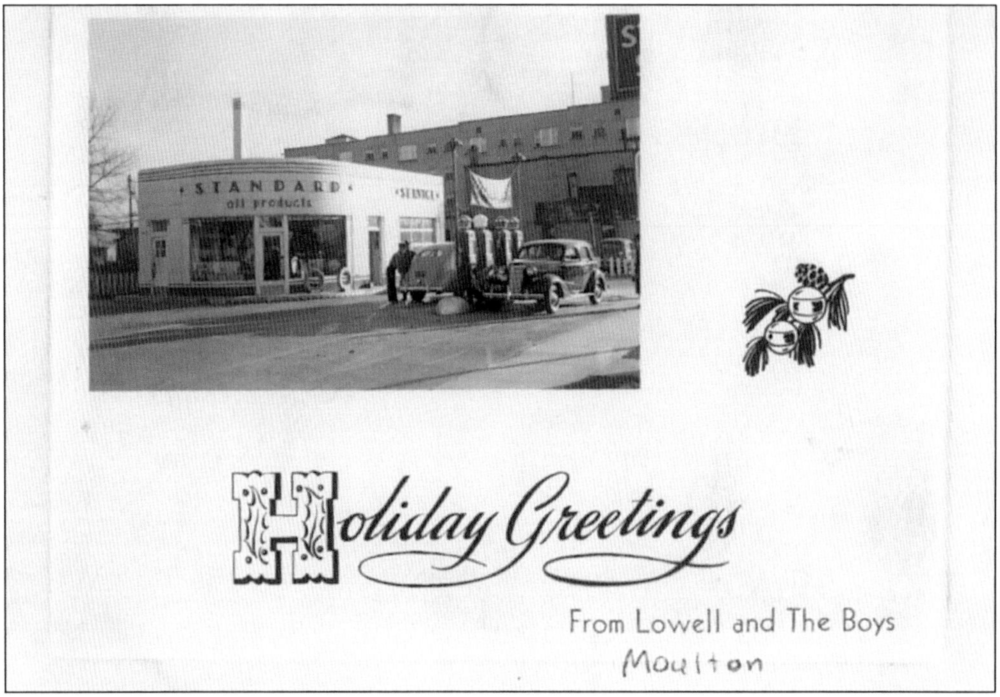

This Standard Oil service station was established on the northeast corner of the intersection of Kemp Avenue and Third Street East, near the Palace Apartments, by 1922. The Art Deco style of the building in this photo from about 1940, suggests that the station was remodeled or rebuilt sometime in the 1930s. The Watertown Senior Citizen Center is now located on the same corner where the service station once was. The Palace Apartments building, visible above the station on the right side of the photo, was built by Robert Schull and completed in 1922.

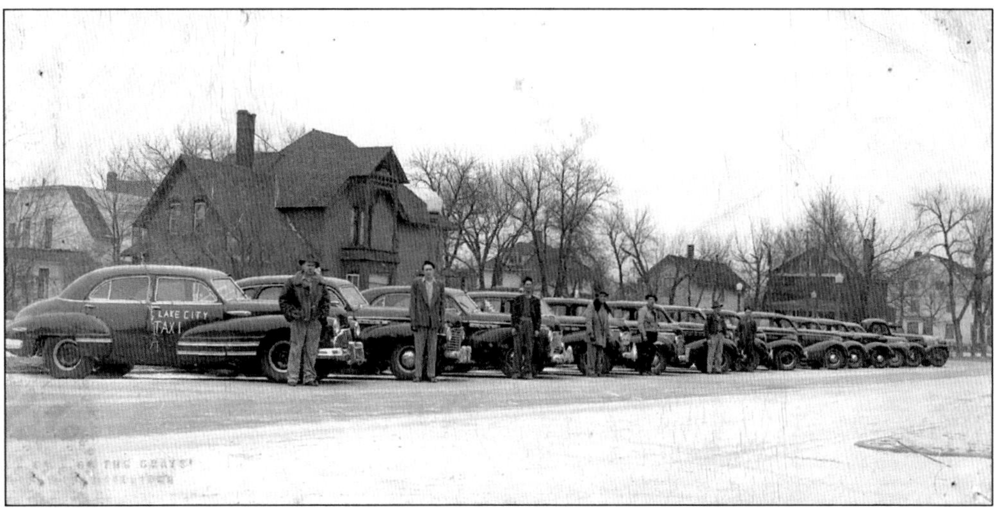

John Binford and Albert Jaehn started the Lake City Taxi company about 1919, at 25 North Maple Street. The taxi fleet is pictured in this photo from the 1940s, on an unidentified street in Watertown. The company was sold to Leo Gartzke and Elias Christianson in the late 1940s and became the Yellow Cab Company for a few years. By 1953, the Yellow Cab Company was no longer listed in the city directory.

Seven

Recreation and Relaxation

An abundance of water led the Winona and St. Peter railroad to first plat Watertown with the name Waterville. The name was promptly changed by early town builders, Oscar and John Kemp, who had the town named after their hometown of Watertown, New York. The name is coincidentally fitting. Area residents took advantage of their proximity to water for survival and recreation. Tourism is currently the second largest industry in South Dakota behind agriculture, and Lake Kampeska and Pelican Lake, currently both within the Watertown city limit, play an important part in the area tourism industry.

Recreation was not something for which most early pioneers had time. There was prairie to break and homes to build, and hunting and fishing were done mostly for survival rather than pleasure. Even though there were not many recreation options for the rural resident, it was still important. Just as people in cities need breaks from work, so too do people in rural areas need a respite from the long hours of demanding farm work. In Watertown and Codington County, much recreation revolves around water. Residents enjoy boating, sailing, swimming, fishing, hunting, and generally being around water.

In addition to aquatic recreation, there are currently 26 parks and recreation areas in Watertown. People also enjoy many forms of seasonal sports, clubs, fraternal orders, bands, museums, and other annual special events. The following photographs show residents and visitors enjoying a variety of local resources and events.

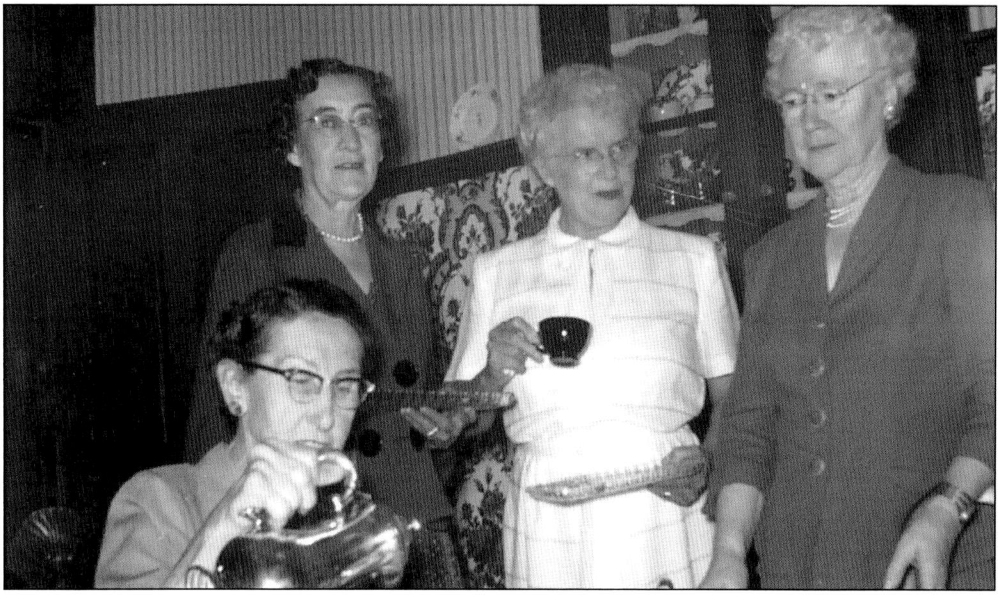

When the home of South Dakota's first governor, Arthur Mellette, at 421 Fifth Avenue Northwest, Watertown, was condemned by the city fire marshal in 1940, concerned citizens Mrs. Andrew Melham, Mrs. F.J. Scholtz, Mrs. R.G. Williams, and Mrs. Walter Miller, left to right in this photo, raised $600 to buy and save the historic home. These women and others formed the Mellette Memorial Association in 1943, and began the mammoth task of restoring the abandoned and dilapidated house to museum condition. Several pieces of original family furniture were given to the Association when Mellette's last son, Arthur Anton, died in Kansas in 1953. This photo was taken in the Mellette House dining room, by a reporter named Bob Travis, in September 1954.

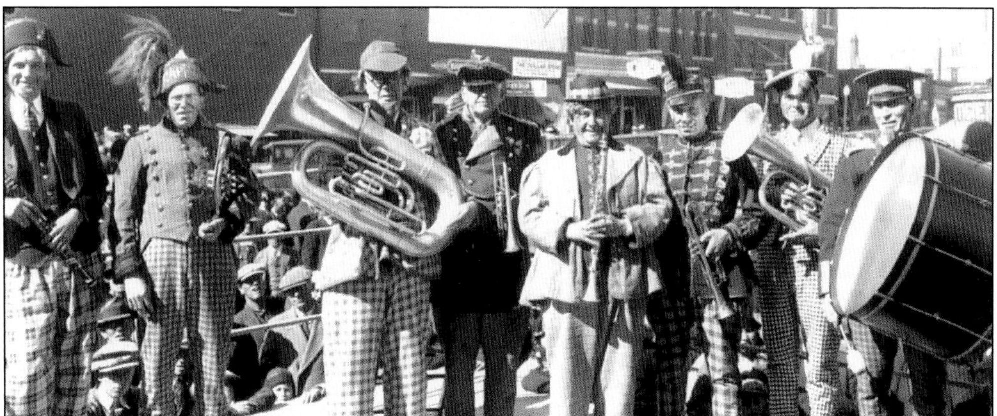

The first annual Play Day in Watertown, designed as a fun day of free entertainment for residents of Codington County and the surrounding area, occurred September 27, 1930. The day before, workmen constructed three large stage platforms on Kemp Avenue at the intersections of Broadway, Maple, and Second Street East. On the day of the fun, the Colonial and Lyric theaters hosted a free movie running every hour, boxing matches were held, vaudeville acts performed, and tugs of war and foot races were played. Watertown's Peck's Band divided into three groups that wandered the streets dressed in black tie, and Italian and German costumes, as pictured here, with Bill Peck, fourth from left, and Paul Krakowski, second from left.

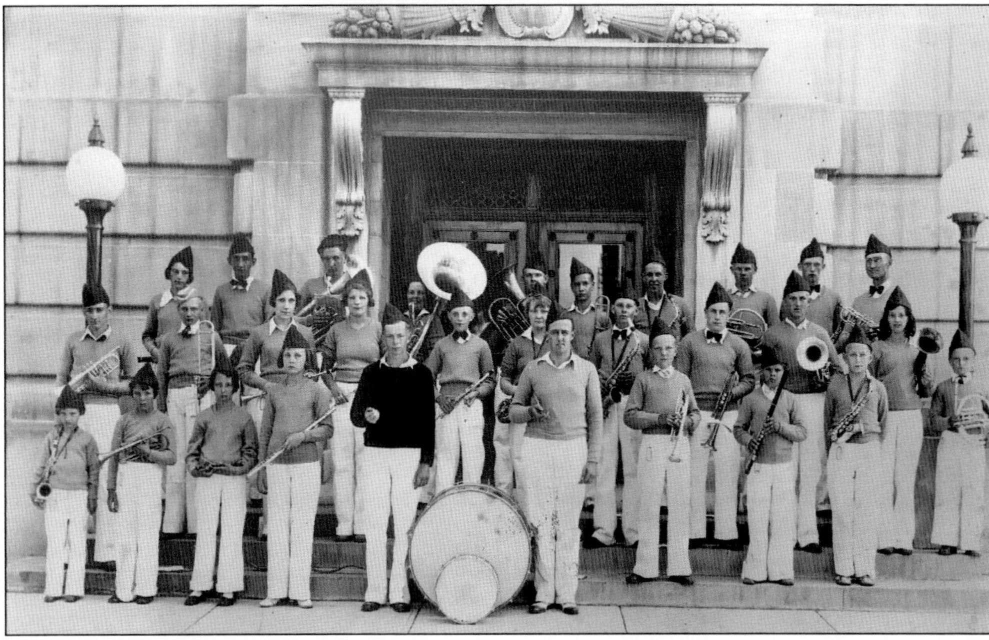

Elmer Carey's Band, pictured here, was one of the bands that played at the dedication of the new Codington County Courthouse, June 19 and 20, 1929. Band members, from left to right, are as follows: (front row) Mardella Schnackenberg, Ida Hoy, Meta Hoy, Marion Melham, Alex Johnson, Crawford, Ken Carey, Bill Guddal, and Wayne Selp; (second row) John Redmond, Harold Baxter, Delores Anderson, Winifred Johnson, Warden Mickelson, Nadine Russel, Al Mielke, Bill French, Gordon Albertson, and Robert Carey; (back row) Myrtle Mitchell, Lawrence Follett, Bill Walsk, Dorothy Dory, Wayne Clausen, Ed Schnackenberg, Emory Wineland, Joseph Wildman, and Elmer Carey. Carey joined the Watertown High School faculty in 1942, as director of instrumental music.

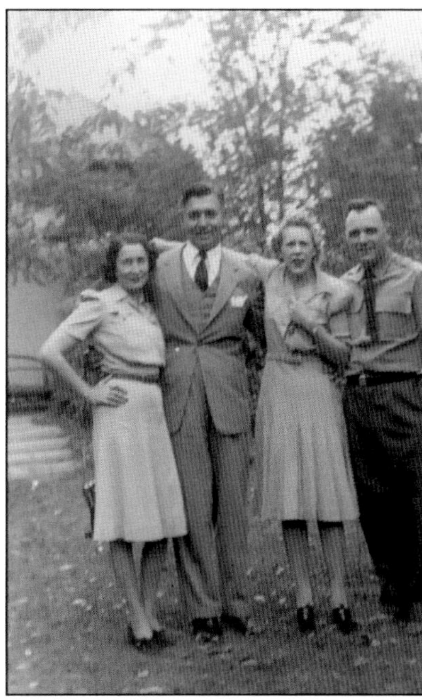

In September 1941, Clark Gable, Carole Lombard, and their friends Nora and Harry Fleischmann made a hunting trip to South Dakota. Through a mutual acquaintance, arrangements were made for the visitors to stay with Dr. Ed Harper in Watertown. Though Gable had just recently filmed "Gone With the Wind," and believed he would need police protection during any public appearance, he received much local attention but was never mobbed. This photo captures Nora Fleischmann, Gable, and Mrs. and Dr. Harper, in the Harper's backyard at 803 First Street Northwest.

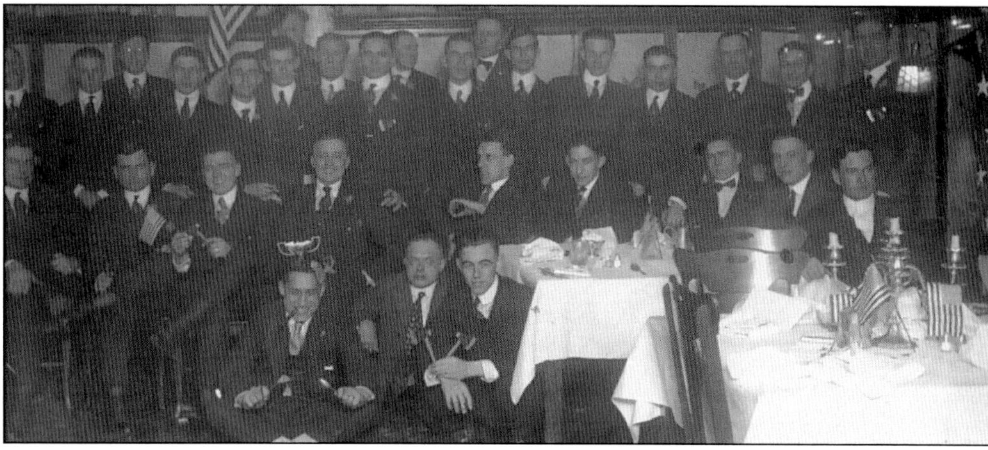

The Raven Club, organized January 1, 1916, held a banquet for its members in the Japanese room of the Kampeska Hotel, February 22, 1917. Decorations for the event had a red, white, and blue theme, in celebration of President Washington's birthday. Attending members in this photo are, from left to right, the following: (standing) Dan Bannister, unidentified, Hal Mann, Harry Hill, Art Wagner, Art English, Ted DeForge, Pete Jacobson, Al Steinmetz, Lloyd Dayton, Clarence Halvorson, Frank Theisen, Roy Sours, Mel Staley, Harold Stanton, Lee Barger, Charlie McNeal, and Bill Prey; (seated) Fred Haberman, Earl Hatts, Howard Curtis, Sig Overus, unidentified, Wally Farl, Don Bannister, Truman Bumford, and Bill Cochrane; (seated in front) Nat Calmenson, Frank Skells, and Frank Neil. The purpose of the Raven Club has not been discovered, but clubs of all types were a popular pastime for men, women, and children, in the first several decades of the twentieth century.

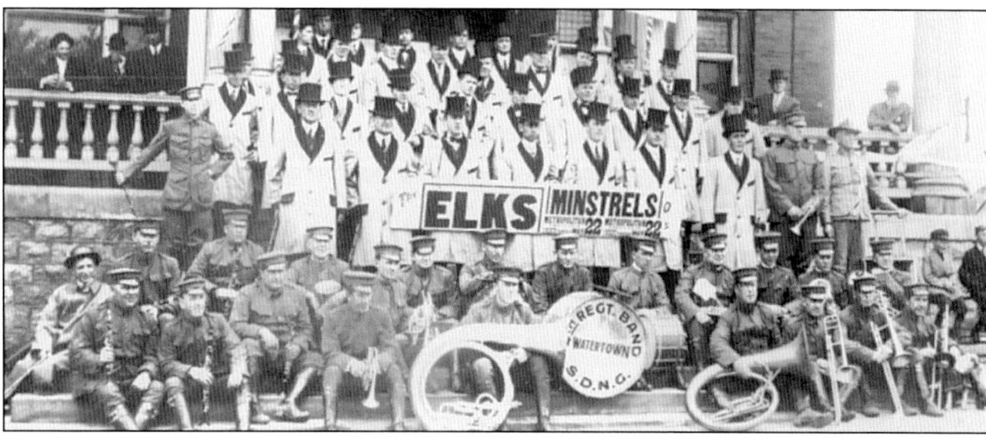

Members of the Watertown Elks club posed with the Fourth Regimental Band of the South Dakota National Guard on the grand porch of Watertown's Elks Lodge at 101 South Broadway. The large sign advertises the "Elks Minstrels," performing at the Metropolitan Theater in the Lincoln Hotel, three nights, beginning Thursday, May 22. The photo postcard is not dated, but is probably from 1913. William S. Peck was hired to take over direction of the Watertown Cadet Band in 1905. The band was mustered into the South Dakota National Guard in 1907 as the Fourth Regimental Band, and played at encampments at Camp Roosevelt near Lake Kampeska and other military events. The band was mustered out in 1915, and became the Codington County Post 17 American Legion Band, but was commonly known as Peck's Band until Elmer Carey became director in 1948. A fire in the Elks Lodge in 2001 extensively damaged the interior. (Courtesy Ken and Lyn Sheldon.)

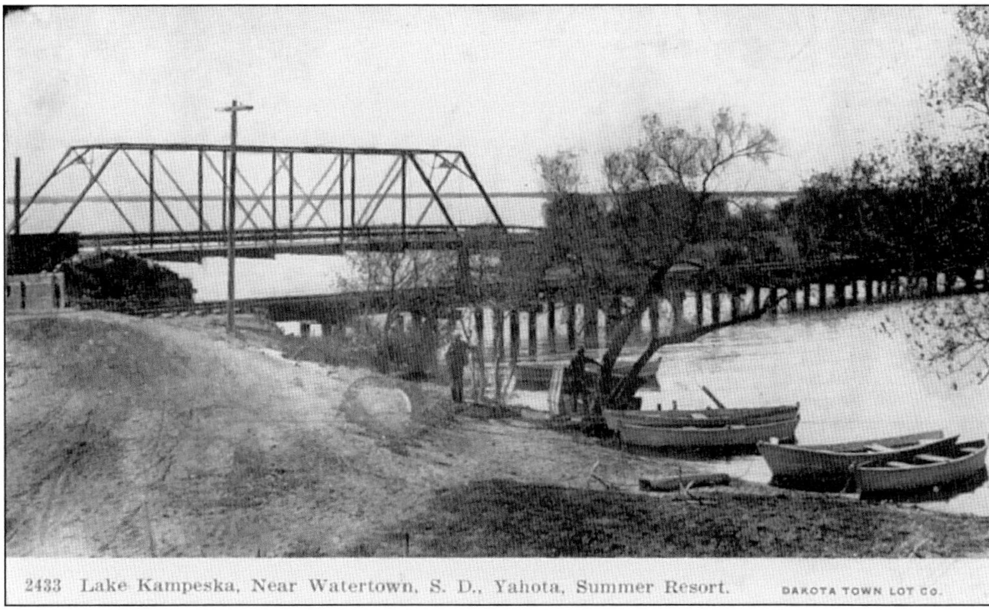

This undated photo shows the Minneapolis & St. Louis Railroad crossing the inlet to Lake Kampeska, close to where the Lake Shore Restaurant is located now. Yahota was platted as a station for the railroad when it extended west from Watertown in 1906. A development named East Yahota was platted southeast of the station along the north shore of Lake Kampeska, and was promoted as a summer resort. Chautauqua programs were held in a tent at this location for several years, beginning in 1908, and the city baseball park, with seating for 3,000, was also located at East Yahota. (Courtesy Bud and Arleen Larson.)

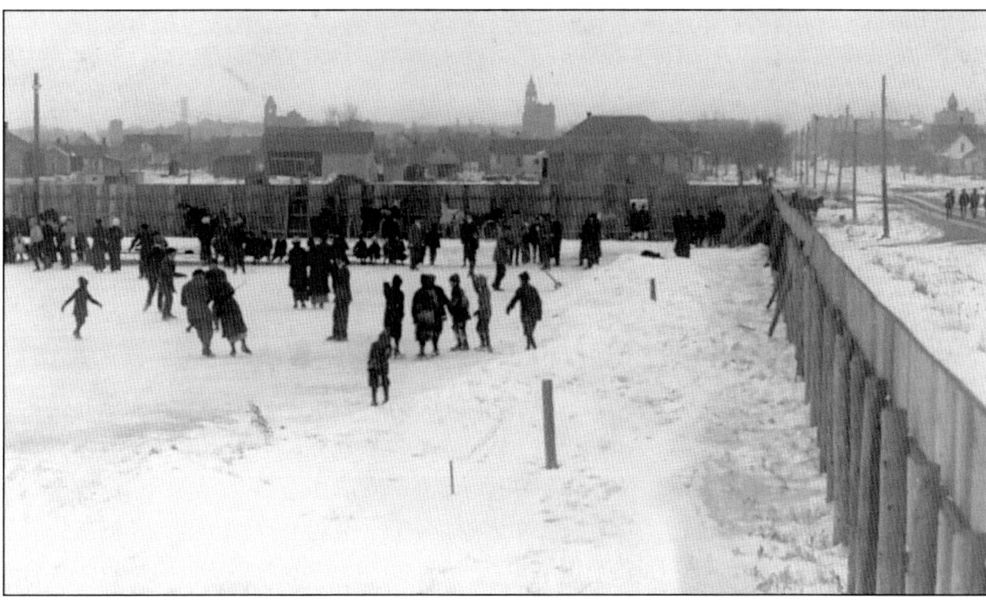

Ice skating in what was known as Bartron field was a popular winter pastime in Watertown. The rink was located on the west side of South Broadway. The three towers visible in the background belong to the Arcade Hotel on the left, City Hall in the center, and the old Codington County Courthouse on the right. The photo dates to about 1910.

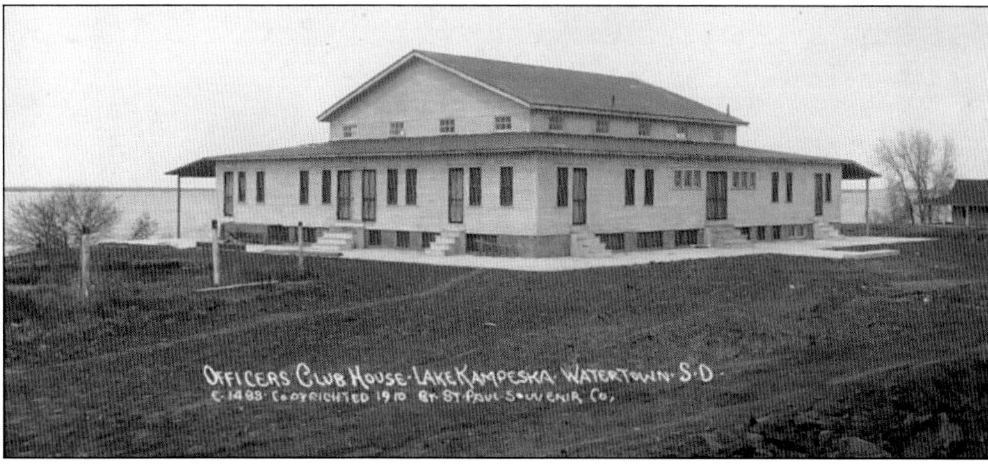

The Officers Club House, on the southeast shore of Lake Kampeska, in this postcard dated 1910, was constructed in connection with the establishment of Camp Roosevelt, the South Dakota National Guard camping grounds. The camp closed in 1912, and the building was remodeled and opened as the first home of the Watertown Country Club in June 1914. A few years later, the country club moved to the south side of the lake, and the city took over its golf course. The clubhouse became the Flamingo dinner club in the 1950s, closed in 1967, and the building was razed about 1973. (Courtesy Ken and Lyn Sheldon.)

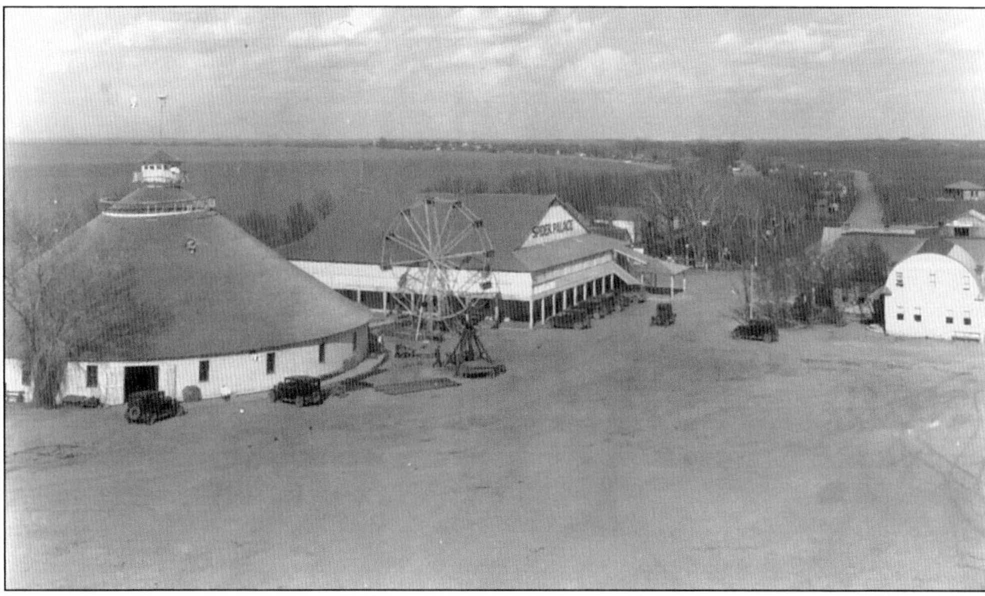

Stony Point at Lake Kampeska began as a tree claim acquired by Charles Williams in 1883. Williams soon opened a small store to cater to the many people who came to the shore to fish and camp. Business continued to grow until it included a bathhouse, trap shoot, a slide that ended in the lake, a barn for horses, and later, an automobile filling station. Charles' son William started the dance hall named Spider Palace, a bowling alley and pool hall, and the roller skating rink called the Spider Web. The Williams family also rented summer cabins located along the lakeshore leading up to Stony Point. Stony Point was the entertainment mecca of Lake Kampeska. All of the old buildings were demolished, but the Williams family still operates The Prop bar and bait and tackle shop on the property.

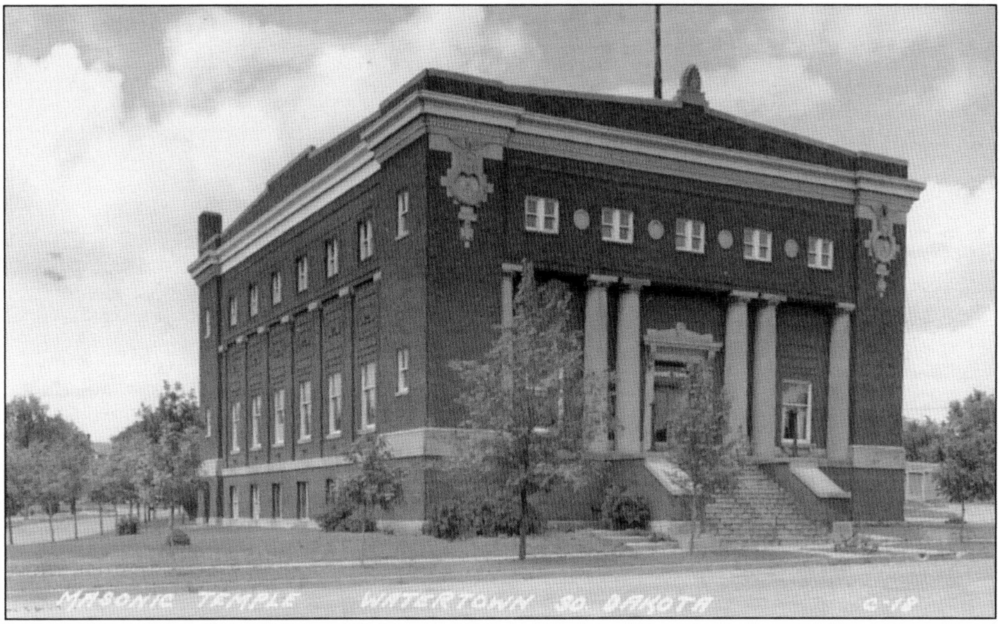

Construction of the Masonic Temple on the southwest corner of the intersection of Broadway and Third Avenue North began in the summer of 1914. The society has recently undertaken a major remodeling project to update the building's interior.

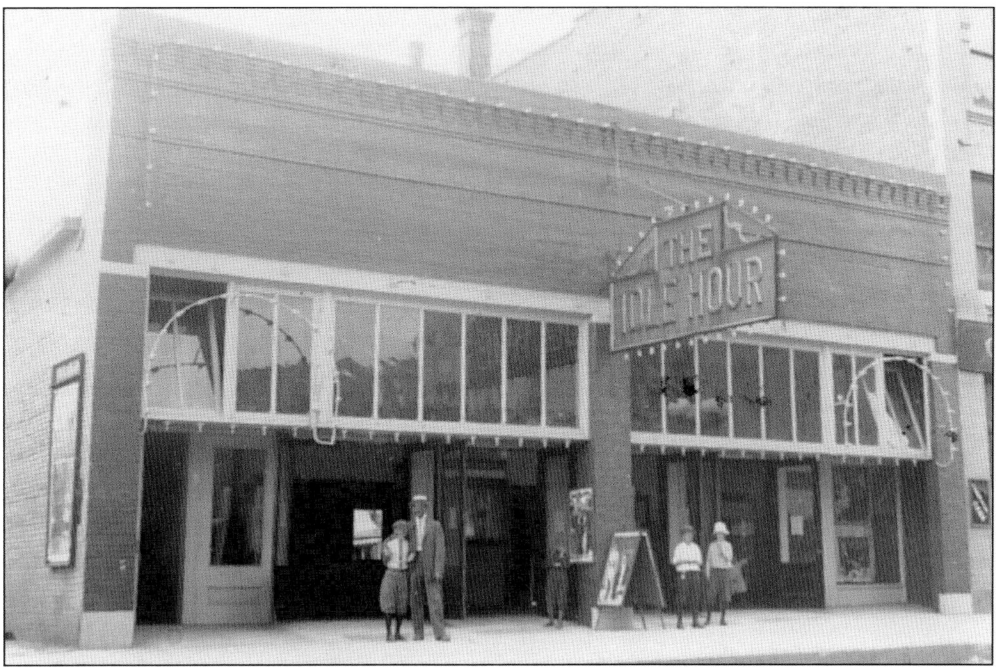

The Idle Hour Theater, at 110 Kemp Avenue East in this photo from about 1916, was opened in 1905 by Ed Drake and Fred Bacon. When Sam Hess and Albert Rau, owners of the Lincoln Hotel and Metropolitan Theater, bought the Idle Hour about 1919, they changed the name to the Lyric Theater, and about 1940 remodeled the facade in the Art Deco style. The theater closed about 1960, and Osco Drug used the building from 1965 to 1978. Klein's Crafts and Hobbies is now there.

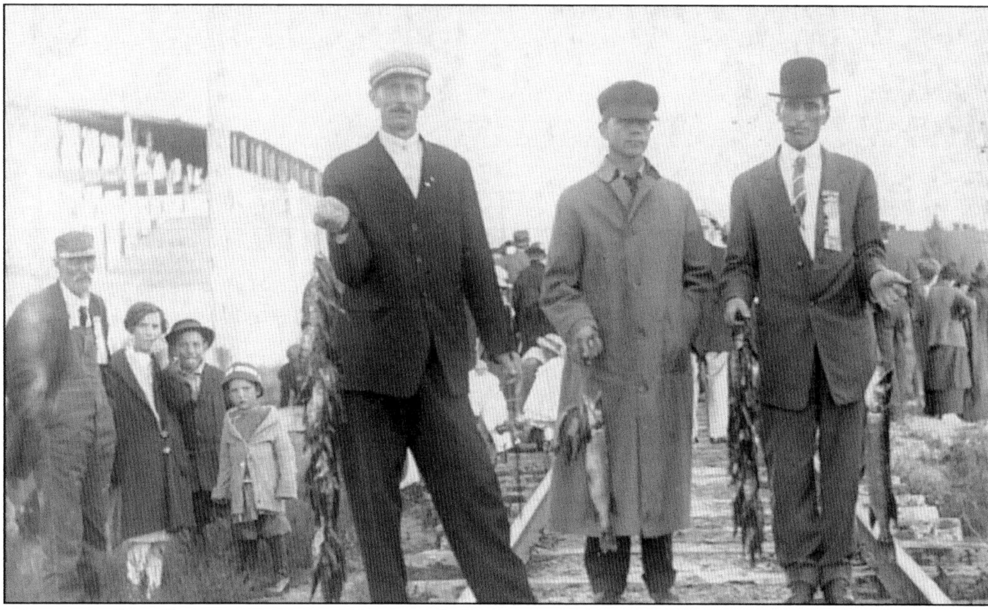

These unidentified men are standing on the Minneapolis & St. Louis railroad tracks near the baseball stadium at the East Yahota resort area on the north side of Lake Kampeska, about 1910. The man at right and the man standing with children at left are wearing ribbons on their lapels that are typical of souvenirs from state club conventions of that time period. Before a flash flood in 1915, Lake Kampeska had large celery beds that provided food for a healthy fish population of pickerel, pike, crappies, bass, and perch. The flood took out part of the dam at the Morrell Plant in Sioux Falls, which allowed carp to enter the Big Sioux River basin, make their way up to Lake Kampeska, and completely consume the celery beds.

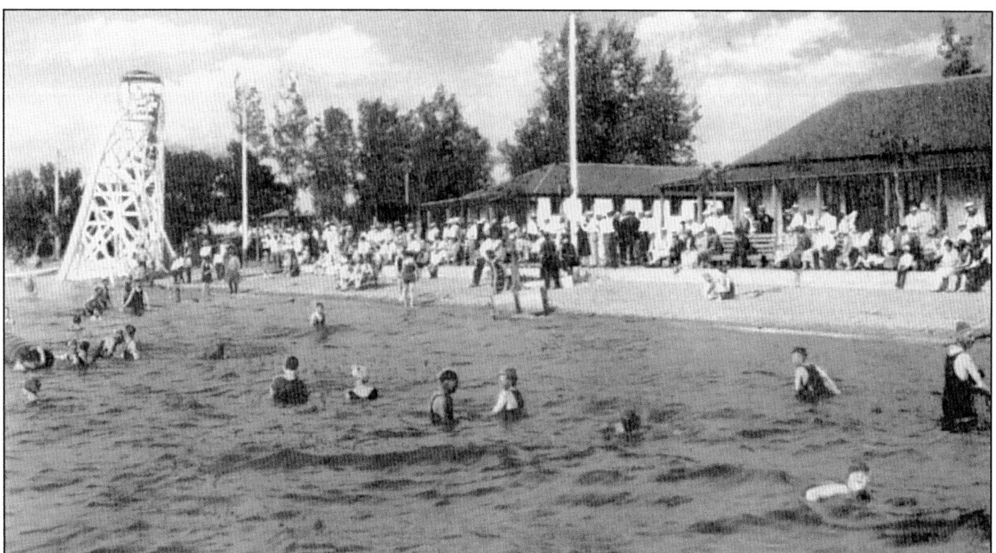

A crowded shore and swimming area from about 1920 are shown on this postcard of City Park on the east shore of Lake Kampeska, which was renamed Stokes-Thomas Park in 1975, in honor of the families who gave the land for the park. The structure on the left is a water slide that had a short life at the park.

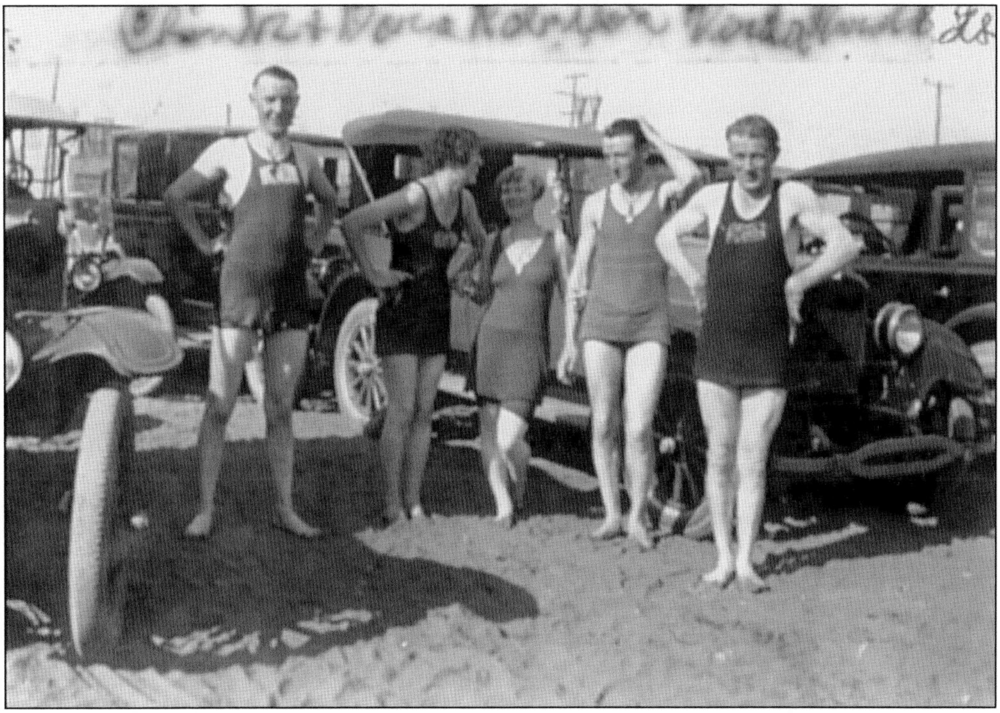

Chink and Dora Robitson or Robilson (handwriting illegible), Verda, Harold, and Ise are identified on this snapshot of 1920s bathing suit fashions from the Mondloch Family collection at the Codington County Heritage Museum. Ise is Isidor Mondloch of Henry, and Verda is probably Verda Hubbard, a teacher and former superintendent of Codington County Schools.

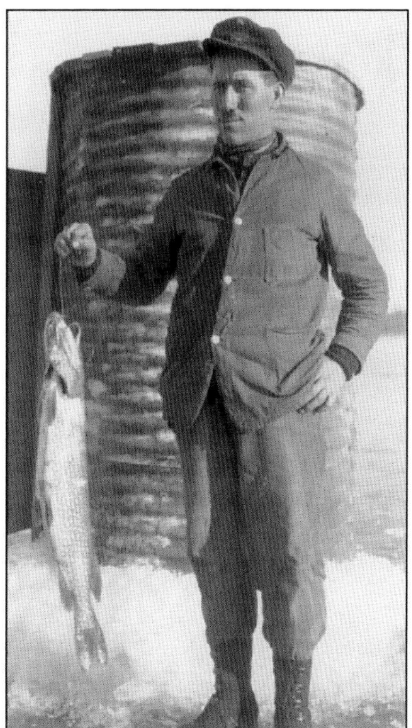

Berthold Loppe, whose widow Amelia is listed in South Shore in a 1916 Watertown city directory, is possibly this man near an ice fishing house on Punished Woman's Lake.

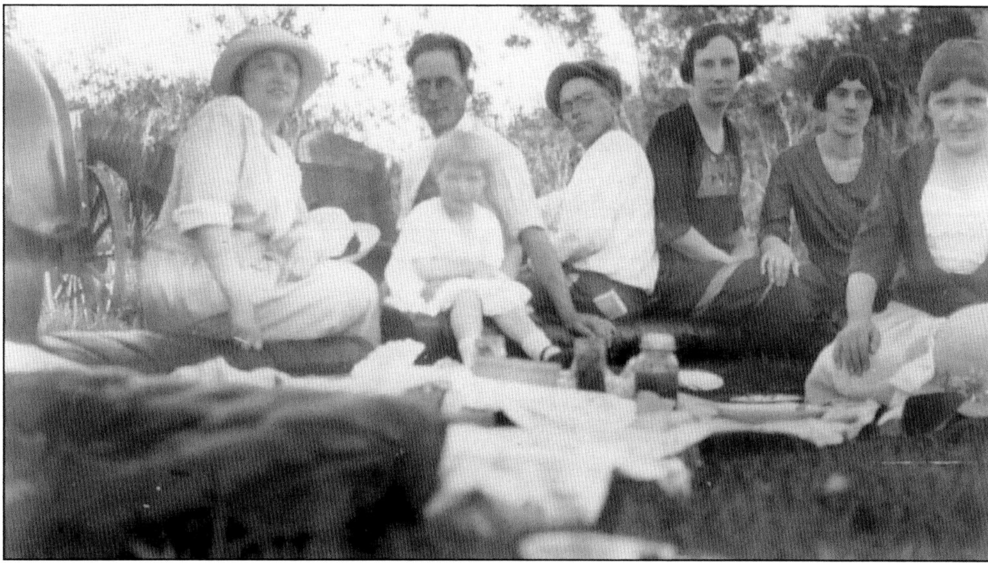

This picnic probably took place near South Shore in the early 1920s. The photo was donated by Hartney Andrisen, but the revelers are unidentified.

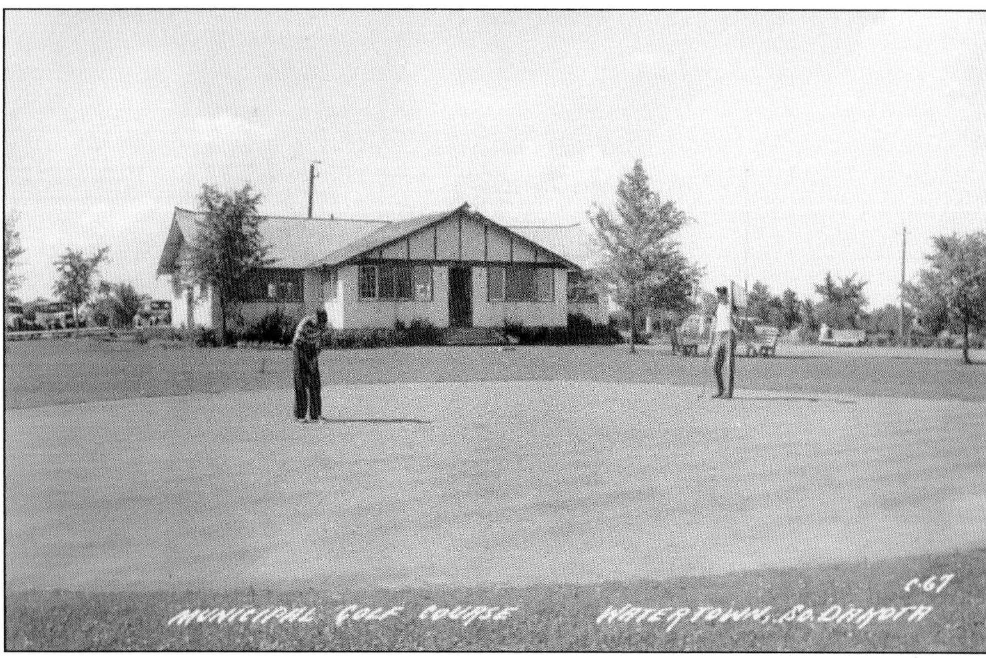

The Municipal Golf Course was established in the 1920s, after the city of Watertown acquired the land previously used by the South Dakota National Guard for Camp Roosevelt, and then developed as a golf course and used for several years by the Country Club. The course sported 18 holes by the 1930s, and an additional 9 holes were added in 2001. (Courtesy Ken and Lyn Sheldon.)

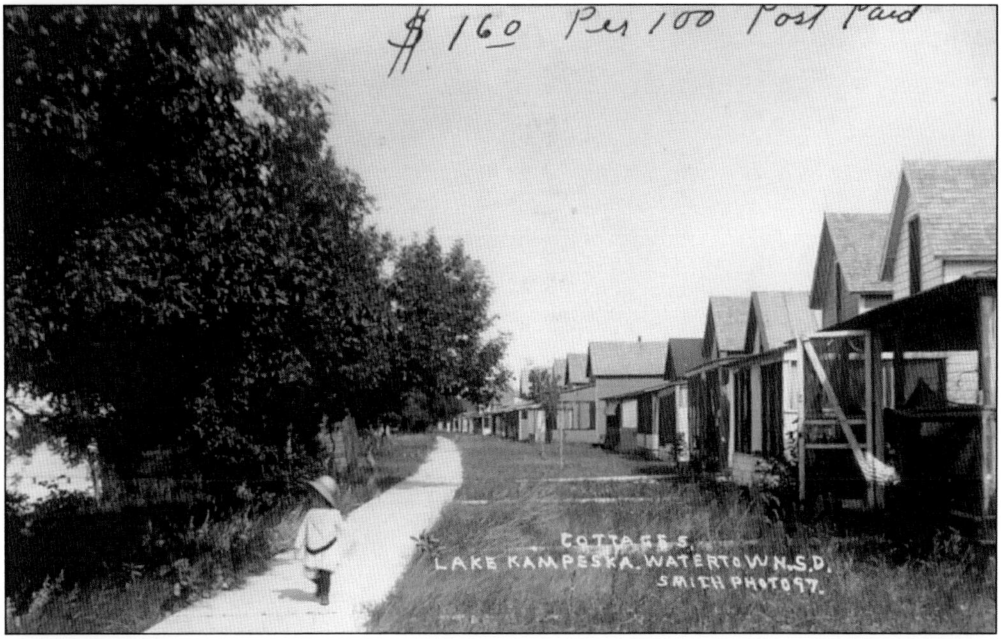

The cottages lining this section of Lake Kampeska shoreline were the ones rented by the Williams family at Stony Point. The Williams built the sidewalk connecting all the cottages, and leading to the store and entertainment at the Point. An identical photo postcard in the Codington County Historical Society collections is postmarked August 9, 1913.

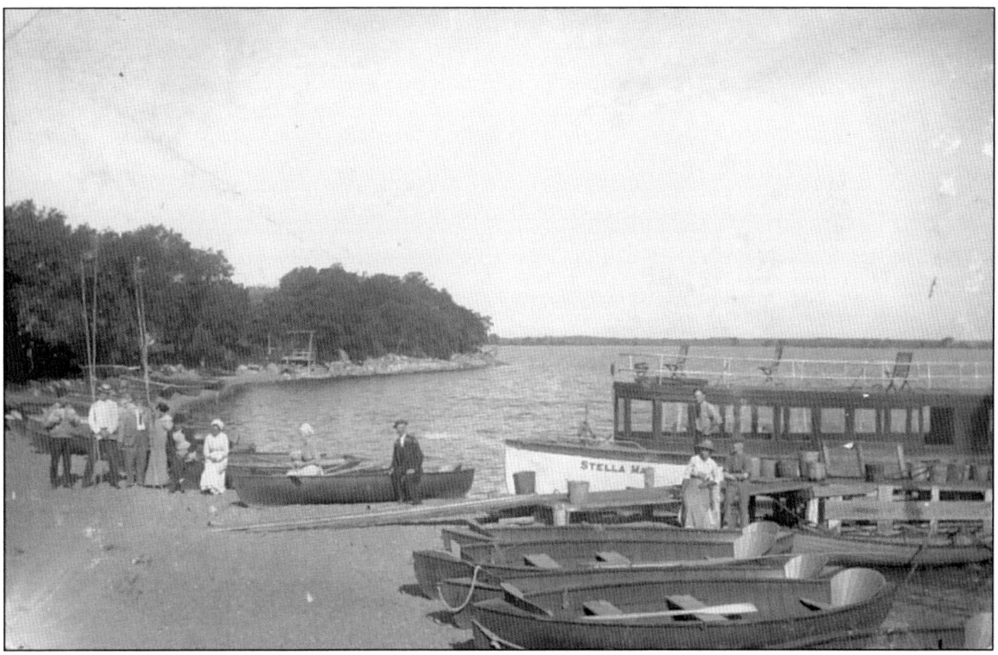

This postcard of boats on the shores of Stony Point is dated June 30, 1910. Charles Williams' son, William, bought the large boat in this photo and named it after his wife, Stella Mae. The boat was used to give tours and pleasure rides around the lake, and Peck's band often played on the upper deck.

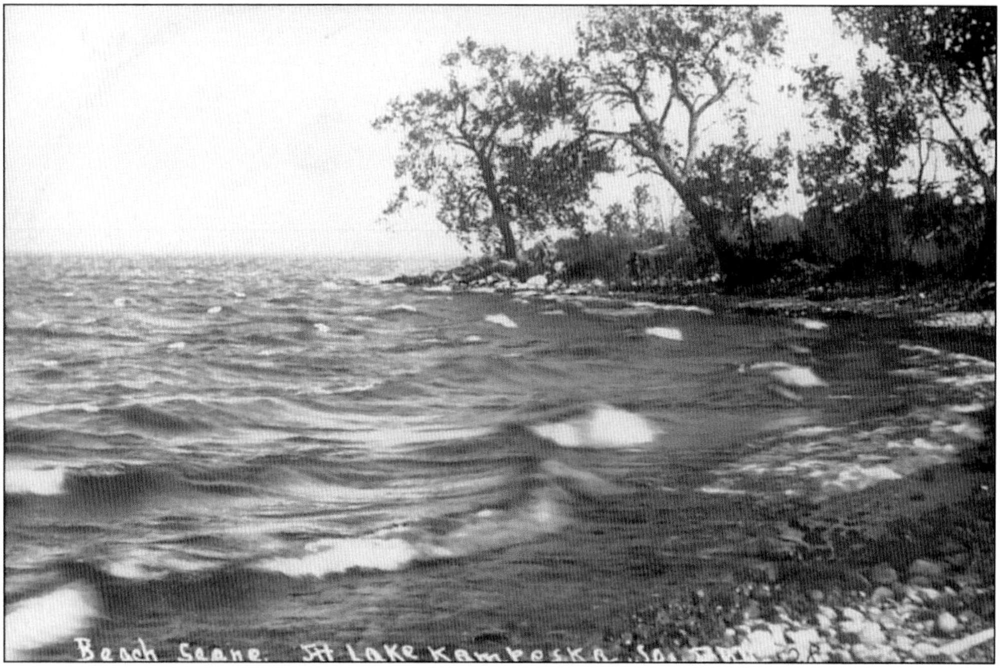

When the first white settlers arrived in Codington County in the 1870s, Kampeska's water was so pure and crystal clear, one could see all the way through it, to its fine sand and gravel floor. This view of a section of Lake Kampeska shoreline dates to about 1913. Pollution and a number of flooding events brought in silt that covered the lake floor and muddied the water; however, the lake continues to be an important resource for recreation, with several parks and camping grounds, a popular race track, two golf courses, and several restaurants, and its shores are almost completely developed with year-round homes.

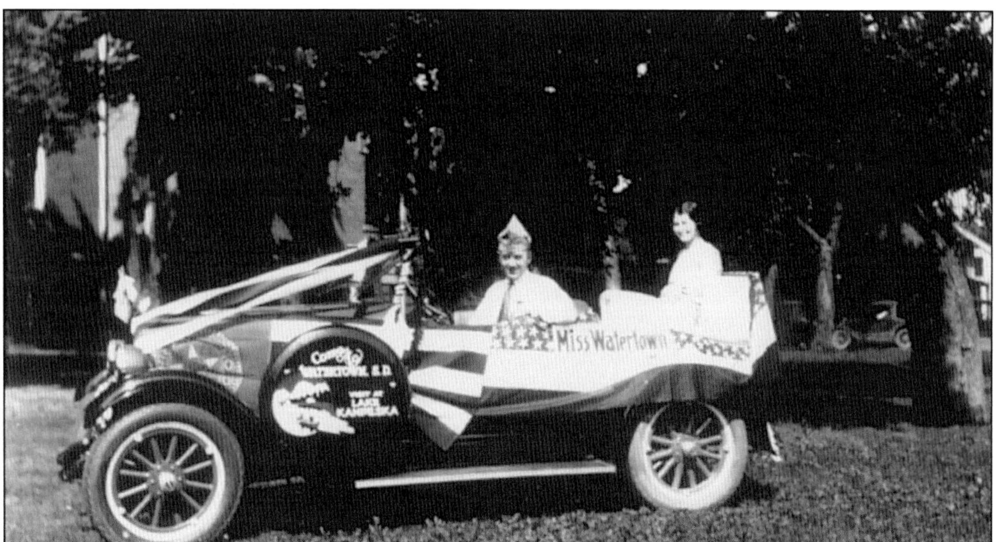

Grace Butcher, pictured here with Carl Argabrite, was Miss Watertown at the 1927 American Legion Convention in Yankton. The spare tire cover on the side of the car reads, "Come to Watertown, S.D., Visit At Lake Kampeska."

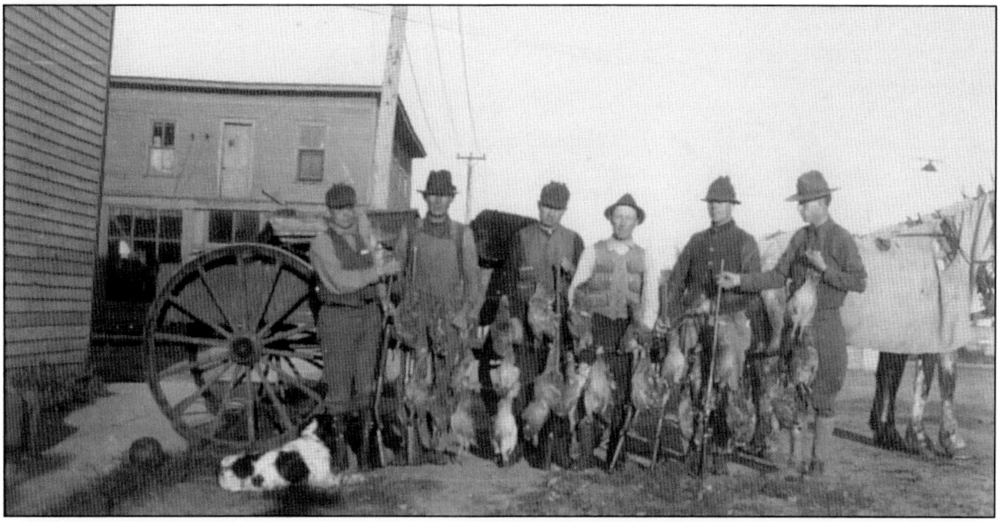

Men from the South Shore area are posed in this undated photo with their bounty from a pheasant hunt. Hunting has been an important part of the economy in eastern and central South Dakota for decades. Famous and wealthy men such as Clark Gable, and Charles Nash, who played a leading roll in the success of Buick and General Motors, came to hunt in the Watertown area. The Lincoln Hotel, among others, went out of its way to accommodate hunters, hosting a "Hunters Stag" party, furnishing lunch kits, and even posting signs suggesting that non-hunting travelers avoid the hotel during the hunting season.

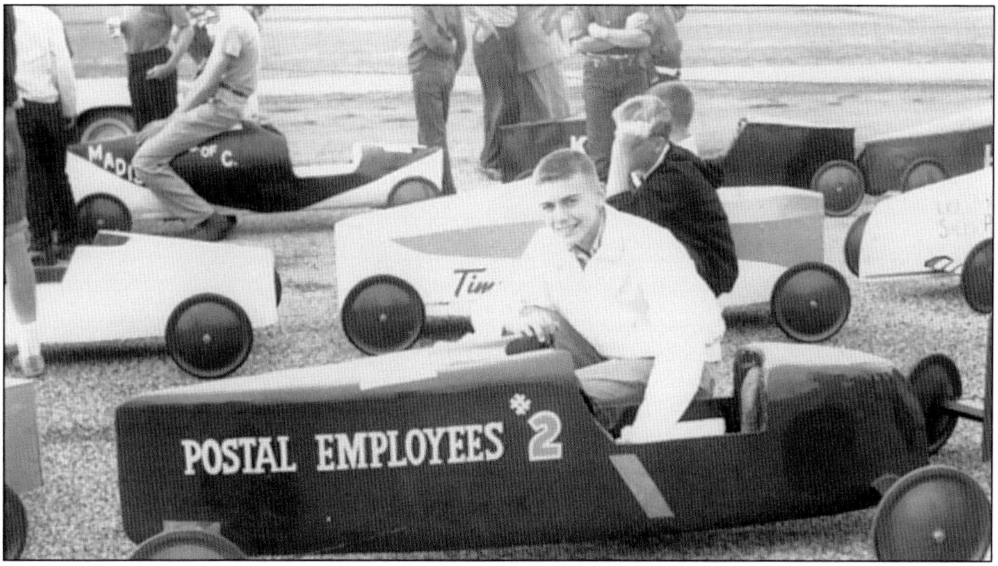

The Watertown Soap Box Derby, pictured in this undated photo, began in 1953 as a project of the Watertown Cosmopolitan Club. The first races, in 1953 and 1954, were held on Carpenter Hill, with Sanders Chevrolet and the *Watertown Public Opinion* as major sponsors. In 1955, the race was held at the new track, designed exactly like the track used for the national races at Akron, Ohio, and built in cooperation with the Codington County Highway Department and National Guard. Though the contest was a good project for young boys who learned the use of tools in the course of constructing their cars, the derby was discontinued in 1973 because of a lack of sponsors.

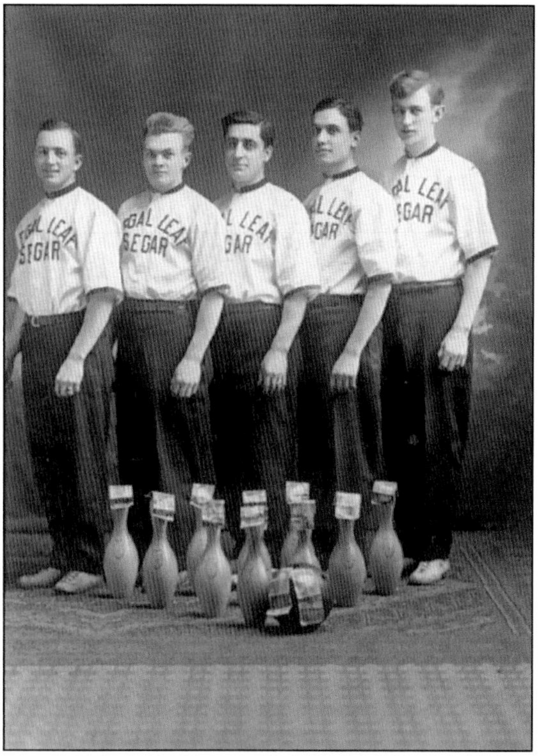

One of Watertown's several cigar manufacturers sponsored the bowling team on this undated postcard, advertising their "Legal Leaf" brand cigar on the team's uniforms. Gray's Photography Studio produced the photo. (Courtesy Ken and Lyn Sheldon.)

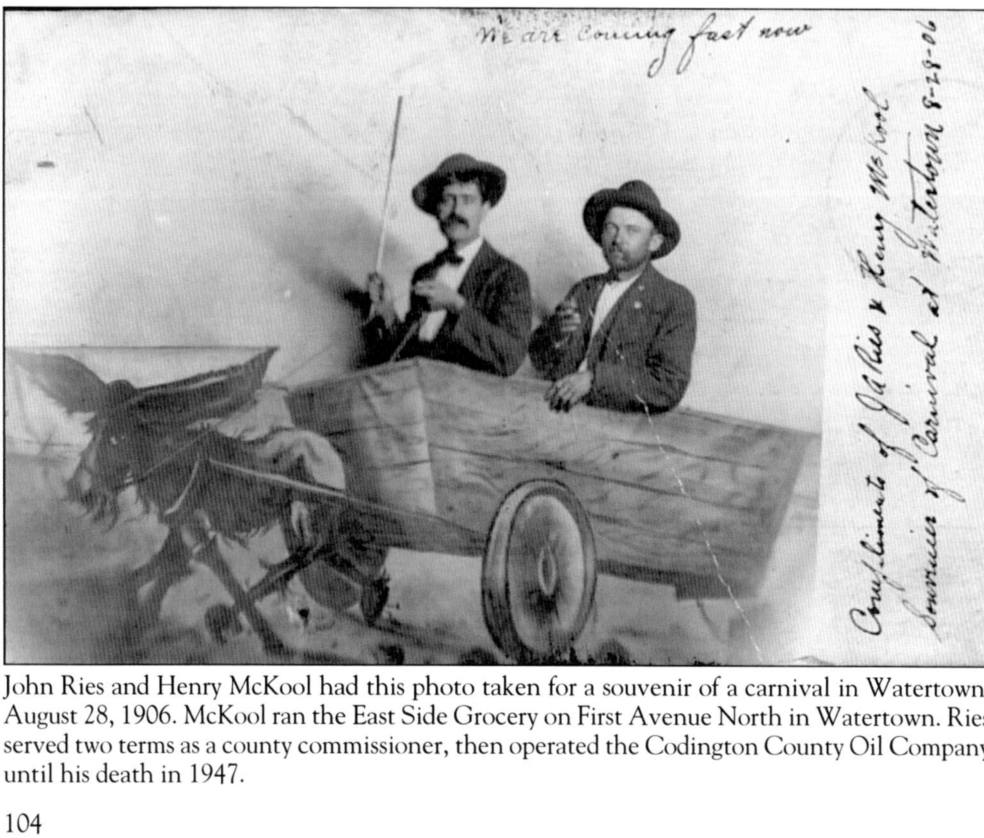

John Ries and Henry McKool had this photo taken for a souvenir of a carnival in Watertown, August 28, 1906. McKool ran the East Side Grocery on First Avenue North in Watertown. Ries served two terms as a county commissioner, then operated the Codington County Oil Company until his death in 1947.

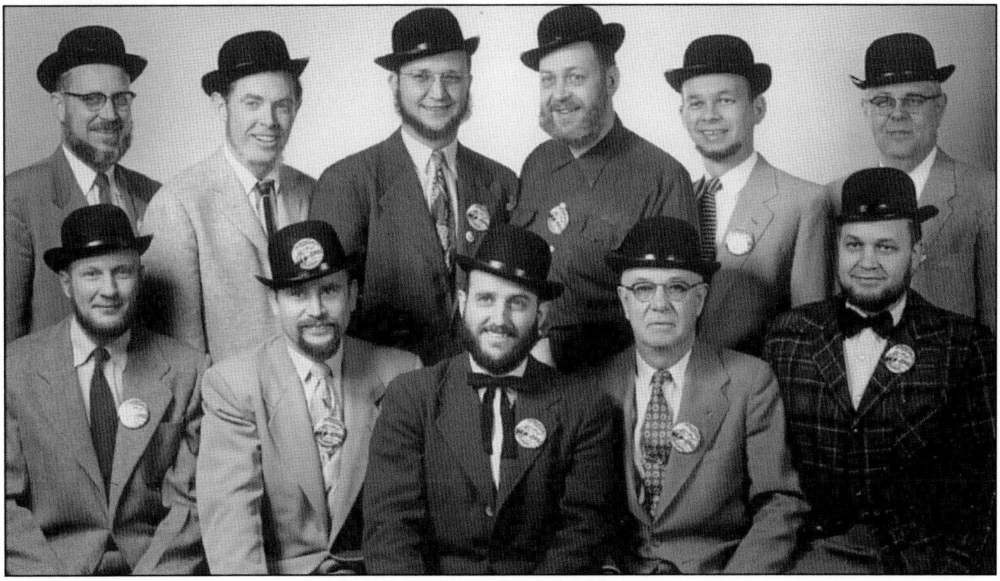

Watertown celebrated its 75th Anniversary in 1954. The men in this photo by Gray's Studio made up the committee to plan activities for the week-long celebration, Sunday, June 20 to Saturday, June 26, which included numerous contests, demonstrations, parades, and the "Kampeska Kavalkade" history pageant. The men are, from left to right, as follows: (front row) Bud Baxter, Lloyd Eastman, Ross Case, Lee Barger, and James Miner; (back row): C.B. Ayers, Harold Gray, Larry Karbo, Dallas Butterbrodt, Howard Gunn, and Dr. Rodney Stoltz. Ross Case, seated, center, was the general chairman for the celebration.

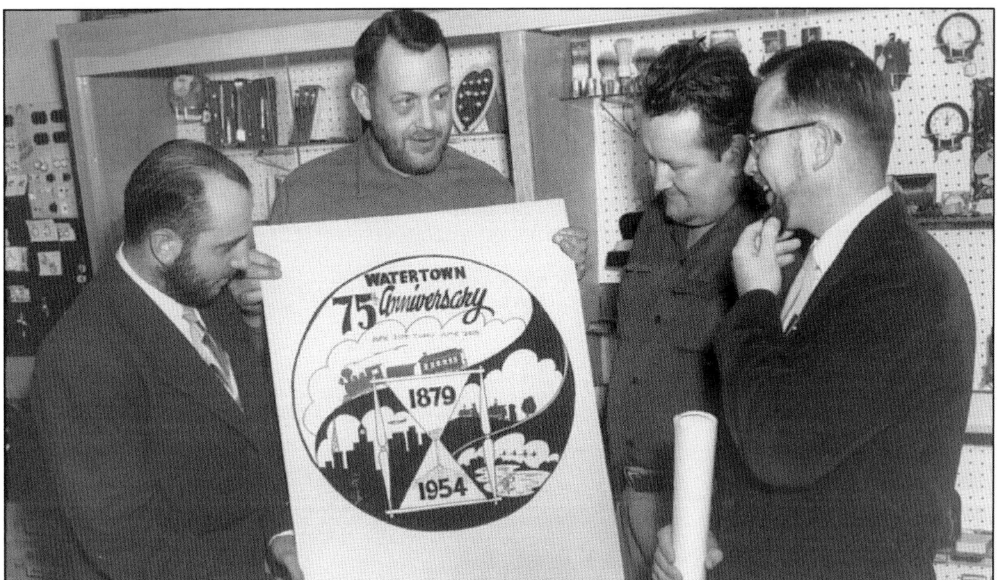

Dallas Butterbrodt and three other gentlemen discuss the logo for Watertown's 75th Anniversary celebration in Butterbrodt's drug store at 11 South Maple Street. According to newspaper accounts, Butterbrodt was one of the most active members of the anniversary committee, and one of the first to start growing a beard for the "Brothers of the Brush" beard-growing contest.

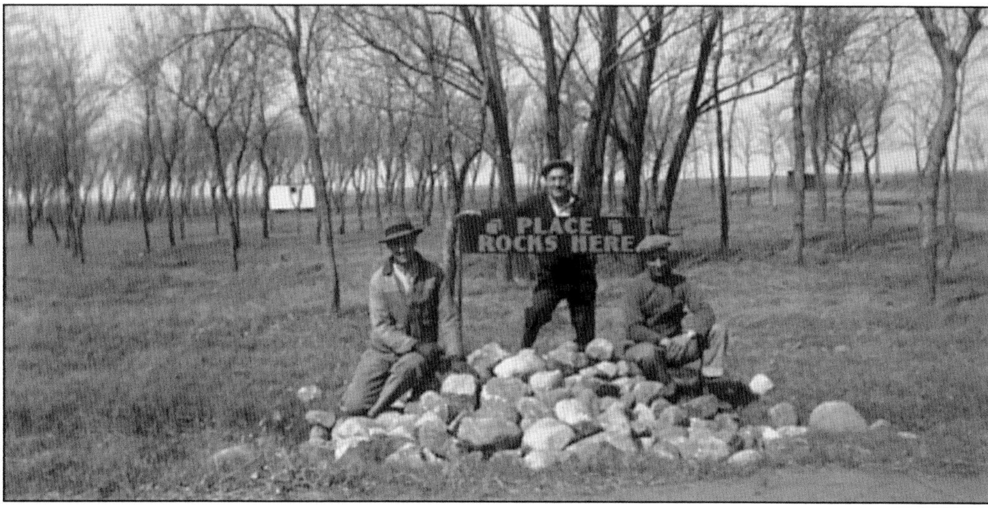

The Codington County American Legion Post No. 17 began collecting rocks early in 1933, for a monument to mark the original site of the city of Watertown, which is where the Stokes-Thomas City Park is located on the east shore of Lake Kampeska. The Winona & St. Peter Railroad, the first railroad in Codington County, mistakenly constructed their line to that point at Lake Kampeska in 1878. The original settlement was named Kampeska and established as the county seat, until it was realized that the railroad's land grant only went as far as the Big Sioux River. Part of the current site of Watertown was then platted, and most of the few buildings at Kampeska moved to the new location. The monument, completed by the Codington County American Legion in June 1933, was placed in the northeast corner of the city park.

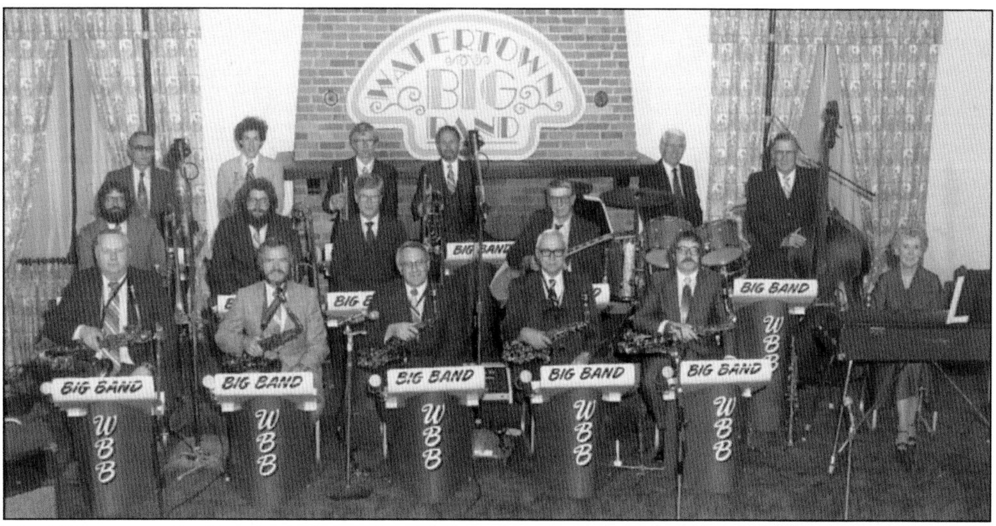

The Watertown Big Band was formed in 1969 and continues to play for events in Watertown. The band gathered for this photo on October 5, 1980, when the South Dakota Public Broadcasting television station produced a show featuring them playing at the Watertown Country Club on South Lake Drive at Lake Kampeska. The band members are, from left to right, as follows: (front row) Dr. Al Wiley, Murph Monahan, Clark Redlinger, Leonard "Shadow" Domonoske, Warren Hattfield, and pianist Pat Amundson; (second row) Rick Herr, Doug Herr, Doug Carpenter, Howard Berge, and Oynie Probart; (back row) Bob Carey, Bill Peterson, Dean Kranhold, Dean DeWall, and Harold "Rip" Collins.

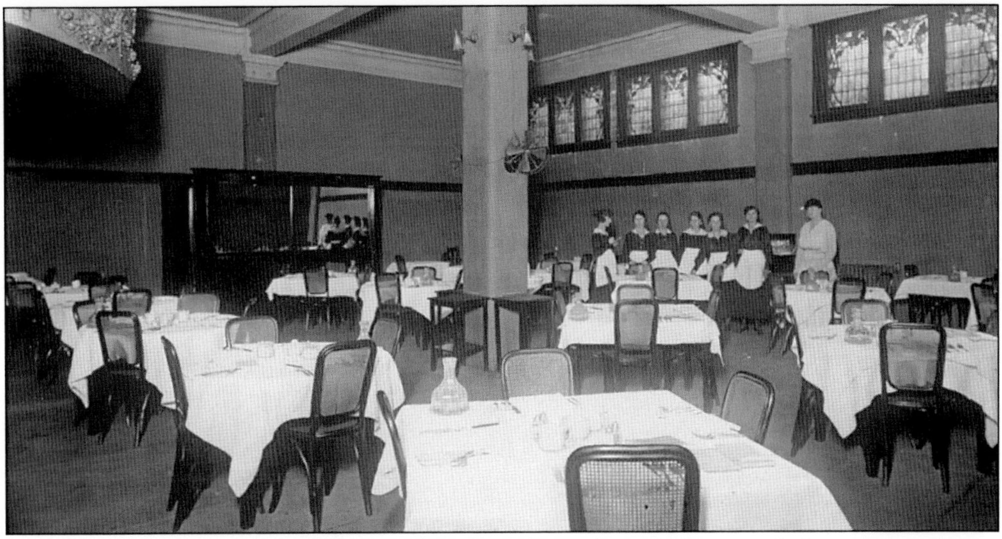

The dining room at Lincoln Hotel, in this photo from about 1920, provided an elegant dining experience, with soft light illuminating stained glass windows designed by local architect Maurice Hockman, and an orchestra playing gently in the balcony at left. The Lincoln Hotel was razed in 1972, and the windows were placed in the dining room and bar of the Guest House Inn on North Broadway.

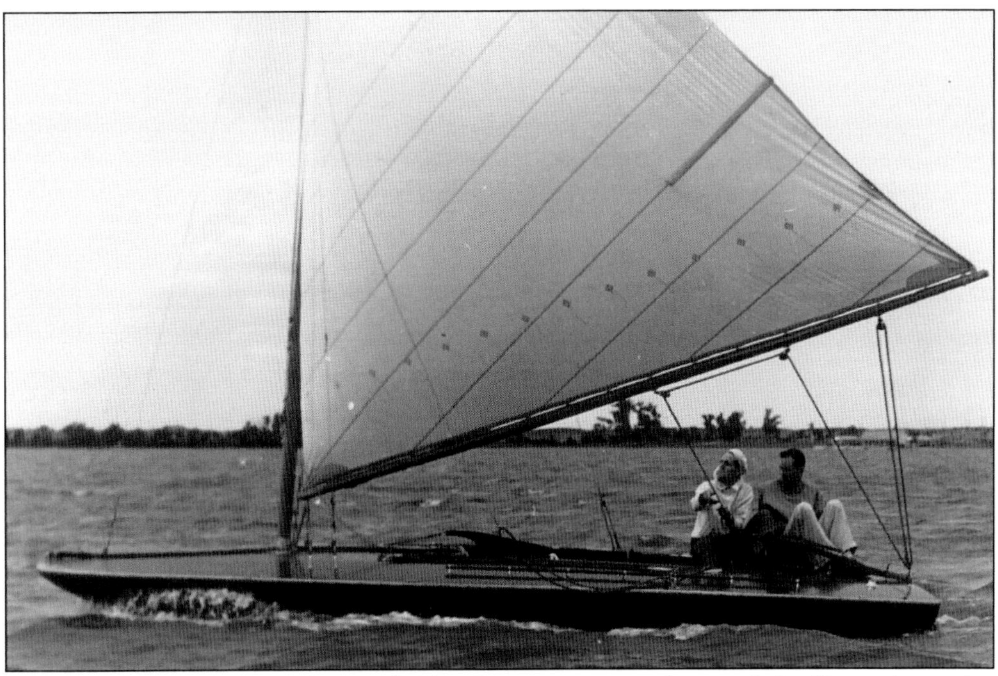

Many years before Harvey Shaw and Glen Patterson were sailing on Lake Kampeska in this photo from 1937, Mark Sheafe, son of General Mark Sheafe, president of the Dakota Loan and Trust Company, and Lorenzo Morris, son of Walter Morris, president of the Citizens National Bank, also owned a sailboat together, about 1900. Sailing was another popular pastime at Lake Kampeska and Lake Pelican in summer and winter; an illustration in an 1889 souvenir book of Watertown shows eight iceboats with large sails.

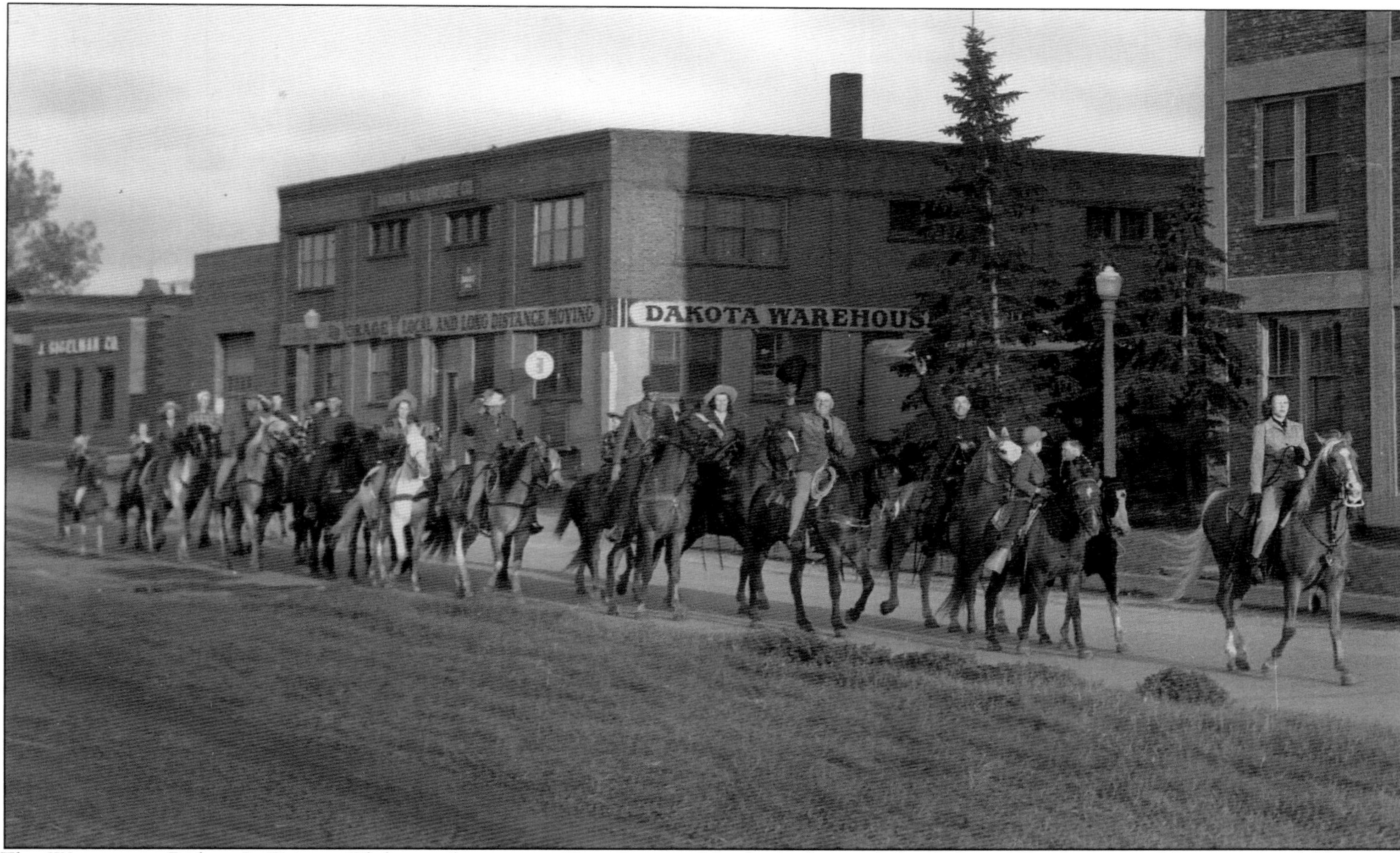

The Watertown Riders & Drivers Club parade west on First Avenue North, in front of the Dakota Warehouse and International Harvester warehouse on Second Street West, in this photo by L.E. Henderson in 1947.

Eight

ACTS OF GOD

Weather is a standard topic of conversation in the Midwest. People are constantly complaining about, commenting on, or predicting the weather.

The Northern Plains are well known for extremes. It is not unusual to have a 120-degree temperature difference between summer and winter. Similar extremes occur with precipitation. Although the area including western Kansas, western Oklahoma, and northern Texas, was known as the "Dust Bowl," South and North Dakota and eastern Montana had a much larger area severely affected by drought in the 1930s. Conversely, the worst flood in recent memory occurred after one of the worst winters. As a result of melting snow and early and heavy spring rain, the Big Sioux River flooded in 1997 causing extensive damage in Watertown.

Watertown and Codington County are situated at the very northern tip of what meteorologists call "Tornado Alley." Although far fewer tornadoes occur here than in Plains states further south, Watertown and Codington County are not immune to the destructive power of tornados.

The Northern Plains are also well known for winter weather. The Blizzard of 1888 was perhaps the worst experienced by early settlers in South Dakota. It was also called the "School Children's Storm" because many of the victims were children who had been released early from school in the hope of getting home before the storm climaxed.

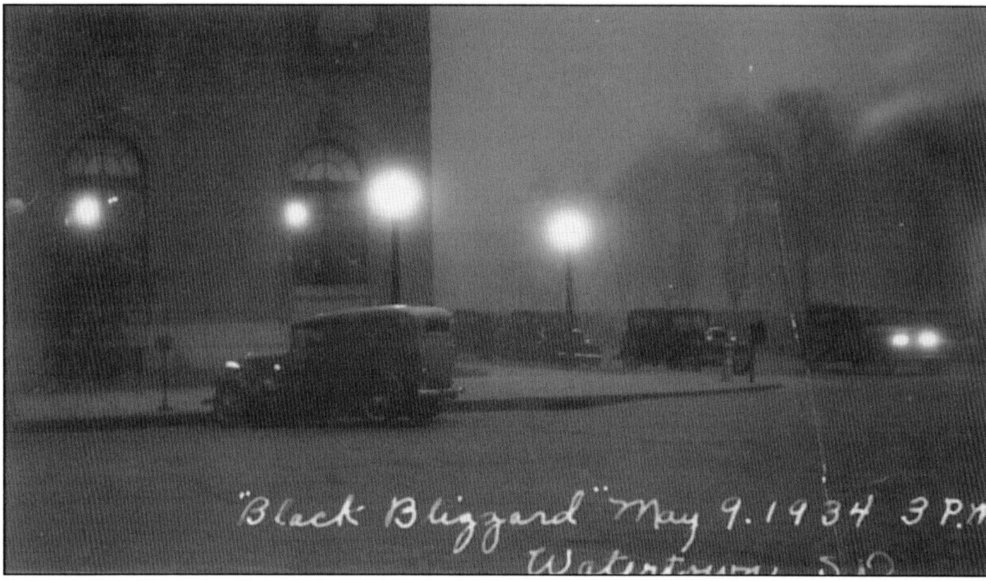

During the afternoon of May 9, 1934, at the height of the Great Depression, a dust cloud formed in western Codington County and soon enveloped Watertown. Visibility became so bad that the streetlights were turned on, and cars were forced to use their headlights. W.C. Gowin shot this photograph of the post office corner at the intersection of Broadway and First Avenue South at 3:00 p.m. The phenomenon is popularly known as the "Black Blizzard."

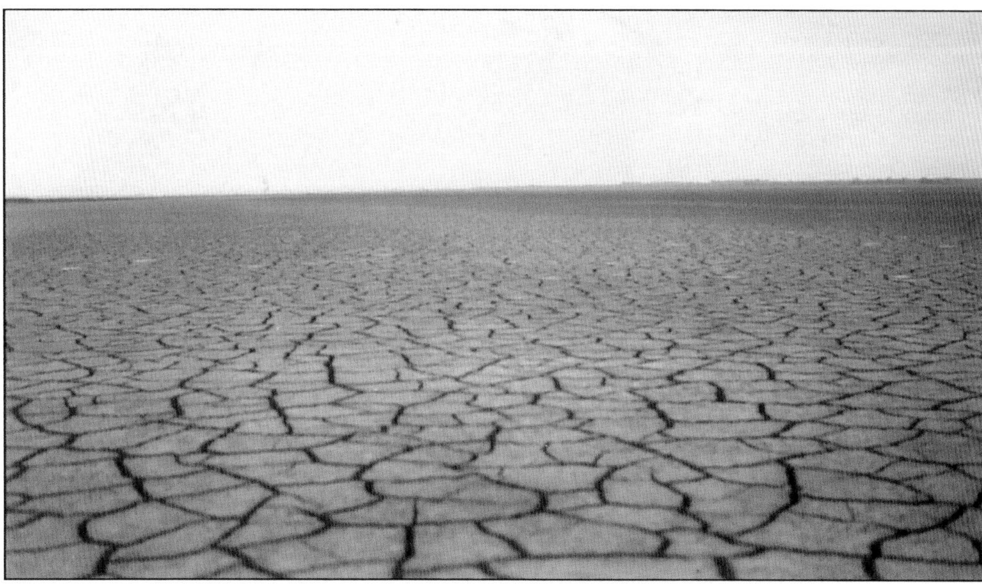

By 1936, Lake Pelican, southwest of Watertown, had dried up almost completely, but the lake did recover, and is now host to a state park and recreation area, and many ice fishermen in winter.

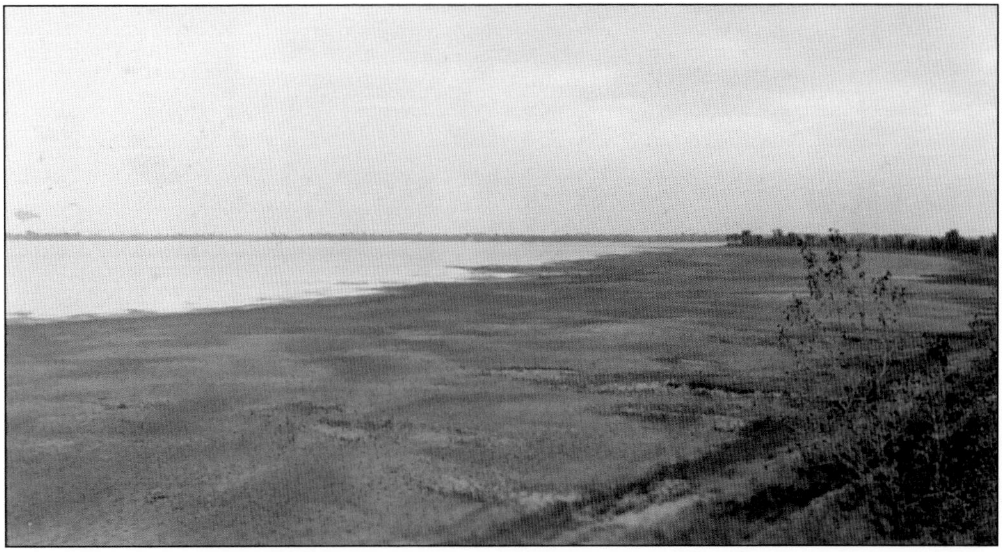

According to Dr. Ward Williams, a respected Watertown citizen, the second stage of Lake Kampeska's decline started in 1936, when the previous winter's large snowfall melted quickly in March. The channel of the Sioux River, which flows into Lake Kampeska, had dried up and filled with silt from the dust storms of the 1930s. Heavy rains followed the rapid melting, and a deluge of mud was swept into the lake. This, in combination with a flash flood in 1915, destroyed the crystal clear water and fine sandy bottom Lake Kampeska had been famous for since settlement began in Codington County in the 1870s.

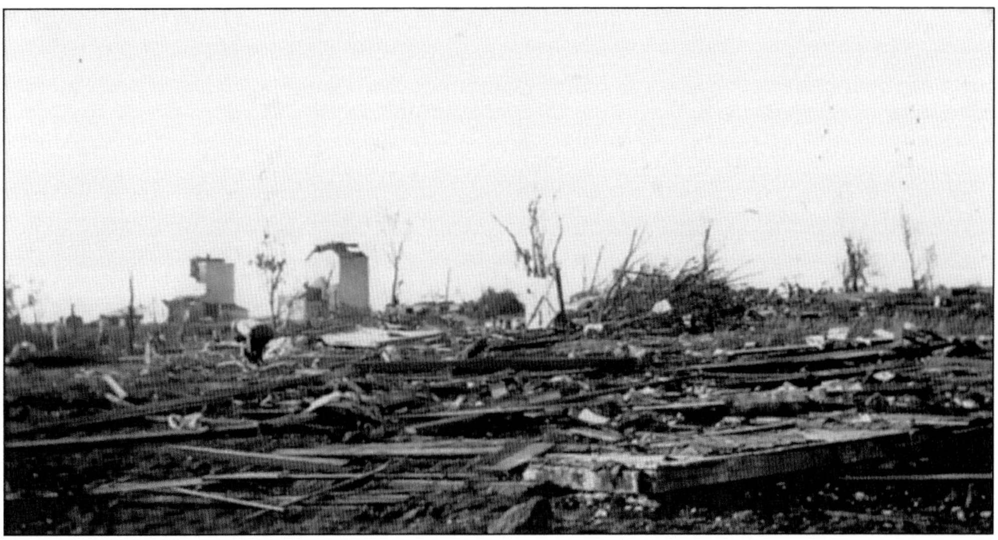

On Saturday afternoon, June 17, 1944, a destructive storm cut across Codington, Grant, Roberts, Brown, and Day counties, producing the worst tornadoes in years, and killing 13 people and injuring more than 75. Mrs. Jennie Larson and Mrs. Ole Kjetland were killed instantly in the tornado, and young Harvey Zirbel, son of Bill Zirbel, died from fatal injuries on the way to a Watertown hospital, after he was pulled out from underneath a pile of broken timber. The most damage from the tornado that hit Florence was done in the southeast part of town, destroying several homes, buildings on several farms, and the Standard Oil bulk tanks, and causing extensive damage to the Farmers Elevator buildings, visible in the left half of this photograph.

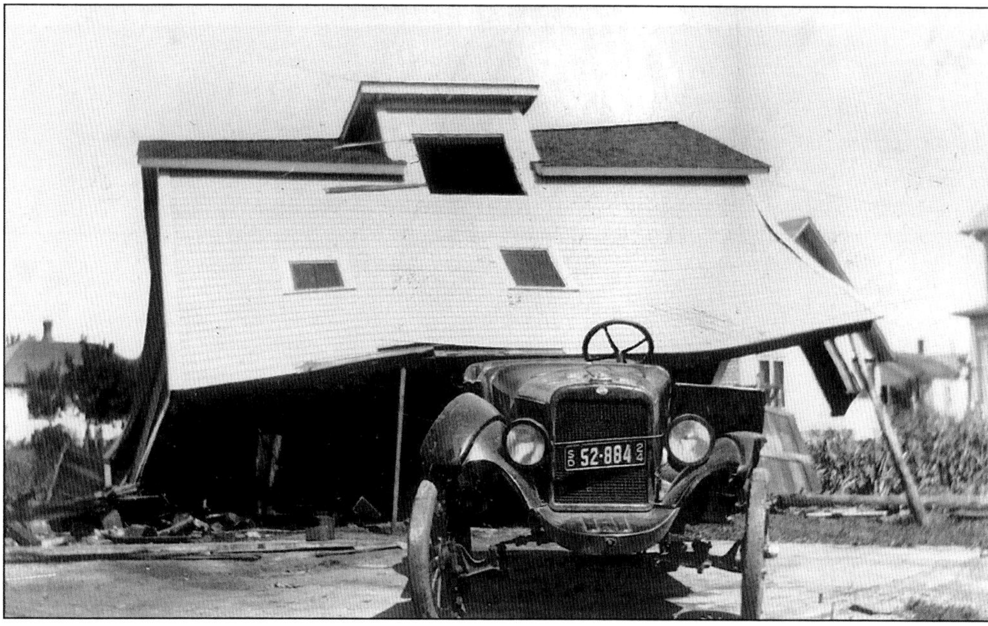

One of the worst tornadoes in the history of Watertown struck the southeast part of town on June 23, 1914. The worst damage from the storm was done between Fourth and Seventh Avenues South and between Broadway and Fifth Street East. Many families were made homeless and many people were injured, some seriously, but none were killed. This photo of part of a house resting on a car is a snapshot, but most of the pictures of the damage that exist today are postcards that were mass produced by a local photographer and sold at a number of stores in the city and county. The Foto Pla and Idle Hour theaters also ran pictures of the tornado for several days following the disaster. The following three images are some of the postcards that were available.

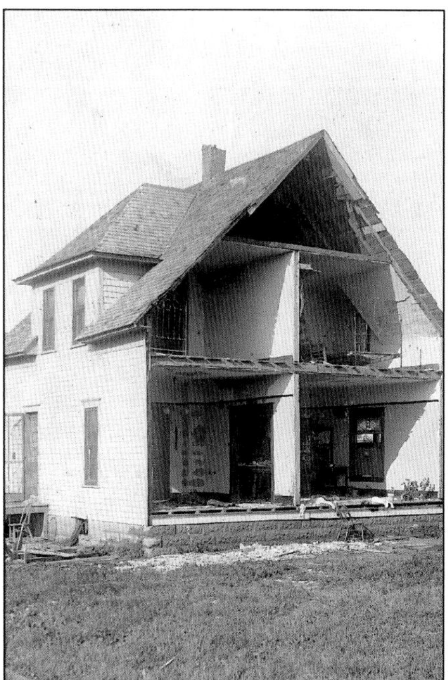

The home of the David Johnson family on Fourth Street Southeast is a peculiar site, with its north wall completely removed by the 1914 tornado, but furniture and other goods still standing inside.

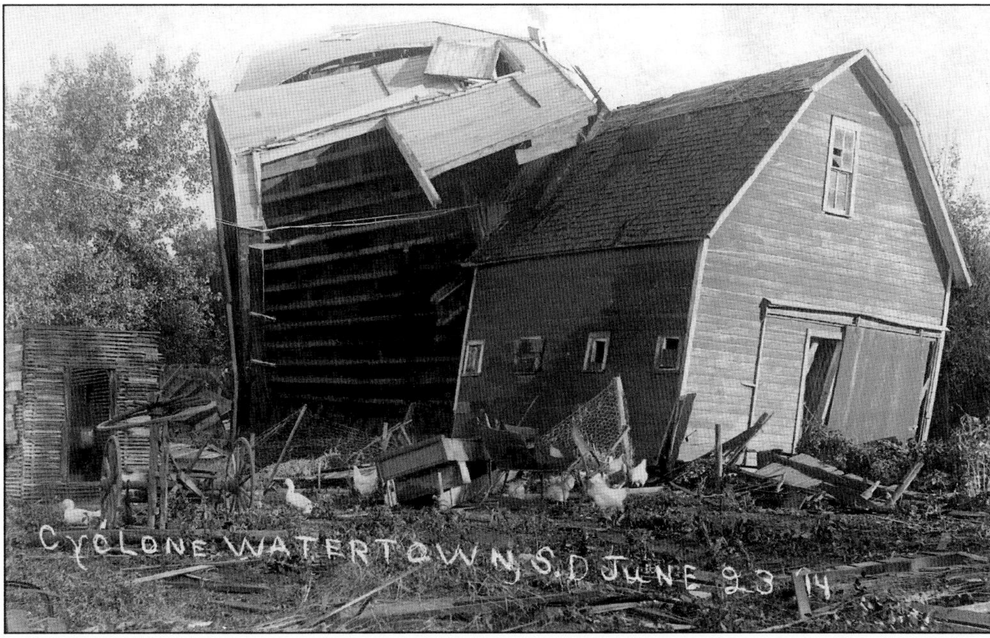

These barns were located on the John King property. The large barn on the left was picked off the ground by the 1914 tornado, and hurled against the adjoining barn.

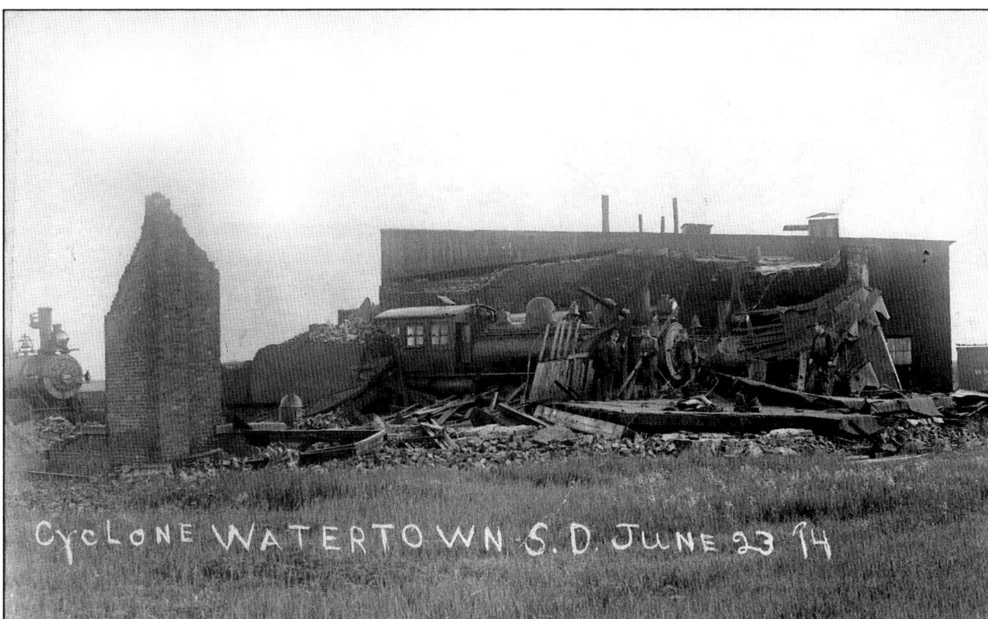

The Minneapolis & St. Louis Railroad round house in east Watertown was destroyed in the 1914 storm and had to be completely rebuilt.

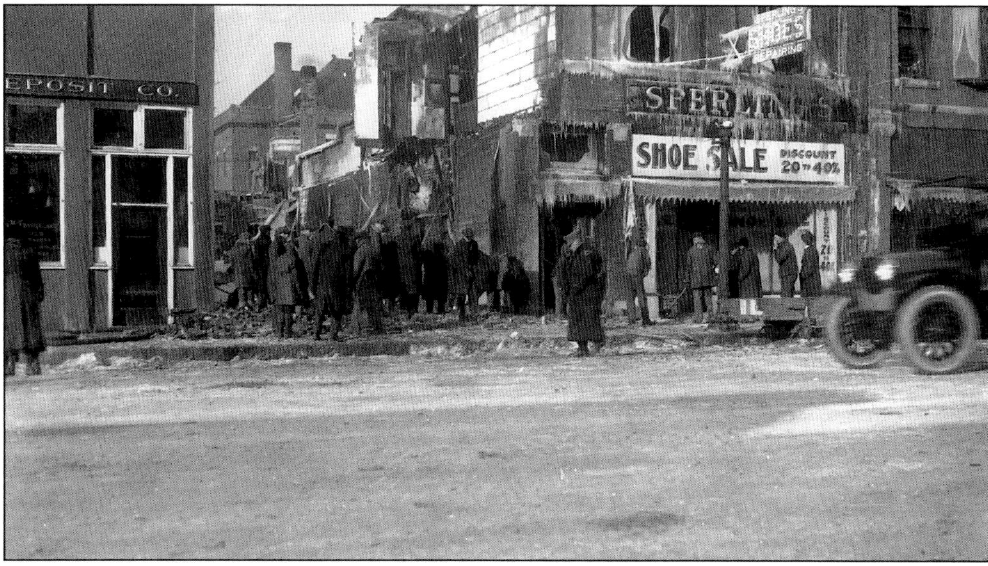

This undated photograph documents a fire in the Sperling Shoe Store at 9 South Broadway. Sperling Shoes recovered from the fire, and was in operation at this location for about 50 years, from about 1920 until 1970.

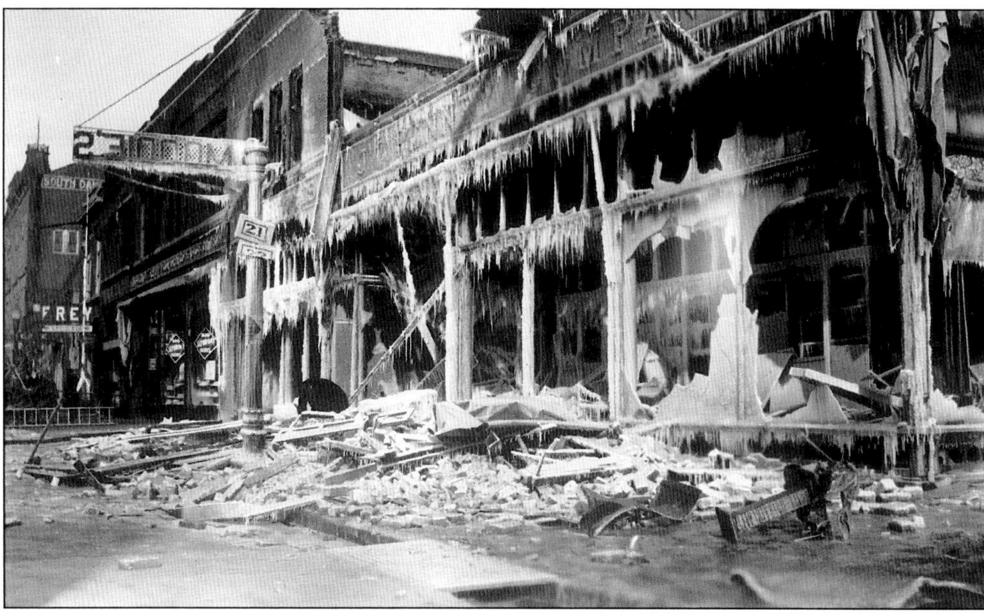

Damage from a fire and subsequent rescue efforts at J.C. Penney, right, and the neighboring Moodie Dry Goods Store, 117–123 East Kemp Avenue, the night of February 25, 1925, was captured on this postcard. The fire started in the rear of the Moodie store and the fire quickly consumed the building, causing all the floors of the two-story structure to fall into the basement. The firemen struggled to reach the flames in the smoke-filled building that night in below-zero temperatures; note the ice-covered remains. (Courtesy Ken and Lyn Sheldon.)

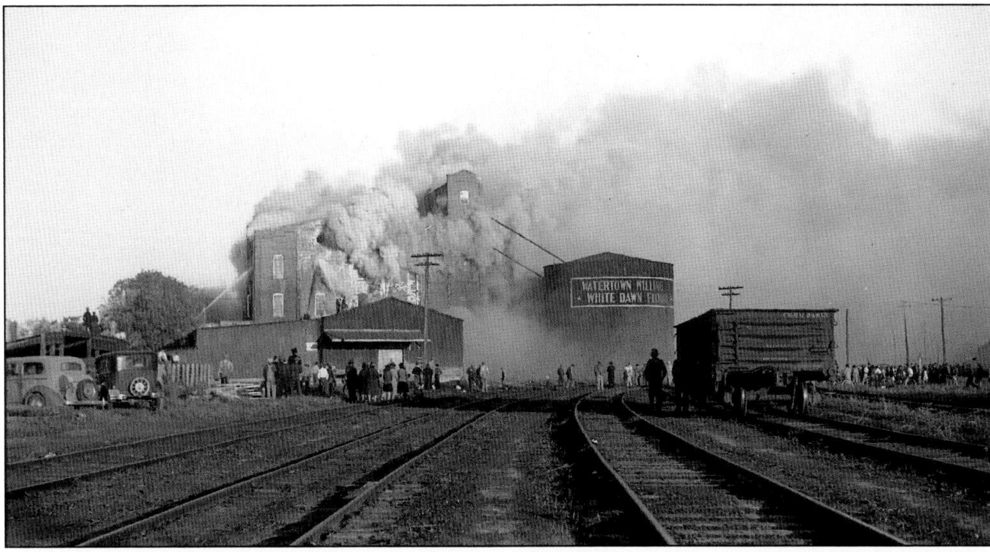

This fire at the Watertown Milling Company in September 1940, was the second fire the mill sustained. The first mill was mostly destroyed in a tragic fire in 1901, but was quickly rebuilt. The Watertown Mill began in 1884 as the Stokes Mill, packaging its own brand of flour, Garland. The current owner, Hubbard Milling Co., which specializes in livestock feed, bought the plant in 1970.

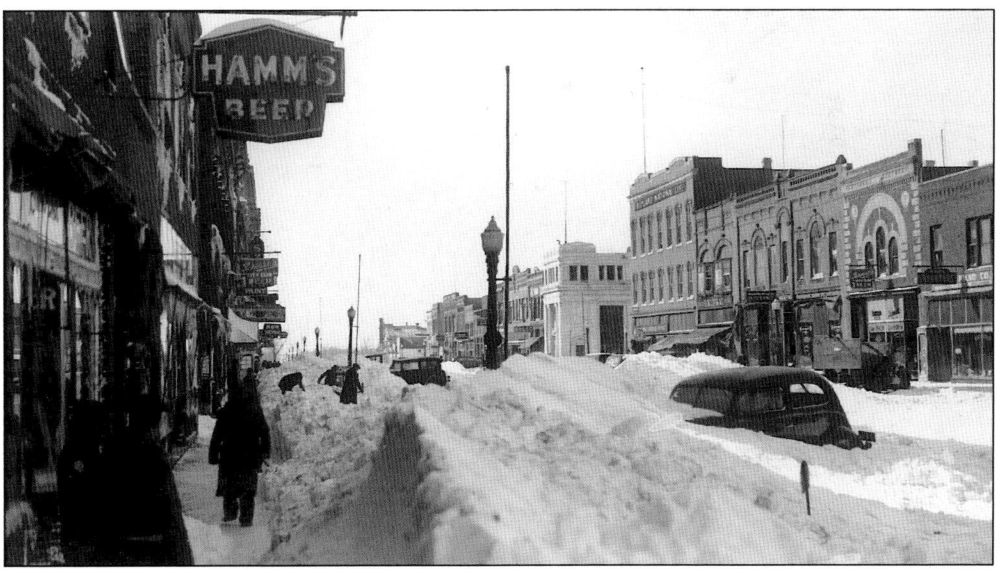

A blizzard in 1936 dumped mountains of snow in Watertown city streets. The last three images in this chapter depict the scenes in town as the clean-up effort began. In this photograph looking south on Broadway from about First Avenue North, cars are buried, and people can be seen on the left shoveling the sidewalks.

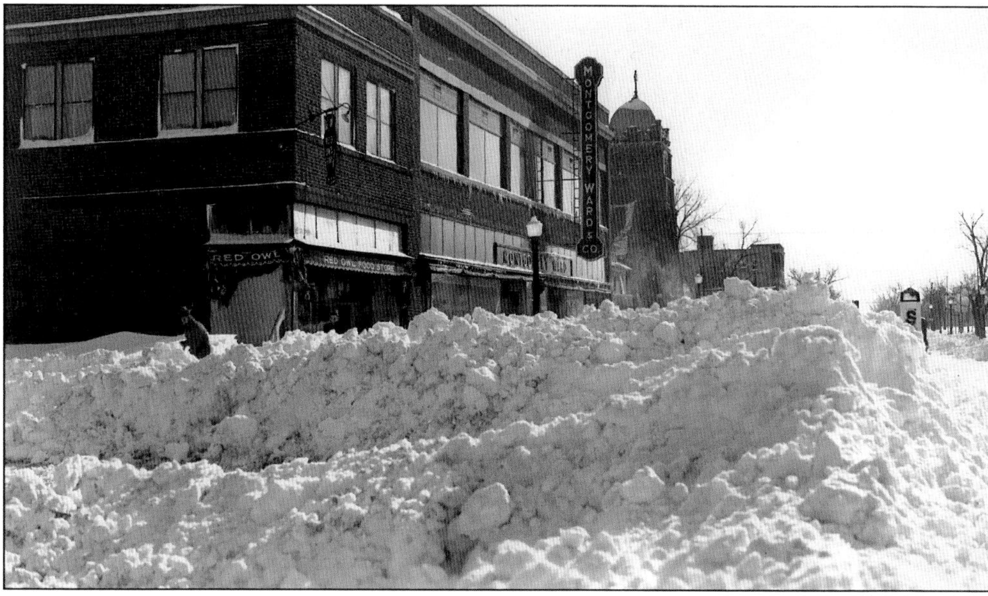

The Red Owl food store and Montgomery Ward at 201 and 203 East Kemp Avenue, are pictured in this view after the 1936 blizzard, looking east on Kemp. Note the Immaculate Conception Church to the right of Montgomery Ward.

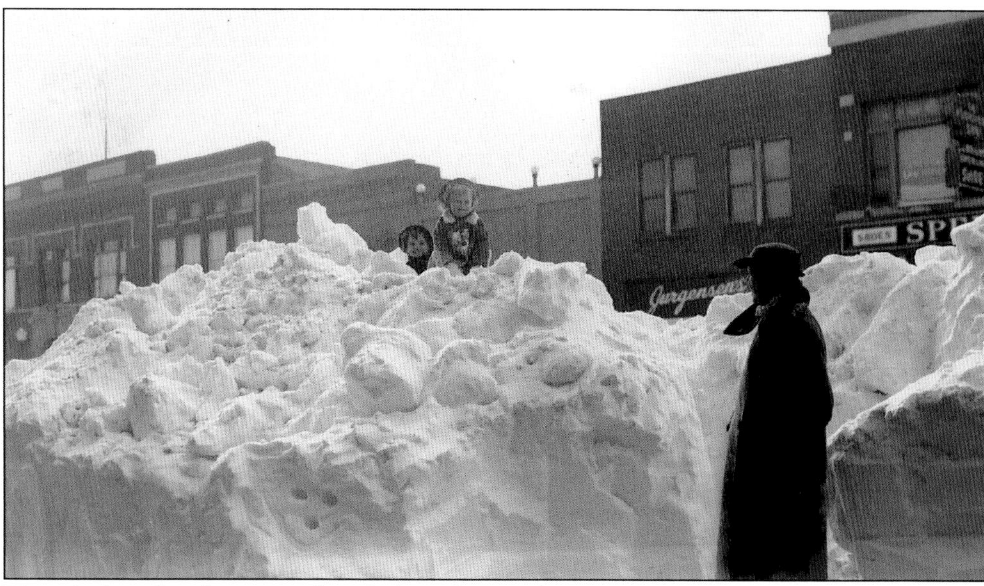

These little girls, who are unidentified, are having fun on a snow bank in front of buildings on the west side of South Broadway, after a 1936 blizzard.

Nine

Promotion and Growth

Even though Watertown did not have a major state institution, early boosters bragged up the town to attract settlers. The following exaggeration was published in the *Watertown Public Opinion* on April 12, 1889:

> *This county, of which Watertown is the county seat, is one of the best in all Dakota. Nestled at the head of the Big Sioux Valley, and bathed with the waters of innumerable lakes, with a soil unequaled in fertility, and with natural advantages for mixed farming and stock raising, Codington County stands first among her sister counties. Farmers in the east who contemplate coming west can find no better soil, no better location, and no better markets in the whole northwest than Codington County presents.*

Apparently the promotion worked because Watertown's largest period of growth was between 1900 and 1913 when the population increased by 45 percent. Since using the motto of the "Live City," Watertown has continued to promote its progressive nature with logos like "City on the Go," and its current slogan, "South Dakota's Rising Star."

The lack of a major showcase institution was outweighed by the greater long-term advantages it brought. Watertown lost the benefits that a showcase institution would have brought, but because the economy became more diversified, the town was able to weather downturns in the economy that deeply affected other communities with major state institutions.

Early promotional postcards and photos illustrating growth and change in Watertown and other county towns are showcased in this final chapter.

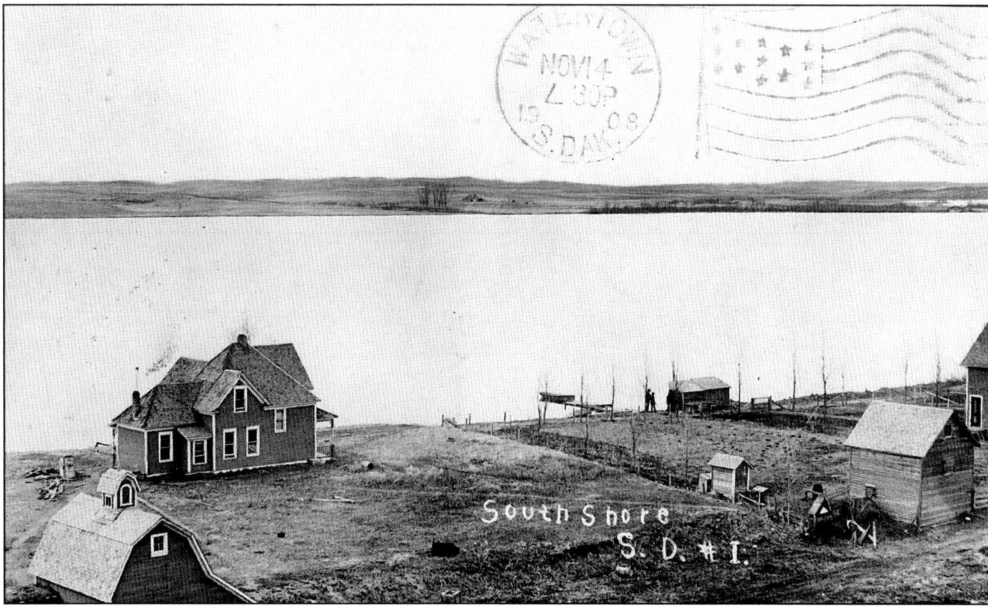

The town of South Shore is just that—a settlement on the south shore of Punished Woman's Lake in northeast Codington County. Two early homes (one at far right) and several outbuildings are subjects of this postcard, postmarked November 14, 1908, on the back of which "Mabel W." invites Lena Lentz of Watertown to a dance in South Shore on Friday night.

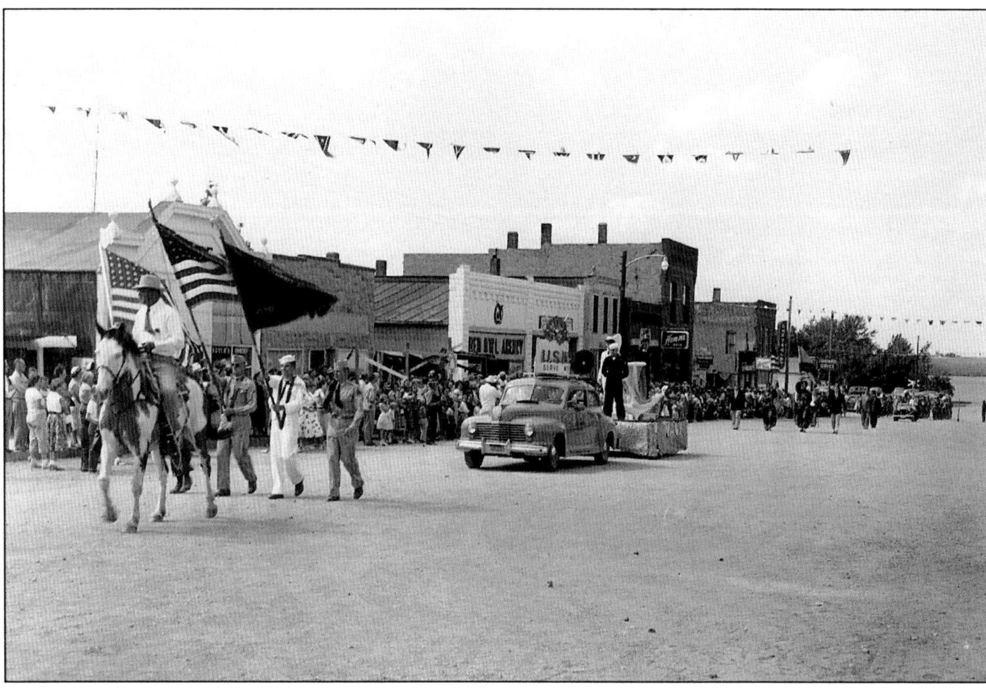

Manley Owens leads this Independence Day parade, headed south on South Shore's Main Street, about 1950. Several devastating fires throughout the history of South Shore claimed many of the town's early commercial buildings. Punished Woman's Lake is just visible at the far right.

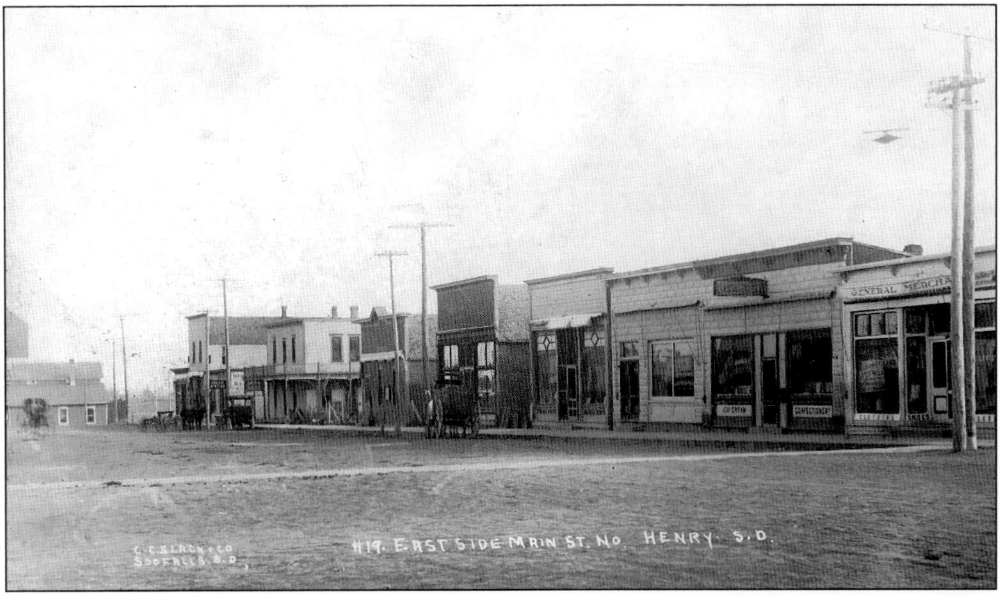

Many businesses lined the east side of Henry's Main Street in this photo postcard from about 1910. A sign for the cream station can be seen on the far left, near the automobile parked in front of the building with a second-story wrap-around porch, which is probably the Commercial House hotel. Further down the street, an ice cream store and confectionery stands next to a store of general merchandise, at the far right.

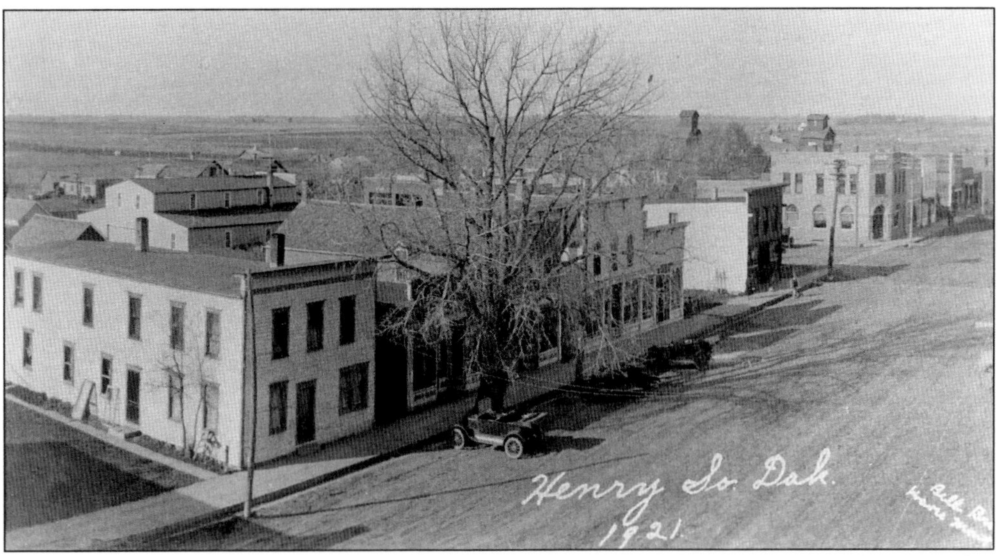

In this view of the west side of Main Street in Henry in 1921, the brick building at right, facing the street corner, was built in 1905, and was home to the Citizens State Bank of Henry until 1926, when the bank closed from economic pressures. The building currently houses the post office and a branch of Watertown's Wight & Comes Funeral Chapel. The frame building across the street, to the left, is the Hubbard Hardware Store, mentioned in Chapter One. The long building in the background at the left of the photo was an implement dealership. Most of Henry's original commercial buildings are now gone, victims of fire and campaigns to simply "clean-up" the town.

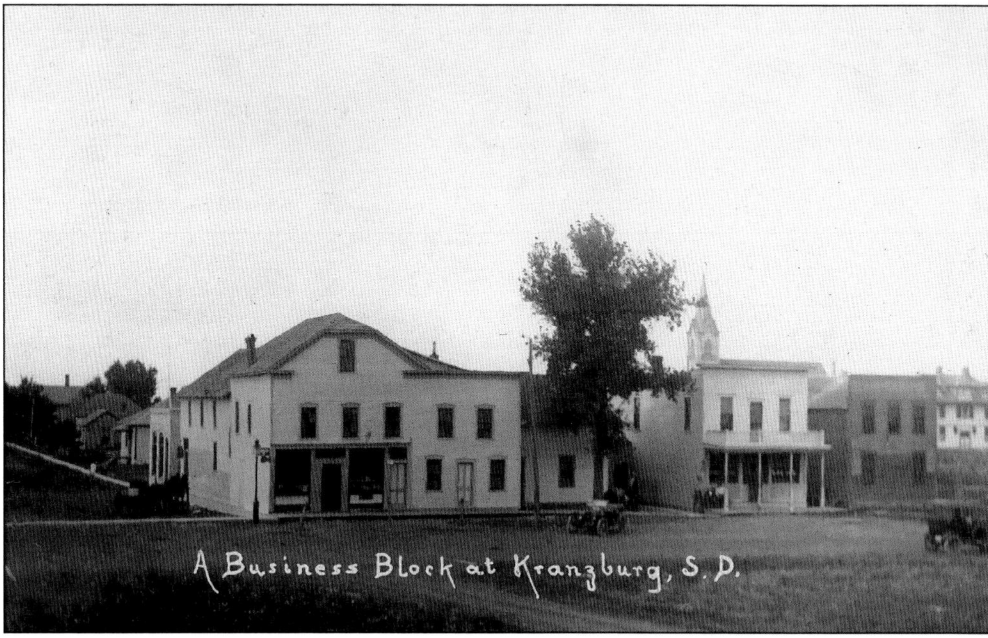

St. Mary Street runs in front of the business block in this undated postcard of Kranzburg. The two-story building on the corner was one of Kranzburg's first business buildings in 1879, and was known as the Matt Kranz Hotel. A general merchandise store and the post office were on the first floor. The building was destroyed by fire before 1920, but was replaced with a garage built by Mike Otto and Pat Heyn. The garage burned in 1953, and a bank was built in its place.

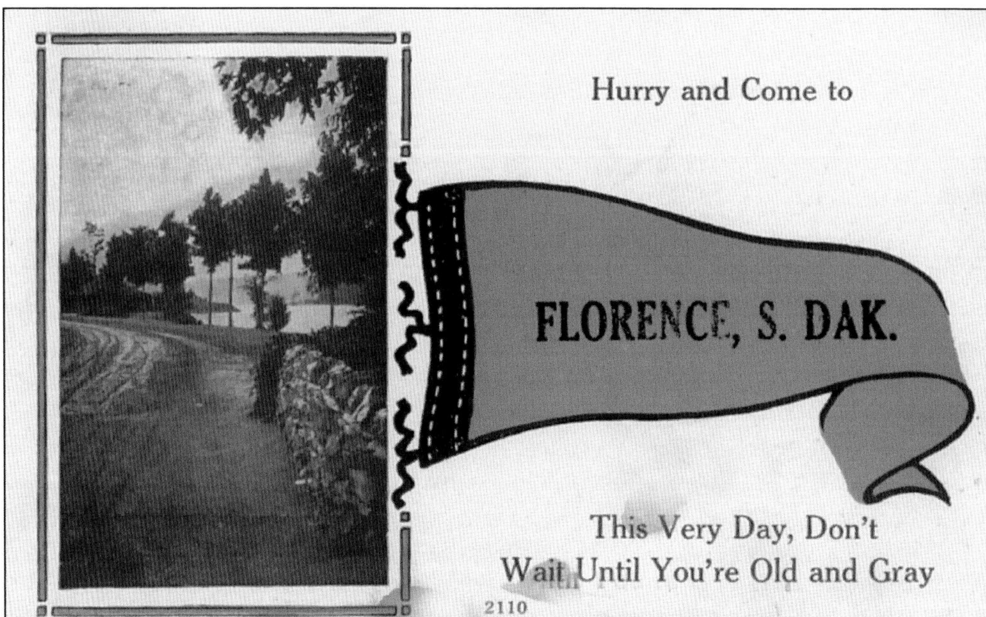

This type of postcard was mass-produced with a standard photograph, not typically of the advertised location. The name of the city or town for which the card was ordered was stamped on. Sent to Lloid Halse, postmarked April 3, 1915.

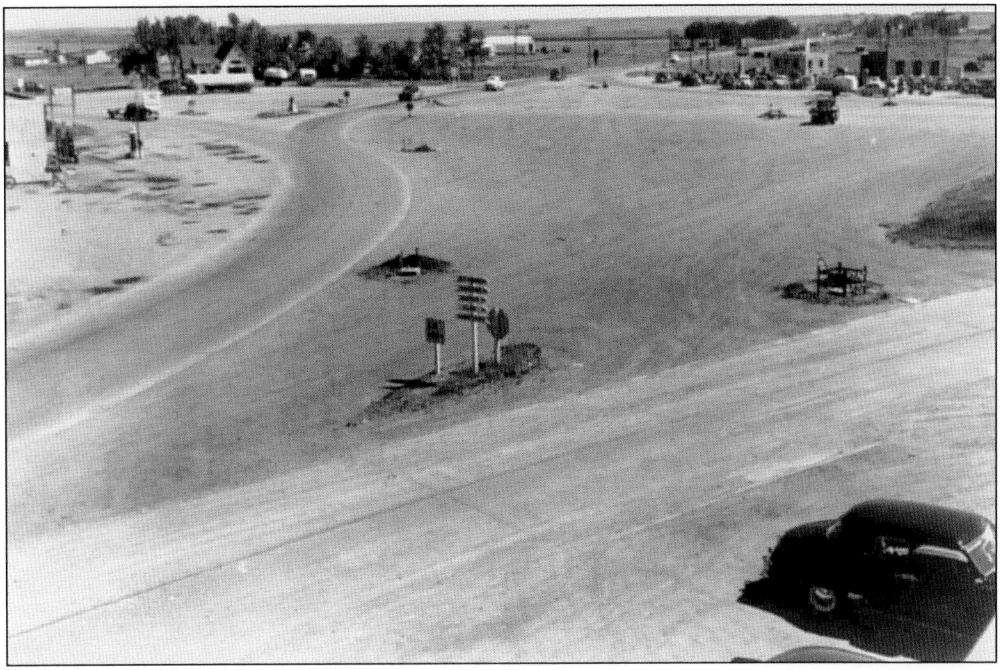

This view of the junction of Highways 81 and 212 in Watertown from about 1950, faces southeast from the top of what is now the Drake Motel, toward the current site of the Cowboy gas station, or what was then the Nelson service station. The Zundel Motor Company is in the upper right corner of the photo, on the southwest corner of the intersection. This junction is now one of the busiest intersections in South Dakota.

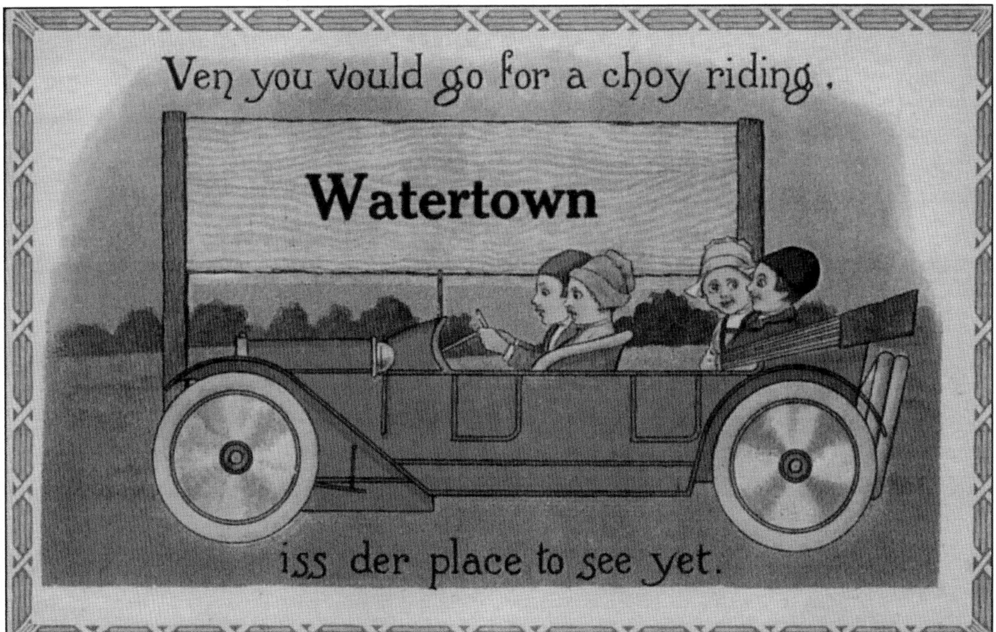

Sent to Miss Martha Emerson in Bryant, from Toronto, South Dakota, postmarked May 7, 1914. (Courtesy Bud and Arleen Larson.)

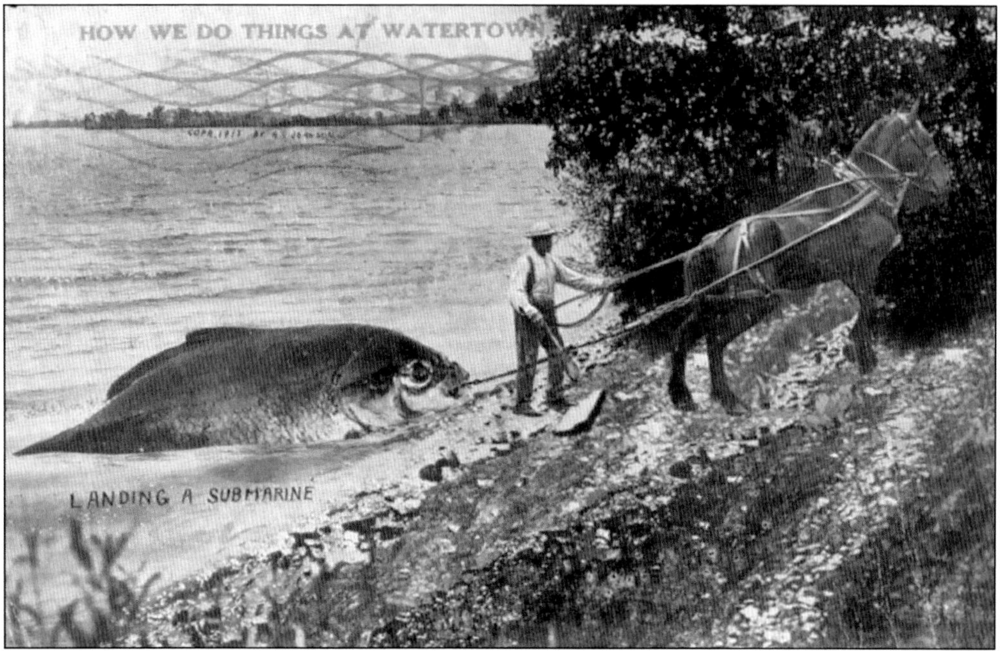

Postcards of giant-sized produce and other resources were a comical way to promote one's hometown. Mrs. O.W. Lundgren sent this card to J.F. Rossiter in Iowa on August 24, 1918. (Courtesy Ken and Lyn Sheldon.)

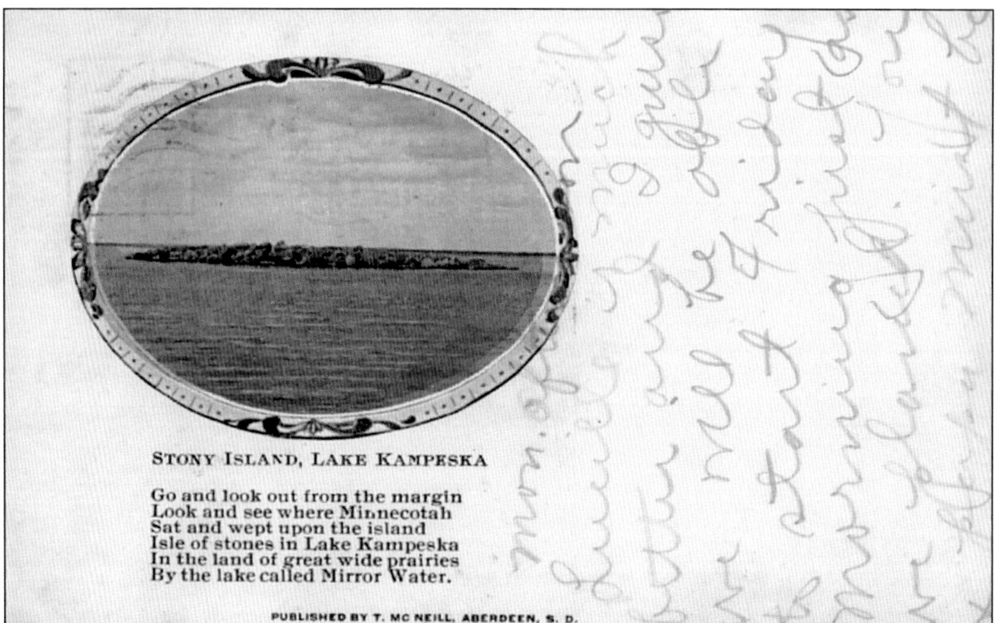

This postcard mentions the legend of Stony Island, also known as Maiden Isle, at Lake Kampeska. The small rocky island was located just off of Stony Point on the southeast side of the lake. The card is postmarked July 13, 1908. (Courtesy Bud and Arleen Larson.)

A photograph of Kemp Avenue was used to illustrate the poem on this card, postmarked August 22, 1913.

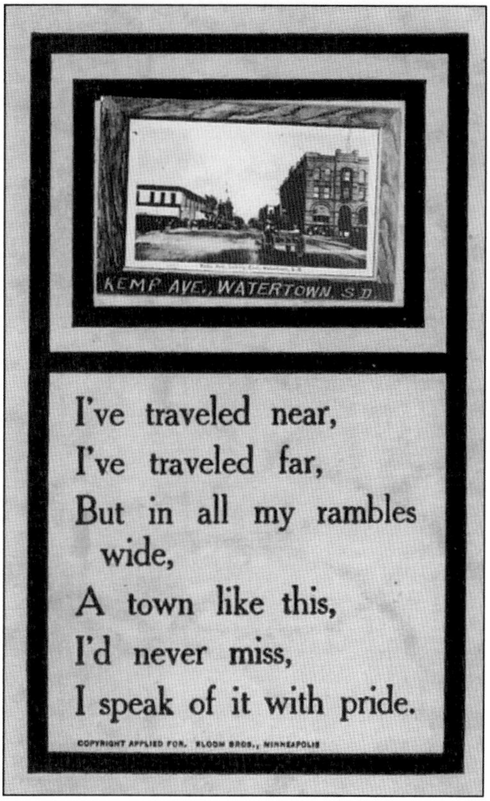

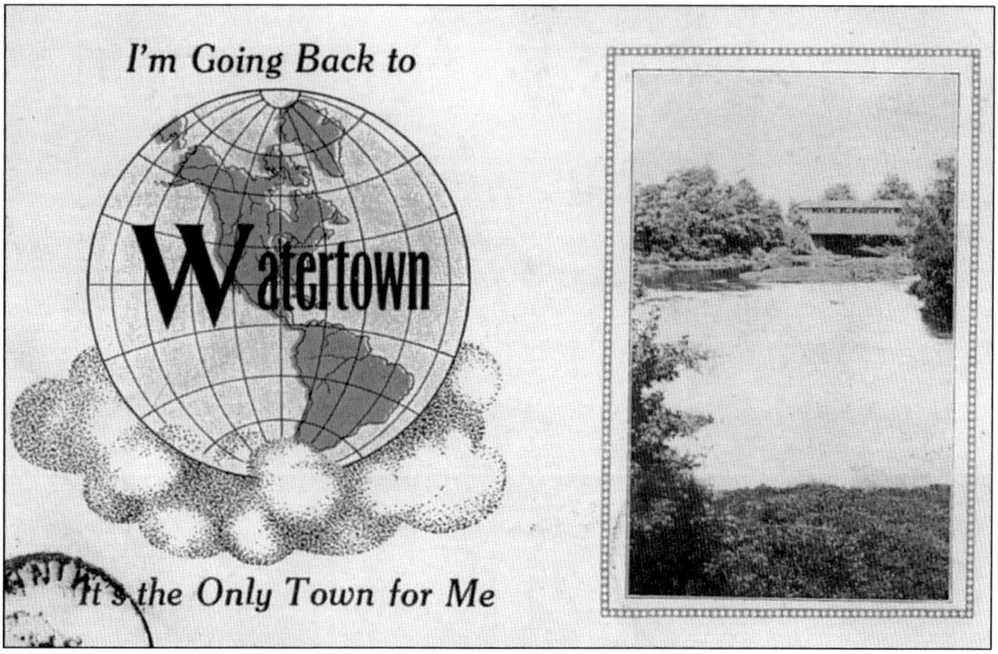

Sent from the town of Hazel, South Dakota, to Miss Emma Giese in Wayzata, Minnesota, postmarked June 12, 1913. (Courtesy Bud and Arleen Larson.)

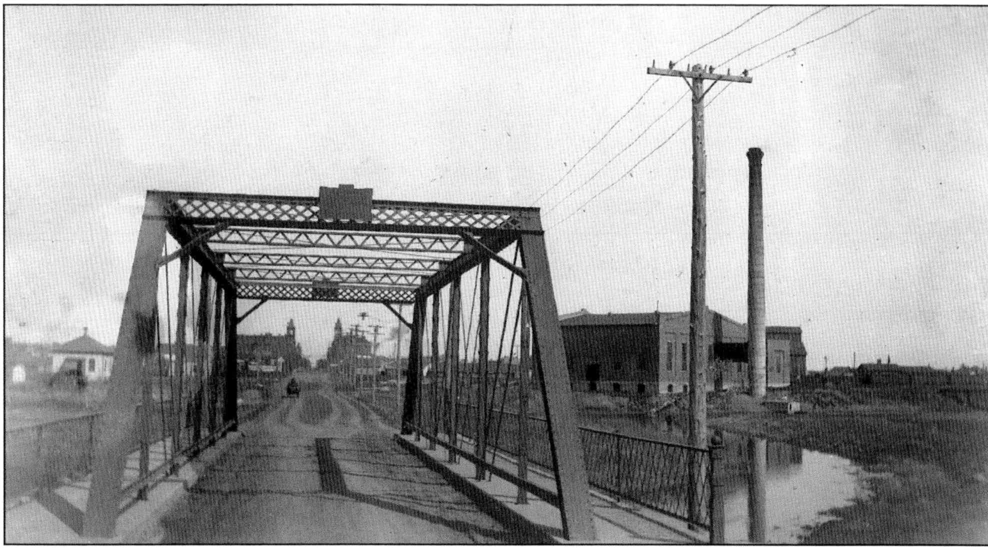

The Watertown Power & Light plant is visible to the right in this undated photo of the bridge over the Big Sioux River on West Kemp Avenue. In 1935, the current bridge of quartzite stone replaced the old steel bridge, which is now part of the monkey exhibit at Bramble Park Zoo in Watertown.

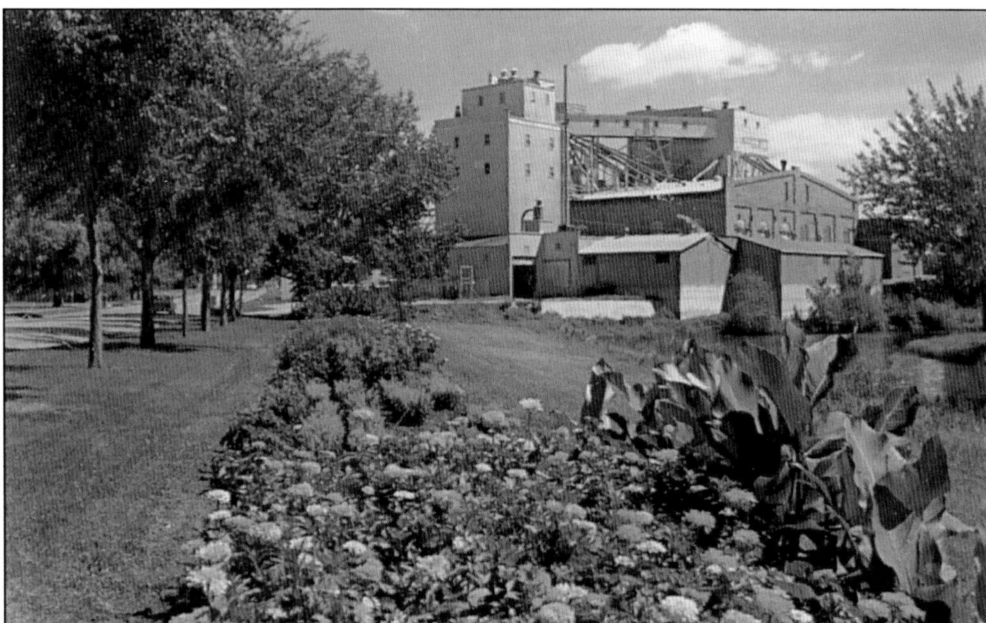

This 1957 view of the Watertown Co-op Elevator was taken from virtually the same vantage point as the view above, of the old Kemp Avenue bridge from about 1910. The Watertown Power & Light Company built the building in 1910 and was put into operation on October 20 of that year. The plant closed in 1929 when the company's franchise with the city ended, and the Watertown Co-op Elevator Association began using the building about 1951. Landmark Builders, Inc. razed the building in 2001, in anticipation of future development. The building was listed on the National Register of Historic Places.

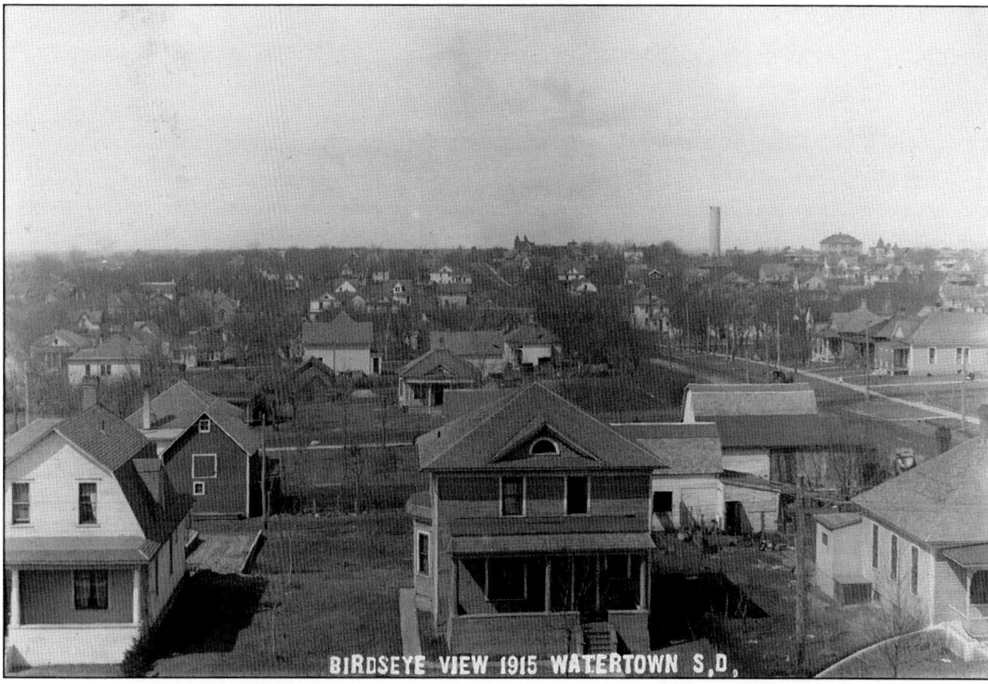

This bird's-eye view of the northern residential section of Watertown was taken in 1915, looking west from the top of Luther Hospital on Fourth Street Northeast. The waterworks standpipe and the old Mellette grade school are visible in the background, in the upper right half of the photo.

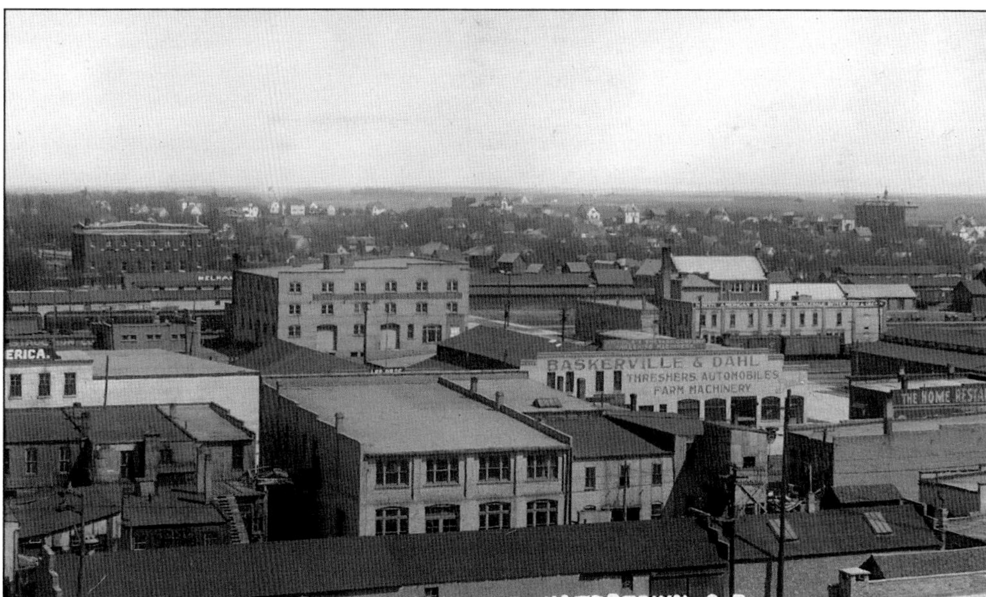

The Luther Hospital, on the upper right side, is virtually the eastern extent of development in Watertown, in this 1915 view of Watertown, facing northeast from the top of City Hall. The Baskerville & Dahl implement, facing First Avenue North in this photo, was in operation until about 1962. Note the Masonic Lodge in the upper left side. (Courtesy Ken and Lyn Sheldon.)

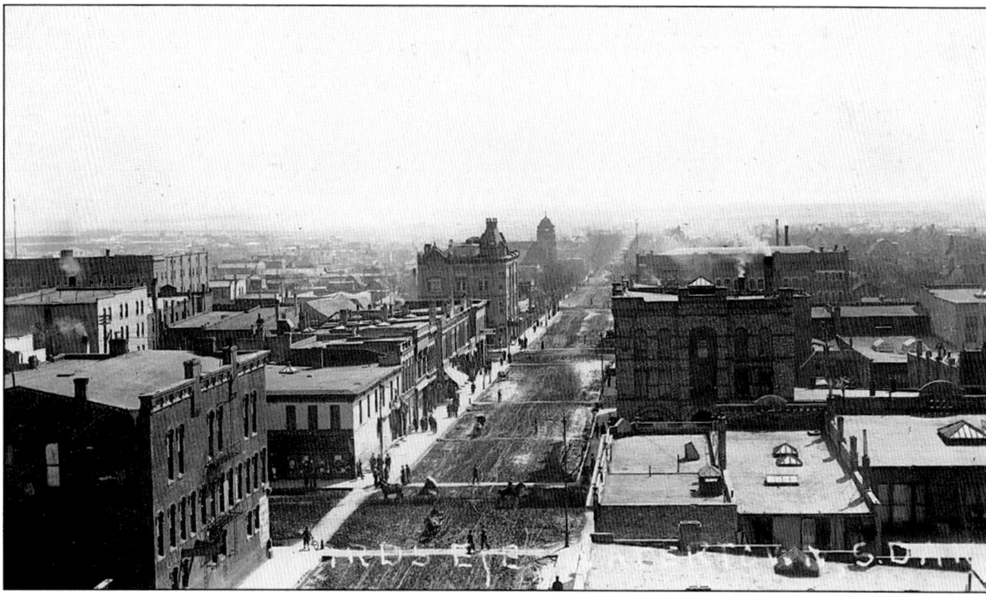

This view of Kemp Avenue, looking east from City Hall, dates to about 1912, when the Lincoln Hotel, on the left side of the photo, opened for business. The Uptown streets were paved in 1914, but the streets in this photo are still dirt. The intersection in the foreground is the junction of Kemp Avenue and Broadway.

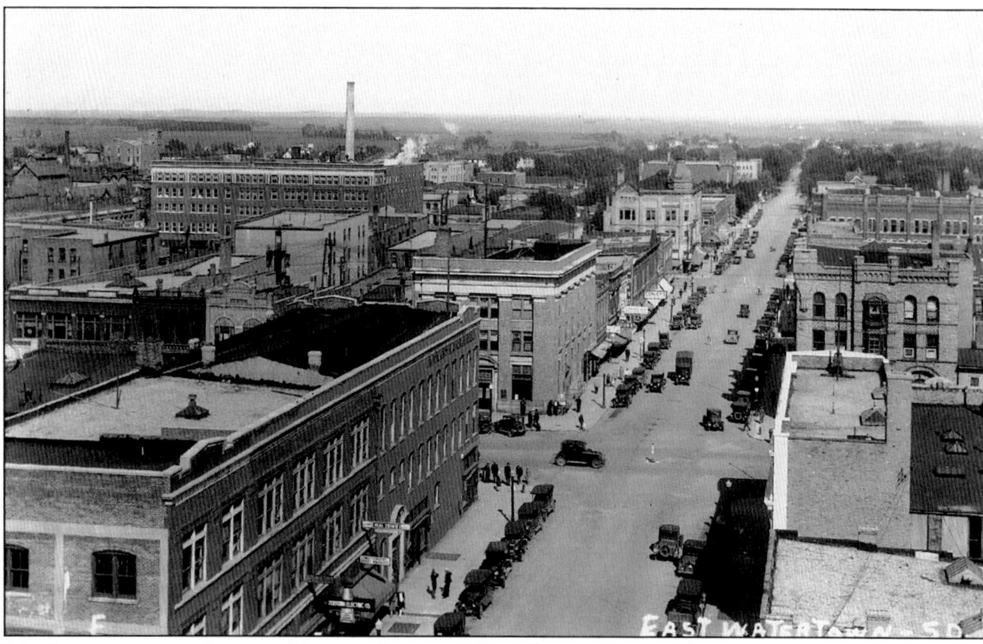

Much progress can be seen 20 years later, in this identical view of Kemp Avenue, looking east from City Hall, about 1930. A fifth floor has been added to the Lincoln Hotel, and a three-story addition built on the west end of the Mellette, also known as the Lamm, building in the lower left corner. The three-story brick and stone Citizens National Bank has also replaced the Rice building on the northeast corner of the Kemp and Broadway intersection.

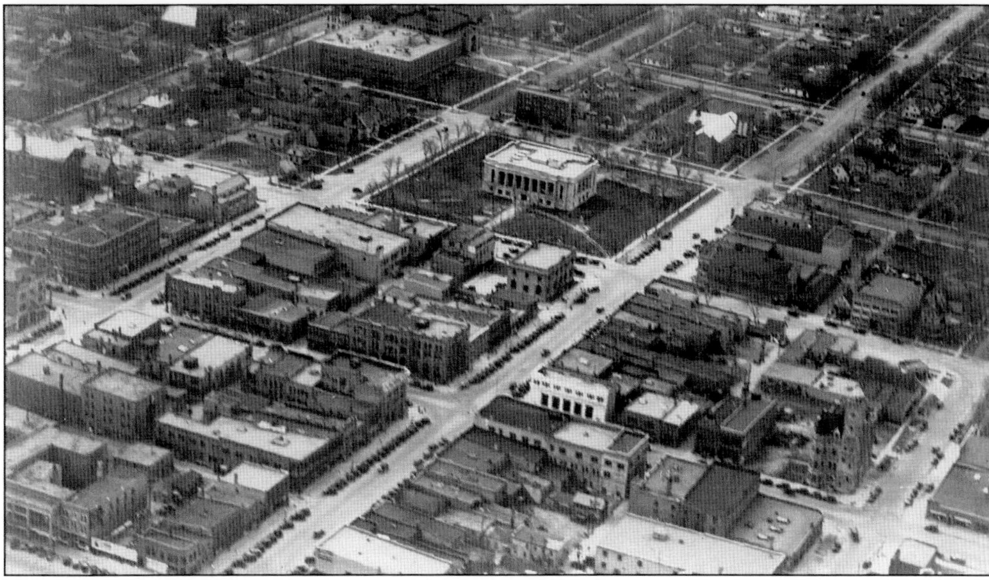

Willard Gowin shot this aerial view of Watertown's main business section about 1930. The photo is bordered by First Avenue North in the bottom left corner, Fourth Avenue South in the upper right corner, Second Street East in the upper left corner, and First Street West in the bottom right corner. The new Codington County courthouse, finished in 1929, is visible almost in the center.

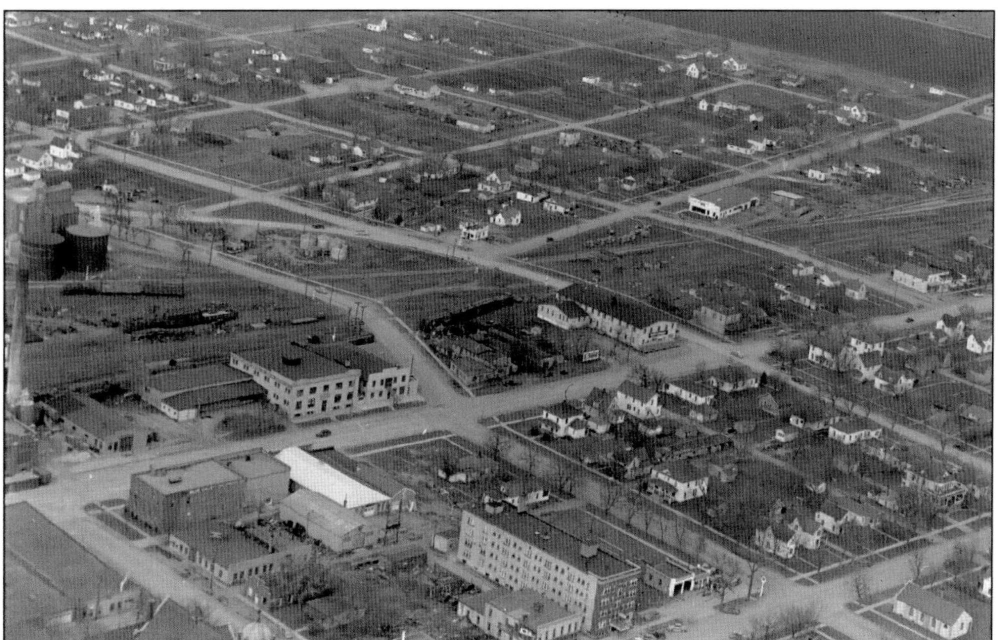

This aerial view of Watertown, of businesses and homes on either side of U.S. Highway 81, running about diagonally from the upper left side of the photo to the lower right, was taken in the spring of 1947. Fourth Street East begins in the bottom right corner and basically parallels Highway 81. The photo is bound by the old Immaculate Conception Church along Third Street East in the bottom left corner, Ninth Street East in the upper right corner, Kemp Avenue in the bottom right corner, and Third Avenue North in the upper left corner.

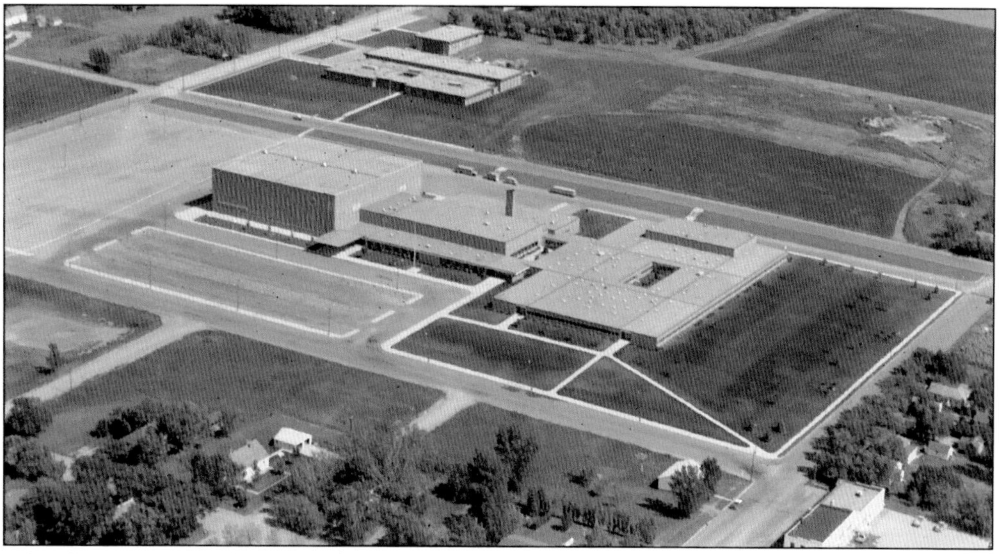

After four tries, a bond issue for $1,500,000 for a new Watertown senior high school was finally passed in the late 1950s. The new High School was finished in 1962, with an adjoining city-owned civic arena. This aerial photo of the new high school grounds was taken September 14, 1968, shortly after the first buildings, just above the high school, were finished for the Lake Area Vocational-Technical Institute, which was founded June 1965. The photo shows that, though the area is now completely surrounded by residential development, the school buildings were constructed, literally, in farmers' fields.

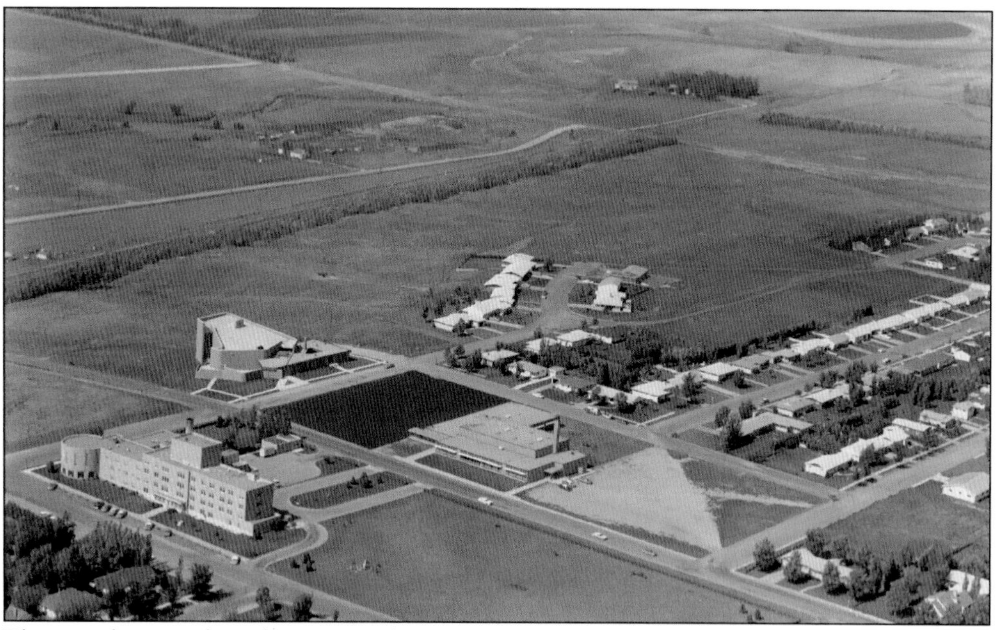

This aerial view, also taken September 14, 1968, shows the northwest area of Watertown, with St. Ann's Hospital, now Prairie Lakes Hospital, in the lower left corner, and Holy Name Church and grade school to the north. A cancer treatment center was constructed on the empty lot to the east of the hospital in this photo, in 1999. The land to the north of the church is now completely filled with homes.